COURT COMPANION ON GENDER-BASED VIOLENCE CASES

Edited by Zarizana Abdul Aziz and Maria Cecilia T. Sicangco

SEPTEMBER 2021

ADB

ASIAN DEVELOPMENT BANK

© 2021 Asian Development Bank
6 ADB Avenue, Mandaluyong City, 1550 Metro Manila, Philippines
Tel +63 2 8632 4444; Fax +63 2 8636 2444
www.adb.org

Some rights reserved. Published in 2021.

ISBN 978-92-9269-046-5 (print); 978-92-9269-047-2 (electronic); 978-92-9269-048-9 (ebook)
Publication Stock No. TCS210340-2
DOI: http://dx.doi.org/10.22617/TCS210340-2

The views expressed in this publication are those of the authors and do not necessarily reflect the views and policies of the Asian Development Bank (ADB) or its Board of Governors or the governments they represent.

ADB does not guarantee the accuracy of the data included in this publication and accepts no responsibility for any consequence of their use. The mention of specific companies or products of manufacturers does not imply that they are endorsed or recommended by ADB in preference to others of a similar nature that are not mentioned.

By making any designation of or reference to a particular territory or geographic area, or by using the term "country" in this document, ADB does not intend to make any judgments as to the legal or other status of any territory or area.

Please contact pubsmarketing@adb.org if you have questions or comments with respect to content, or if you wish to obtain copyright permission for your intended use that does not fall within these terms, or for permission to use the ADB logo.

Corrigenda to ADB publications may be found at http://www.adb.org/publications/corrigenda.

Notes:
In this publication, "$" refers to United States dollars and "PRs" refers to Pakistan rupees.
ADB recognizes "Bangalore" as Bengaluru.

Printed on recycled paper

Contents

Tables, Figures, and Boxes ix

Foreword xi

Acknowledgments xiii

Abbreviations xv

Preliminary Notes xvii

INTRODUCTION 1

Chapter 1 THE COURTS—CONSTITUTIONAL MANDATE AND RIGHTS 5
FRAMEWORK

I. Introduction 5
   A. Judicial Effectiveness and State Mandate 5
   B. Fundamental Rights: Constitutional Rights Approach 8
   C. Human Rights Approach 10
II. Women's Human and Fundamental Rights 11
III. Cases from Pakistan That Applied International Law 15
IV. Cases from Other Common Law Countries That Applied International Law 16
V. Access to Justice 18
VI. Conclusory Remarks: Gender-Based Violence Courts 20

Chapter 2 BARRIERS TO WOMEN ACCESSING JUSTICE 23
I. Introduction 23
II. Lack of Confidence in the Police and Judicial Process 23
III. Problematic Interpretation and Implementation of the Law 25
   A. Lack of Gender Understanding 25
   B. Demystifying Gender and Sex and Gender Stereotyping 26
   C. Lack of Sensitivity to Gender-Based Violence 29
   D. Understanding Unconscious and Implicit Bias 30
IV. Risk Factors for Judges 30
   A. Emotional States 30
   B. Ambiguity 31

C.   Distracted or Pressured Decision-Making Circumstances   31

D.   Low-Effort Processing   31

E.   How Can Judges Reduce Unconscious Bias   31

V.   Social Barriers   32

VI. Types of Culturally Sanctioned Crimes against Women   34

A.   Honor Killings   34

B.   Domestic Violence   34

C.   Bride Price, *Sarpaisa, Watta Satta*   35

D.   Compensation and Child Marriages   35

VII. Delayed Reporting or Non-Reporting   36

A.   Coercion and Resiling and Fear of Retribution   37

B.   A Horrific Example of Coercion in a Rape Case   37

C.   Autonomy, Mobility, Financial Resources, Shelter, Interim Maintenance,   37
     and Housing

VIII. Conclusory Remarks   38

Chapter 3   **UNDERSTANDING GENDER-BASED VIOLENCE AGAINST WOMEN**   **41**

I.   Introduction   41

II.   What Is Gender-Based Violence?   42

III. Causes and Impact of Gender-Based Violence   43

IV.   Gender-Based Violence Offenses   45

V.   Gender-Based Violence: Violation of Constitutional Rights   47

Chapter 4   **MANIFESTATIONS OF GENDER-BASED VIOLENCE:**   **51**
SEXUAL ASSAULT, ACID ATTACKS, AND ONLINE GENDER-BASED
VIOLENCE

I.   Rape and Sexual Assault   51

A.   Ascertaining Consent   52

B.   Vitiating Consent   53

II.   *Zina*   55

III. Acid Attacks   58

IV.   Online Gender-Based Violence   59

Chapter 5   **MANIFESTATIONS OF GENDER-BASED VIOLENCE:**   **65**
FAMILY-RELATED GENDER-BASED VIOLENCE

I.   Introduction   65

II.   Domestic Violence (Intimate Partner Violence)   65

III. Economic Violence   69

A.   Denial of Women's Inheritance Rights   70

IV.   Femicide on the Pretext of "Honor"   73

V. Forced and Early Marriage of Women and Girls   76

   A. Child Marriages   76

   B. *Watta Satta*   77

   C. *Ghag*   77

   D. Marriage to the Holy Qur'an   78

   E. *Badla-e-Sulha, Swarra, Wanni, Sung Chatti*   78

VI. Conclusory Remarks   79

Chapter 6   UNDERSTANDING GENDER DISCRIMINATION AND GENDER EQUALITY   81

I. Introduction   81

II. Gender Discrimination   81

   A. General Principles   81

   B. Who Is the Comparator?   83

   C. Protected Characteristics   84

   D. Intersectional Discrimination   85

   E. Gender Discrimination Violates the Right to Life   85

III. Gender Equality   86

   A. General Principles   86

   B. Special Measures   88

IV. Culture and Gender Ideology   90

V. Discrimination Based on Gender Identity   93

Chapter 7   UNDERSTANDING AND INTERACTING WITH VICTIMS DURING THE CRIMINAL PROCESS   95

I. Introduction   95

II. Before Coming to Court   95

   A. Police   96

   B. Medical Personnel   99

III. Protection Orders and Restraining Orders   101

   A. Protection Orders under Pakistan Law   101

   B. Domestic Violence Laws: Case Examples   106

IV. Legal Aid   108

V. Conclusory Remarks   109

Chapter 8   THE COURT ENVIRONMENT   111

I. Introduction   111

II. Gender-Based Violence Specialized Courts   111

   A. Overview of Specialized Gender-Based Violence Courts in Pakistan   112

   B. Gender-Based Violence Court Guidelines and Practice Notes   114

	C.	Who Is Covered and for What Offenses?	114
	D.	Fast Tracking Trial Dates and Finalization with Strict Hearing Schedules	115
	E.	Attending to Victims When They Arrive at the Court Precinct	115
	F.	Courtroom Set Up and Design	115
	G.	Hearing in Camera	118
	H.	Set Up and Use of the e-Courtroom	118
III.	Role of Judges in Gender-Based Violence Courts	119
	A.	Judicial Role: Before Evidence Commences	119
	B.	Settling the Victim and Witnesses	119
	C.	Settling a Child Victim or Witnesses	120
	D.	Settling Persons with Disability	120
	E.	Interpreter or Communication Assistant for Victims or Witnesses	120
	F.	Conduct in the Courtroom	121
	G.	General Observations about Language and Questioning of Victims	121
	H.	Cross-Examination of Victims by Defense Counsel	122
	I.	A Good Practice to Obtain Truthful Evidence	123
	J.	Conclusory Remarks on the Role of Judges	123
IV.	Role of Prosecutors in Gender-Based Violence Courts	124
	A.	Preparing for Trial	125
	B.	The Trial Process	125
	C.	Conclusory Observations on the Role of Prosecutors	125
V.	Role of Defense Counsel in Gender-Based Violence Courts	125
VI.	*Amicus Curiae*	126
VII.	Conclusory Remarks	127

Chapter 9   EVIDENCE AND CREDIBILITY   129

I.	Introduction	129
II.	Police Evidence	130
	A. Cases from Pakistan	130
	B. Cases before Regional Courts or Commissions	131
	C. Police Good Practice	132
III.	Corroboration: Concept and Application	133
IV.	Corroboration: Credibility of Women's Evidence in Gender-Based Violence Cases	134
	A. International Case Examples of Corroboration of Women's Evidence	135
	B. Pakistani Case Examples of Corroboration of Women's Evidence in Sex Cases	138

V.   Court Processes Impacting on the Credibility of Women Victims   140

    A.   Character Attacks   140

    B.   Virginity Testing   141

VI.   Conclusory Remarks   145

Chapter 10   JUDGMENT WRITING   147

I.   Introduction   147

II.   Content   147

III.   Gender-Sensitive Language   148

    A.   The Importance of Gender-Sensitive Language   148

    B.   Gender-Sensitive and Gender-Insensitive Language   150

IV.   Victim Blaming   153

V.   Disparaging Language   154

VI.   Language Favoring Males   155

VII.   Burden of Proof in Gender-Based Violence Offenses   156

VIII.   Conclusory Remarks   157

Chapter 11   SENTENCING, COMPENSATION, AND FORGIVENESS   159

I.   Introduction   159

II.   Punishment   160

III.   *Jinayat* and Forgiveness   161

IV.   *Jinayat*: State's Interest and Victim's Interest   164

V.   Impact of Forgiveness   166

VI.   Reparation   170

Chapter 12   RESILING AND ATTRITION   175

I.   Introduction   175

II.   What Is Meant by Attrition?   177

III.   International Experience on Attrition   178

    A.   Victim-Related Factors   178

    B.   System-Related Factors   179

IV.   Why Attrition Matters   179

V.   Attrition and Resiling in Pakistan   179

VI.   Good Practices to Increase Conviction Rates and Reduce Attrition and Acquittal Rates   183

    A.   The Practice Notes: Approach of the Court When Resiling Occurs   183

    B.   Victimless Prosecution   184

    C.   Pro-Prosecution: No Drop Policy   185

    D.   Witness Tampering and Protections for Witnesses   186

VII.   Conclusory Remarks   187

Chapter 13   INSTITUTIONAL PRACTICES, EVALUATION, AND MONITORING   191

    I.   Introduction   191
    II.   Overarching Themes and Strategies   191
    III.   Data Collection, Monitoring, and Evaluation   193
           A. Court Data   193
           B. Prosecution Data   195
           C. Police Data   197
    IV.   Creating Specialized Agencies   197
           A. Special Judges for Gender-Based Violence Courts   197
           B. Special Prosecutors   197
           C. Special Police Cells/Investigators   197
    V.   Capacity Building and Training on Gender Equality and Gender Promotion   198
    VI.   Capacity Training on Gender Sensitization and Gender-Based Violence 199
    VII.   Proactively Improving Investigation and Protection in Gender-Based   201
           Violence Cases
    VIII. Proactively Improving Court Processes and Case Management   201
    IX.   Developing Cooperative Approaches between the Courts, Police,   202
           Prosecutors, and Civil Society
    X.   Conclusory Remarks   202

APPENDIXES   203

    1   Guidelines to Be Followed in Cases of Gender-Based Violence (GBV)   204
    2   Practice Note for the Model Gender-Based Violence Cases Court, Lahore   208
    2A   Updated Practice Note Incorporating Underlined Refinements Suggested   215
         by the District and Sessions Court Judges in Lahore
    3   Questioning of Child Witnesses in Court—Some Helpful Hints Using   222
         Best Practices
    4   Suggested Procedure for Cross–Examination of the Victim   227
         by the Defense Counsel
    5   Direction to Police to Investigate Resiling Witnesses   229
    6   Direction to Establish a Gender-Based Violence Police Cell at   232
         Investigation Headquarters District Lahore

GLOSSARY   237

ABOUT THE AUTHORS AND CONTRIBUTORS   241

Tables, Figures, and Boxes

TABLES

2.1	Traditional Gender Stereotypes	28
2.2	Gender Stereotypes and Gender Roles	28
3.1	Common Reactions to the Behavior of a Man and a Woman	44
3.2	List of Cases Referred to Gender-Based Violence Courts	46

FIGURES

2.1	Usual Treatment of Women at the Police Station	24
2.2	Application of a Gender Lens	27
3.1	Categories of Gender-Based Violence	42
3.2	Violence against Women vs. Violence among Men	45
5.1	Repetitive Nature of Domestic Violence	68
5.2	Ownership of Assets by Women and Men Age 15–49	70
6.1	Formal Equality vs. Substantive Equality	88
7.1	Obstacles to Women Reporting	102
8.1	Layout of a Gender-Based Violence Court	117
8.2	Video Facilities in e-Courtrooms	118
8.3	e-Courtrooms for Child Witnesses	119
9.1	Interlocking Elements Affecting Gender-Based Violence Claims and Outcomes	129
9.2	Tweets by the World Health Organization on Virginity Testing	144
11.1	Types of Offenses in *Fiqh* (Islamic Jurisprudence)	161
12.1	Convictions vs. Acquittals and Cases Consigned to Record in Violence against Women Cases in Punjab, 2017	175
12.2	Disposal of Rape Cases in Punjab, 2017	176

13.1   Seven Linked Strategies to Protect the Victim's Rights in Court   192

13.2   Training Manuals for Judges and Prosecutors Handling Gender-Based Violence Cases   200

BOXES

5.1   Pakistani Case Law on Women's Inheritance Rights   72

5.2   Perspective of a Compensation Marriage Bride   78

Foreword

The right to life is the right to live with dignity. This right is protected under our Constitution. In *Atif Zareef v. The State*, the Supreme Court of Pakistan emphasized that the right to dignity under Article 14 of the Constitution is an absolute right:

> Every person has the right to live, and the right to live means right to live with dignity. A person should live as "person" and no less. Human dignity hovers over our laws like a guardian angel; it underlies every norm of a just legal system and provides an ultimate justification for every legal rule, [...] making human worth and humanness of a person a far more fundamental right than the others, a right that is absolutely non-negotiable.[a]

The right to life is also protected under international law. Article 3 of the Universal Declaration of Human Rights states, "Everyone has the right to life, liberty and security of person." Similarly, Article 6 of the International Covenant on Civil and Political Rights (ICCPR) begins with this statement: "Every human being has the inherent right to life." The right to life, Article 4 of the ICCPR emphasizes, is non-derogable.

Yet, our lived reality that is reflected in the everyday practice of law and the judicial process appears not to bend to the will of the Constitution and the law, but the will of those intent to demean the sanctity of life.

When reports of violence against women, sexual assault, rape, domestic violence, and sexual harassment are lodged, they are withdrawn due to compromises and settlement. When the law prohibits such compromises, women are compelled by their male relatives to resile and recant, contributing to the erroneous stereotype that women 'lie' when alleging violence or that Pakistan is free of gender-based violence.

Bizarre concepts of *ghairat* or 'honour' are used to justify violence against women. Let us be clear. Dishonour belongs to the perpetrator of a crime, not the victim. There is nothing honourable about killing, or beating a woman, or splashing acid on another. As my fellow Supreme Court judge said in *Muhammad Abbas v. The State*, it is more accurate to translate the trait of *ghairat* as 'arrogance.'[b]

In fact, the honour of our society hangs in the balance when perpetrators are not held accountable. The duty of judges is to dispense justice, to protect the disempowered, and punish the aggressor. When the legal and judicial processes break down, chaos ensues. Prevention and punishment of violence must be the foundation of our judicial system. We have to do more to ensure that crimes against women do not take place, and to punish perpetrators when they do.

---

[a] PLD 2021 SC 550, per Syed Mansoor Ali Shah J.
[b] PLD 2020 SC 620, per Qazi Faez Isa J.

Courts cannot be swayed by notions of inequality whereby only some are entitled to dignity while others may be subjected to violence. They must function within the frame of constitutionalism and the rule of law. The idea is for judges to make the clarion call that emphatically takes a stance against gender-based violence—to issue wide-reaching jurisprudence that is capable of changing mindsets, creating a society ingrained with the conviction of human worth and humanness.

When I discussed with the Asian Development Bank (ADB) the possibility of taking proactive measures to increase access to justice by victims of violence, I had hoped that our efforts would bring about some measure of change. In Punjab, where I was then Chief Justice, there were hardly recorded convictions for gender-based violence against women. Indeed, this sad state of affairs was replicated throughout Pakistan.

But the outcome was beyond expectations. We trained over 600 judges and prosecutors, as well as established Gender-Based Violence Courts—the first in Lahore and subsequently throughout Pakistan. This was a first in Asia and I am very proud to have spearheaded the process of bringing about this change. And my gratitude to ADB and its team of amazing experts and trainers. I would also like to congratulate the team for publishing this *Court Companion for Gender-based Violence Cases*, which should be a constant companion on the desk of every judge in Pakistan.

As I conclude this foreword, the coronavirus disease (COVID-19) pandemic has caged humans with self-isolation and global lockdown. Studies have shown that the isolation has brought unprecedented spikes in gender-based violence, amplifying risk factors of violence against women, and creating a "pandemic within a pandemic." As we turn to digital communication technology to ameliorate the impacts of quarantines, lockdowns, and movement restrictions, we are also witnessing increased online gender-based violence. There remains much work to be done and we must continue to be ever vigilant.

Indeed, the establishment of Gender-Based Violence Courts does not signal the pinnacle of our work but the beginning of a new era. It is important to be open to new ideas and embrace change with open arms. As Allama Iqbal, our national poet, said:

آئین نو سے ڈرنا، طرز کہن پہ اڑنا

منزل یہی کھٹن ہے قوموں کی زندگی میں

To be afraid of the new ways, to insist on the old ones
This is the only difficult stage in the life of nations.

SYED MANSOOR ALI SHAH
Justice
Supreme Court of Pakistan
Islamabad
15 August 2021

Acknowledgments

Overview and supervision: **Irum Ahsan**

Principal editor: **Zarizana Abdul Aziz**

Secondary editor: **Maria Cecilia T. Sicangco**

Authors and contributors of chapters: **Zarizana Abdul Aziz, Saima Amin Khawaja, Robyn Layton, Samar Minallah Khan, Maria Cecilia T. Sicangco,** and **Sohail Akbar Warraich**

The invaluable assistance and contributions of the following are deeply appreciated—and all those who have facilitated, assisted, and contributed in one way or another to this endeavor.

- **Justice Syed Mansoor Ali Shah**, Supreme Court Justice of Pakistan and former Chief Justice of Lahore High Court;

- **Justice Asif Saeed Khan Khosa**, former Chief Justice of the Supreme Court of Pakistan;

- **Justice Syed Yawar Ali, Justice Sardar Muhammad Shamim Khan**, and **Justice Mamoon Rashid Sheikh**, former Chief Justices of the Lahore High Court;

- **Justice Ayesha Malik** and **Justice Aalia Neelum**, and **Justice Jawad Hassan**, Lahore High Court Justices;

- **Uzma Chugtai, Mahrukh Aziz, Abdul Sattar**, and **Habib Ullah Amir**, former Directors General of the Punjab Judicial Academy;

- **Jazeela Aslam**, **Shazia Shah**, and the entire administration and faculty of the Punjab Judicial Academy;

- **Hayat Ali Shah**, former Director General of the Federal Judicial Academy;

- **Muhammad Raheem Awan**, former Secretary of Pakistan's National Judicial (Policy Making) Committee and his staff;

- **District and Sessions Judge Lahore Abid Hussain Qureshi**, Additional Sessions Judges, **Judge Rehmat Ali** and **Judge Tajammul Shahzad Chaudry**;

- **Asiya Yasin**, Prosecutor, Lahore GBV Court;

- **Robyn Layton**, Asian Development Bank (ADB) principal capacity development specialist (consultant) and former Justice of the Supreme Court of South Australia, for her expert assistance in setting up the model Gender-Based Violence Court in Lahore, Punjab;

- **Humaira Masihuddin** for her contributions to this publication and the judicial capacity building conducted in Pakistan in 2019;

- Former ADB general counsel **Christopher Stephens** and current general counsel **Thomas M. Clark** for their support for the *Legal Literacy for Women* and *Promotion of Gender-Responsive Judicial Systems* technical assistance projects;

- **Christina U. Pak**, principal counsel and team leader, Law and Policy Reform Program, for overseeing the *Court Companion on Gender-Based Violence Cases* to publication;

- **Maria Cecilia T. Sicangco**, whose support and assistance went above and beyond the call of duty during both the 2017–2019 capacity building programs and the publication process of this *Court Companion on Gender-Based Violence Cases*;

- **Ma. Celeste Grace A. Saniel-Gois, Gladys Sangalang**, and **Francesse Joy J. Cordon-Navarro** for their assistance and support during the 2017–2019 capacity building programs;

- **Ryah Zendra M. Sanvicente** and **Imelda Alcala**, for assisting with the publication process;

- **Khalid Hussain** for the hand-drawn illustrations and **Khuda Bakhsh Abro** for the cover graphic; and

- **ADB Department of Communications team** for guidance on design and publishing; and **Judy Yñiguez** and other service providers for printing and publishing support.

Abbreviations

ADB	Asian Development Bank*
CCPO	capital city police officer
CEDAW	Convention on the Elimination of All Forms of Discrimination against Women*
CNIC	computerized national identity card
CRC	Convention on the Rights of the Child*
CrPC	Criminal Procedure Code*
DPO	District Police Office
DSC	District and Sessions Court
FIR	first information report
GBV	gender-based violence*
IACHR	Inter-American Commission on Human Rights
ICCPR	International Covenant on Civil and Political Rights
ICESCR	International Covenant on Economic, Social and Cultural Rights
ICT	information and communication technology
LHC	Lahore High Court*
NGO	nongovernment organization
ODI	Overseas Development Institute
PCSW	Punjab Commission on the Status of Women
PECA	Prevention of Electronic Crimes Act, 2016
PPC	Pakistan Penal Code 1860*
PTSD	post-traumatic stress disorder
QSO	Qanun e-Shahadat Order 1984*
UDHR	Universal Declaration of Human Rights*
UN	United Nations*
UNDP	United Nations Development Programme
UNESCO	United Nations Educational, Scientific and Cultural Organization

UNICEF	United Nations Children's Fund
US	United States
VAW	violence against women*
VCLT	Vienna Convention on the Law of Treaties
WHO	World Health Organization*

---

*   These terms are further defined in the Glossary on p. 237.

Preliminary Notes

Whom the Companion Is For

The *Court Companion on Gender-Based Violence Cases* is for judges, prosecutors, and the police. It also caters to anyone seeking to understand the workings of the law in relation to gender-based violence (GBV), such as medical officers, civil society advocates working with GBV victims, paralegals assisting victims to access justice, defense counsels, and victims who wish to access the justice system.

The idea for the *Court Companion* came about after the completion of 3 years of judicial and prosecutorial training and capacity building programs conducted by the Asian Development Bank (ADB) team led by Irum Ahsan, then principal counsel at the Office of the General Counsel and currently advisor, Office of the Compliance Review Panel. The team members are Zarizana Abdul Aziz, Saima Amin Khawaja, Robyn Layton, Humaira Masihuddin, Samar Minallah Khan, and Maria Cecilia T. Sicangco. The team also undertook training of trainers, worked to embed the training modules in the curriculum of judicial training academies, and provided technical assistance in setting up the first GBV Court (in Lahore) and subsequent GBV Courts. This *Court Companion* complements the capacity building programs and serves as an easy and accessible reference for all those who are interested in pursuing justice, holding perpetrators accountable, and providing effective redress and reparation for victims.

A Note on Language

Throughout this *Court Companion*, the term 'victim' instead of 'survivor' is used when referring to persons who have suffered GBV. While these persons are also survivors of violence and discrimination, the term 'victim' is used in this publication for the sake of clarity and cohesiveness as that is the language used in legislations, and because this *Court Companion* will be used in courtrooms. Readers are, however, encouraged to regard the victims as survivors.

A Note on Religious References

In this *Court Companion*, all quotes related to religion and spirituality do not in any way reflect the beliefs of ADB or imply that ADB subscribes to a particular religious belief. Article 227 of the Constitution of the Islamic Republic of Pakistan provides that all laws shall be in conformity with the injunctions of Islam. Article 203D provides that the Federal Shariat Court may "examine and decide the question whether or not any law or provision of law is repugnant to the injunctions of Islam, as laid down in the Holy Qur'an and Sunnah of the Holy Prophet" and "if any law or provision of law is held to be repugnant to the injunctions of Islam," such or provision of law shall be amended to bring it into conformity or cease to have effect. Under the circumstances, references and quotes related to religion and spirituality are included in good faith by the authors as they resonate with and support the law or a specific legal provision, approach or norm.

Girls from South Punjab, Pakistan. More than one-fourth of women in Pakistan are married before they reach the age of 18. A study conducted by UN Women states, "Education of young women is the key factor for delaying early marriages as only 4% of women with graduation and above education were married before age 18 years; however, 35% of the women who are illiterate or have less than primary education were married before age 18 years" (photo by Samar Minallah Khan). Source: UN Women. 2020. Young Women in Pakistan—Status Report 2020. Islamabad.

INTRODUCTION

In 2016, out of 2,353 rape cases before the courts in Punjab, only 100 cases resulted in convictions.[1] That makes a conviction rate of 4.25%. These did not include the vast majority of cases that were withdrawn before court listings for one reason or another. In response, the then Chief Justice of the Lahore (Punjab) High Court requested the Asian Development Bank (ADB) to provide technical assistance in developing the capacity of the judiciary and key court officers, culminating in the setting up of the first Gender-Based Violence (GBV) Court in Pakistan.

An assessment undertaken by the ADB team indicates that there was an ingrained and widespread belief that false rape claims were common (though this belief was not confined only to Pakistan). Further inquiry revealed that firstly, complainants and victims recanted or resiled after reporting in almost all cases. Secondly, male family members who had invariably reached a 'compromise' with and/or received compensation from the alleged perpetrators outside of the court proceedings were responsible for pressuring women to recant or resile.

Understanding and addressing gender bias in court was critical. Imposing counsels, the loud environment in court, and the proximity of the victim to the perpetrator all serve to intimidate and traumatize the victims.[2] The Supreme Court guidelines on victims testifying in sexual assault cases were generally not implemented.

After a series of trainings, the first GBV Court was set up in Lahore. The physical court layout was revamped. The victim and witness were provided a seat and a screen. Female support staff was appointed. Provisions were made to enable complainants and vulnerable witnesses such as children to wait in a separate room and give evidence through videoconferencing facilities. New practice notes were drawn up. Case management skills training was also conducted. Other than specialized judges, specialized prosecutors were identified and likewise provided training. Specialized police units to investigate GBV cases were also established.

Continued monitoring and evaluation of the GBV Court found that prosecutors, victims, and defense counsels received the changes well. After a year, the conviction rate for rape cases heard in the specialized court rose to 16.5%.[3] Subsequently, the Supreme Court directed that specialized GBV Courts be set up in each of Pakistan's 116 districts.

---

[1] Punjab Commission on the Status of Women (PCSW). Gender Management Information System.

[2] The term 'victim' is used in this publication for the sake of clarity and cohesiveness as that is the language used in legislation and in courtrooms. See Note on Language on page xvii.

[3] Data from Judge of GBV Court, Lahore.

The success of the program lies in its addressing all issues—including sensitive issues—boldly and thoughtfully, as well as integrating and customizing international norms and good practices to the national context. In 2020, the Committee on the Elimination of Discrimination against Women, in reviewing Pakistan's implementation of the Convention on the Elimination of All Forms of Discrimination against Women, commended the Government of Pakistan for setting up the GBV Courts. At the same time, the Committee stressed that more can be done to improve access to justice by ensuring nondiscrimination, removing economic barriers, and implementing further capacity building measures.

The training of judges and prosecutors and the establishment of specialized GBV Courts have transformed the judicial landscape in Pakistan. The changes implemented serve as proof of how political will and capacity development can make justice more accessible to GBV victims by enhancing judicial capacity and streamlining the judicial process.

This *Court Companion on Gender-Based Violence Cases* captures and makes available the knowledge gained from the research and training materials developed by ADB.[4] It serves as an important component of a broader framework that aims to address and reduce GBV. The *Companion* lays out ways to distill facts from myths, stereotypes, and negative perception of women. It underscores judicial integrity by challenging unconscious bias. It is grounded in the Constitution, international law derived from treaties to which Pakistan has acceded/ratified, and relevant international good practices. In so doing, it simultaneously integrates all six principles stipulated in the Bangalore Principles of Judicial Conduct, namely independence, impartiality, integrity, propriety, equality of treatment, as well as competence and diligence.

Zarizana Abdul Aziz

Principal editor, *Court Companion on Gender-Based Violence Cases*; and principal capacity development specialist (consultant), Asian Development Bank (2017–2020)

---

[4] The laws referred to in this *Companion* are the laws in effect as of 20 April 2021. There have been initiatives to amend the law, one of which is the Anti-Rape (Investigation and Trial) Ordinance 2020 (Ordinance No. XVI of 2020). The Ordinance was tabled at the National Assembly on 1 February 2021. However, as of August 2021, the ordinance has not been promulgated into law.

Puppetry as a legal empowerment tool.
ADB held a series of puppet shows on the rights of women and girls, such as the right to receive inheritance, the right to marry only with their free and full consent, and the right to education (photo by Samar Minallah Khan).

Gender disparities in education. Human Rights Watch data indicate that girls represent a disproportionate number of out-of-school youths in Pakistan. By sixth grade, 59% of girls no longer attend school, versus 49% of boys. Secondary school statistics are worse—by ninth grade, 87% of girls are out of school (photo by Sara Farid/ADB).

Chapter 1

THE COURTS— CONSTITUTIONAL MANDATE AND RIGHTS FRAMEWORK

I. Introduction

> "
> The failure to prosecute and convict the perpetrator [...] is an indication that the State condones the violence [...]. The condoning of this situation by the entire system only serves to perpetuate the psychological, social, and historical roots and factors that sustain and encourage violence against women. [...]
>
> That general and discriminatory judicial ineffectiveness also creates a climate that is conducive to domestic violence, since society sees no evidence of willingness by the State, as the representative of the society, to take effective action to sanction such acts.
>
> Source: *Maria Da Penha v. Brazil*, Case 12.051, Inter-American Commission on Human Rights, Report No. 54/01 (2000).

Access to justice is predicated on the efficacy of the judicial legal institutions and the law. Its foundational premise is certainty of the law—that every individual is guaranteed due process, that the law and judicial-legal institution are fair, impartial and neutral, and equally accessible to all.

A. Judicial Effectiveness and State Mandate

Judicial effectiveness in delivery of justice for victims of violence is an integral part of the State's commitment to eliminating violence against women. In a United Nations (UN) study of 10,000 men who commit sexual violence, on average, half of those interviewed reported using physical and/or sexual violence against a female partner and nearly a quarter of men admitted to raping a woman. Of those men who had admitted to rape, the vast majority (72% to 97% in most places) did not face any legal consequences.[1] When courts do not hold perpetrators accountable, society is more inclined to associate violence against women as part of its cultural identity.

Furthermore, any inappropriate conduct exhibited by the police can create or increase the risk of violence to the victim.[2] An example is a comment made by the most senior police official in Lahore to the media which implied that a woman who was gang-raped was partly to blame because her car had stalled at a motorway.[3] Such thinking serves to embolden those who commit violence. It also implies that violence is 'understandable' if not 'acceptable' and 'forgivable.' This points to a breakdown of societal order.

Further, the presumption that the law is neutral is inherently problematic because it ignores the fact that lawmakers are products of their environment and incorporate their latent perspectives and biases into the formulation of the law. Anatole France (1894) states, "[t]he law in its majestic equality, forbids the rich as well as the poor to sleep under bridges, to beg in the streets, and to steal bread."[4] Similarly the presumption that the courts are equally accessible to every victim is inherently problematic.

Conviction rates for rape cases are low. For example, in 2016, out of 2,353 rape cases before the courts, only 100 cases resulted in convictions.[5] A total of 2,183 cases resulted in acquittals and 70 cases were consigned to record (footnote 5). That makes a conviction rate of 4.25%. These numbers do not include the vast majority of cases that were withdrawn before court listings for one reason or another (as elaborated in Chapter 12). In addition, in Islamabad between 2008 and 2012, there was a 0% conviction rate of 103 rape cases.[6]

On the other hand, as noted by Justice Haziqul Khairi, while male rapists enjoy impunity, 1,600 women had been accused of adultery with not a single man accused alongside the women, even though men were similarly involved in the act.[7]

So how prevalent is violence against women? According to 2018 estimates by the World Health Organization (WHO), globally, 31% of women aged 15–49 years have experienced either physical and/or sexual intimate partner violence or non-partner sexual violence and 26% of women who have been in a relationship report that they have experienced violence by their intimate

---

[1]   E. Fulu et al. 2013. *Why Do Some Men Use Violence against Women and How Can We Prevent It: Quantitative Findings from a United Nations Multi-Country Study on Men and Violence in Asia and the Pacific.* Bangkok: UNDP, et al.

[2]   See *Okin v. Cornwall-on-Hudson Police Department, 577* F.3d 415 (2d Cir. 2009).

[3]   I. Gabol. 2020. Suspect in Motorway Rape Surrenders to Punjab Police, Denies Involvement. *Dawn.* 13 September.

[4]   A. France. 1894. *Le Lys Rouge (The Red Lily).* Paris: Calmann-Lévy. Chapter 7.

[5]   Punjab Commission on the Status of Women (PCSW). Gender Management Information System.

[6]   See Statement of Objects and Reasons in 'A Bill Further to Amend the Pakistan Penal Code, 1860, the Code of Criminal Procedure, 1898 and the Qanoon-e-Shahadat Order, 1984' filed by Senator Syeda Sughra Imam with the Senate of Pakistan on 13 January 2014.

[7]   Justice Haziqul Khairi (retired), former chief justice of the Federal Shariat Court and a former justice of the Sindh High Court, speaking on "Iqbal's concept of a state" at a contest sponsored by the Pakistan Women's Foundation for Peace. See A. Datta. 2017. Iqbal's Dream of a State with Social and Economic Justice has been Shattered. *The News.* 23 November.

partner.[8] That makes one in three women in the world who has experienced either physical or sexual violence at some point in their lives, mostly from someone close to them. In South Asia, including Pakistan, the estimate of women who have experienced intimate partner violence rises to 35% (footnote 8). The Human Rights Commission of Pakistan reports that four women are raped every day, half of them minors.[9]

As shocking as these figures are, they may still not reflect the actual number of women experiencing gender-based violence (GBV). As the World Bank notes, "Violence against women, and especially sexual violence (whether by a partner or non-partner), remains strongly taboo and stigmatizing such that disclosure may be particularly challenging in societies where victims and survivors are likely to be blamed for it; this results in underreporting and therefore underestimation of the prevalence."[10]

The Islamabad High Court denounced cultural norms that not only tolerate but support violence against women:

> In defiance of the explicit commands of Islam, child marriage, rape and honour killings are not uncommon in our society today. Women are forced into marriage against their will. Heinous traditions of *Karokari*, *Swara*, *Wani* and other forms of exploitation are being practiced in a State where 97% of the population professes to be Muslim. The tribal and other societal norms seem to have taken precedence over the Islamic injunctions. Female children are not safe and there cannot be a more offensive illustration than the unimaginable pain and agony suffered by the little innocent "Zainab." The alarming aspect is that there is no outrage against the practices and mindsets which are a blatant violation of the unambiguous injunctions of Islam. The practices and attitudes highlighted above are prevalent in our society and are public knowledge. Evidence of these practices are the female victims whose heartrending stories are heard by the Courts across the country on a daily basis. These norms are not only offensive but blasphemous.[11]

Gender-Based Violence

The prevalence of GBV against women, coupled with low reporting and conviction rates, requires immediate and robust interrogation of the efficacy of the legal-judicial processes as well as societal norms and practices. It is not viable that domestic judicial decisions demonstrate "a lack of efficacy and a certain degree of tolerance, and had no noticeable preventive or deterrent effect."[12] The former UN Secretary-General Ban Ki-Moon stated, "There is one universal truth, applicable to all countries, cultures and communities: violence against women is never

---

[8] WHO, on behalf of the United Nations Inter-Agency Working Group on Violence against Women Estimation and Data (VAW-IAWGED). 2021. *Violence against Women Prevalence Estimates, 2018: Global, Regional and National Prevalence Estimates for Intimate Partner Violence against Women and Global and Regional Prevalence Estimates for Non-Partner Sexual Violence against Women*. Geneva.

[9] Human Rights Commission of Pakistan. 2016. *State of Human Rights in 2015*. Lahore.

[10] Footnote 8, p. 10.

[11] *Imran Javed Aziz v. Federation of Pakistan through Secretary, Ministry of Interior*, Writ Petition No. 753/2020, per Athar Minallah CJ.

[12] *Opuz v Turkey*, Application No. 33401/02, [2009] ECHR 870.

acceptable, never excusable, never tolerable."[13] These strong condemnations of GBV do not, however, appear to be reflected in the investigation, arrest, prosecution, and punishment of perpetrators of violence.

Findings by the UN indicate that, "[e]xperiences of complainants/survivors with court personnel in regular courts suggests that such personnel frequently do not have the necessary gender-sensitivity or comprehensive understanding of the various laws that apply to violence against women cases; may not be sensitive to women's human rights; and may be overburdened with other cases, resulting in delays and increased costs to the complainant. Specialized courts [...] have been effective in many instances as they provide a stronger possibility that court and judicial officials will be specialized and gender-sensitive regarding violence against women, and often include procedures to expedite cases [...]"[14]

B.   Fundamental Rights: Constitutional Rights Approach

The avoidance and prevention of violence constitute the basic purpose of law making. The rule is so fundamental that "if a legal system did not have them there would be no point in having any other rules at all."[15]

The Constitution of Pakistan entrenches several fundamental rights. The 'fundamental rights' theory posits that every person has basic rights that must be constitutionally protected by the courts, including the following:

> Article 8(1). Any law, or any custom or usage having the force of law, in so far as it is inconsistent with the rights conferred by this Chapter, shall, to the extent of such inconsistency, be void.

> Article 8(2). The State shall not make any law which takes away or abridges the rights so conferred and any law made in contravention of this clause shall, to the extent of such contravention, be void.

The Constitution of Pakistan has several critical articles that form the foundational understanding of the imperative to end GBV against women:

> Article 25.
>
> 1. All citizens are equal before law and are entitled to equal protection of the law.
> 2. There shall be no discrimination on the basis of sex.
> 3. Nothing in this Article shall prevent the State from making any special provision for the protection of women and children.[16]

> Article 9. No person shall be deprived of life or liberty save in accordance with the law.

[13]   United Nations Department of Public Information, News and Media Division. 2008. *Secretary-General Says Violence against Women Never Acceptable, Never Excusable, Never Tolerable, as He Launches Global Campaign on Issue*. Press Release. 25 February.

[14]   UN Department of Economic and Social Affairs. 2010. *Handbook for Legislation on Violence Against Women*. New York.

[15]   H.L.A. Hart. 1958. Positivism and the Separation of Law and Morals. *Harvard Law Review*. 71(4). pp. 593–629.

[16]   This exception does not detract from the gender equality principle and will be dealt with in Chapter 6.

Other fundamental rights include, but are not limited to, the right to property and protection of property rights (Article 23), freedom of speech (Article 19), freedom of movement (Article 15), right to education (Article 25A), and freedom from slavery (Article 11).

It has been assumed that constitutional matters are decided and applied only by superior courts and have no relation to the cases that come before the District and Sessions Courts. Faqir Hussain laid this assumption to rest when he said, "Constitutional rights are not only upheld and decided by superior courts. The District and Sessions Courts play a critical role in enforcing constitutional safeguards whether they be substantive or procedural safeguards. For example, due process, equal protection of the law, prohibition of torture."[17]

The existence of these fundamental rights indicates the fact that not only is GBV against women prohibited under statute, but it is also a matter of high constitutional concern. Superior courts and law commissions across the world have repeatedly emphasized the principle that GBV against women is a constitutional issue.

- *India: The State duty is not only to apprehend and punish but also to prevent GBV.*

  The Verma Committee was convened by the Government of India following a public outcry against the brutal rape and murder of a young woman in New Delhi.[18] The Committee concluded that, "[t]he right to be protected from sexual harassment and sexual assault is, therefore, guaranteed by the Constitution and is one of the pillars on which the very construct of gender justice stands. [...] Crimes against women are an egregious violation of several human rights demanding strict punishment with deterrence to prevent similar crimes in future by the likeminded."[19]

- *Kenya: Failure to conduct prompt, effective, proper, and professional investigations is in violation of the Constitution.*

  The petitioners in the '160 Girls' case sought to hold the Government of Kenya accountable for failure to prosecute sexual offenses.[20] The High Court at Meru found that the police "[failed] to conduct prompt, effective, proper and professional investigations... [and] infringed the petitioners' fundamental rights and freedoms under [...] the Constitution of Kenya 2010 and the general rules of international law" (footnote 20).

---

[17] F. Hussain. 2015. *The Role of District Judiciary in Protection of Human Rights*. Islamabad Federal Judicial Academy.

[18] Four of the rapists have since been convicted and sentenced. See *BBC News*. 2020. Profiles: Who Were the Delhi Gang Rape Convicts? 20 March.

[19] J.S. Verma, L. Seth, and G. Subramanium. 2013. *Report of the Committee on Amendments to Criminal Law*. pp. 2–3.

[20] *C.K. (A Child) through Ripples International as Her Guardian and Next Friend & Ors v. The Commissioner of Police/Inspector General of the National Police Service & Ors*, Petition No. 8 of 2012, High Court of Meru, [2012] eKLR. The case seeks, among other things (i) a declaration to the effect that the neglect, omission, refusal and/or failure of the police to conduct prompt, effective, proper and professional investigations into the petitioners' respective complaints violates the Universal Declaration of Human Rights, UN Convention on the Rights of the Child, African Charter on the Rights and Welfare of the Child, and African Charter on Human and People's Rights; and (ii) mandamus [that the respondents conduct prompt effective investigations and formulate a national policy framework in compliance with the Constitution on sexual offenses].

The High Court at Meru continued, "The respondent's ongoing failure [...] created a 'climate of impunity' for commission of sexual offences and in particular defilement. [...] This to me makes the respondents responsible [...] because of their laxity and their failure to take prompt and positive action to deter defilement" (footnote 20).

- *South Africa: The State has direct constitutional obligations to deal with domestic violence and protect every individual's right to be free from domestic (or private) violence.*

The State is under a series of constitutional mandates, which include the obligation to deal with domestic violence: "to protect both the rights of everyone to enjoy freedom and security of the person and to bodily and psychological integrity, and the right to have their dignity respected and protected, as well as the defensive rights of everyone not to be subjected to torture in any way and not to be treated or punished in a cruel, inhuman or degrading way."[21]

- *South Africa: The State is constitutionally obliged to afford citizens protection from violence.*

In *Suzette Irene Elmarie Nelson v The Minister of Safety and Security & Another*, the High Court of South Africa held that the "State is constitutionally obliged to afford its citizens protection from violence. Defendants' servants must fulfill not only constitutional duties but also statutory duties. Plaintiff is not liable as joint wrongdoer."[22]

Many of the national constitutions drawn up after the Second World War include similar provisions to those found in the Universal Declaration of Human Rights (UDHR) (1948). Consequently, the interpretations of fundamental rights under the Constitution and under human rights in international law can be mutually reinforcing.

C.   Human Rights Approach

Human rights is the idea that each individual has inherent inalienable and indivisible rights under the Constitution. Its foundational belief is that all human beings are equal.

The first article in the UDHR entrenches the equality in rights and dignity of all human beings. The second article specifically prohibits distinctions in rights based on race, color, sex, and other differences:

Article 1. All human beings are born free and equal in dignity and rights. They are endowed with reason and conscience and should act towards one another in a spirit of brotherhood.

Article 2. Everyone is entitled to all the rights and freedoms set forth in this Declaration, without distinction of any kind, such as race, colour, sex, language, religion, political or other opinion, national or social origin, property, birth or other status.

---

[21]   *S v Baloyi and Others*, 2000 (1) BCLR 86 (CC), per Sachs J.

[22]   *Suzette Irene Elmarie Nelson v The Minister of Safety and Security & Another*, [2006] ZANCHC 88.

These rights include the prohibition of discrimination against women.

In addition to the UDHR, the prohibition against gender discrimination and the right to gender equality is entrenched in the following international instruments:

(i)   International Covenant on Civil and Political Rights (ICCPR), Article 26;[23]

(ii)   International Covenant on Economic, Social and Cultural Rights (ICESCR), Article 2;[24] and

(iii)   Convention on the Elimination of All Forms of Discrimination against Women (CEDAW).[25]

The most detailed information can be found in CEDAW, which is the second most ratified/ acceded human rights convention in the world. It had 189 States Parties as of July 2021. The rights contained in CEDAW are regarded as fundamental human rights.

II.   Women's Human and Fundamental Rights

The rights entrenched in both the Pakistan constitution and international human rights are fundamental rights and human rights. As such, it allows women's lives and realities to be expounded through a gender lens. It also elevates women's rights as issues of fundamental and human rights.

Today, GBV against women is treated as a violation of women's human right and constitutes a form of discrimination against women, which is prohibited under international human rights. CEDAW further obligates States to protect women against violence of any kind occurring within the family, at the workplace, in the community or in any other area of social life.[26]

---

[23]   *International Covenant on Civil and Political Rights*, New York, 16 December 1966, United Nations Treaty Series, Vol. 999, No. 14668, p. 171. Art. 26 of the ICCPR states:
> All persons are equal before the law and are entitled without any discrimination to the equal protection of the law. In this respect, the law shall prohibit any discrimination and guarantee to all persons equal and effective protection against discrimination on any ground such as race, colour, sex, language, religion, political or other opinion, national or social origin, property, birth or other status.

[24]   *International Covenant on Economic, Social and Cultural Rights*, New York, 16 December 1966, United Nations Treaty Series, Vol. 993, No. 14531, p. 3. Art. 2 of the ICESCR states:
> 1. Each State Party to the present Covenant undertakes to take steps, individually and through international assistance and co-operation, especially economic and technical, to the maximum of its available resources, with a view to achieving progressively the full realization of the rights recognized in the present Covenant by all appropriate means, including particularly the adoption of legislative measures.
> 2. The States Parties to the present Covenant undertake to guarantee that the rights enunciated in the present Covenant will be exercised without discrimination of any kind as to race, colour, sex, language, religion, political or other opinion, national or social origin, property, birth or other status.
> 3. Developing countries, with due regard to human rights and their national economy, may determine to what extent they would guarantee the economic rights recognized in the present Covenant to non-nationals.

[25]   *Convention on the Elimination of All Forms of Discrimination against Women*, New York, 18 December 1979, United Nations Treaty Series, Vol. 1249, No. 20378, p. 13.

[26]   UN Committee on the Elimination of Discrimination against Women, *General Recommendation No. 12: Violence against Women*, Eighth Session (1989).

The CEDAW Committee (a committee of experts who assist in the interpretation and implementation of CEDAW) interprets GBV against women as discrimination within the meaning of Article 1 of CEDAW, which impairs or nullifies the enjoyment by women of human rights and fundamental freedoms under general international law or under human rights conventions.[27] In fact, violence against women is one of the most extreme and pervasive forms of discrimination against women, severely impairing and nullifying the enforcement of their rights.[28]

Yet, GBV against women was only formally recognized as part of the human rights agenda at the World Conference on Human Rights, held in Vienna, Austria in 1993. The Vienna Declaration and Programme of Action states that GBV against women includes cultural prejudices and sexual harassment, and called for the elimination of violence against women through legal action.[29] This has helped in systemically mainstreaming gender equality in the international system (footnote 29).

In 1996, Pakistan acceded to CEDAW with the following declaration and reservation:

> Declaration: "The accession by [the] Government of the Islamic Republic of Pakistan to the [said Convention] is subject to the provisions of the Constitution of the Islamic Republic of Pakistan."

> Reservation: "The Government of the Islamic Republic of Pakistan declares that it does not consider itself bound by paragraph 1 of [A]rticle 29 of the Convention."[30]

By ratifying or acceding to a treaty, the State agrees to be bound by the obligations provided in the treaty. The State also agrees to comply with the treaty's provisions in good faith. This is the principle of *pacta sunt servanda*, codified in Article 26 of the Vienna Convention on the Law of Treaties (VCLT).[31] In fact, in several instances, Pakistan courts have underscored Pakistan's obligations to comply with CEDAW.

---

[27] UN Committee on the Elimination of Discrimination against Women, *General Recommendation No. 19: Violence against Women*, Eleventh Session (1992); UN Committee on the Elimination of Discrimination against Women, *General Recommendation No. 35 on Gender-Based Violence against Women, Updating General Recommendation No. 19*, Sixty-seventh Session (2017); and UN Committee against Torture, *General Comment No. 2: Implementation of Article 2 by States Parties*, CAT/C/GC/2 (24 January 2008).

[28] *Jessica Lenahan (Gonzales) v. United States*, Case 12.626, Inter-American Commission on Human Rights, Report No. 80/11 (2011). para. 110. See also Articles 1 to 5 of CEDAW (footnote 25), which discuss the meaning of discrimination, both direct and indirect, substantive equality, and State obligations.

[29] *Vienna Declaration and Programme of Action*, Vienna, 25 June 1993. p. 7, para. 18.

[30] Art. 29(1) of CEDAW states:
Any dispute between two or more States Parties concerning the interpretation or application of the present Convention which is not settled by negotiation shall, at the request of one of them, be submitted to arbitration. If within six months from the date of the request for arbitration the parties are unable to agree on the organization of the arbitration, any one of those parties may refer the dispute to the International Court of Justice by request in conformity with the Statute of the Court.

[31] *Vienna Convention on the Law of Treaties*, Vienna, 23 May 1969, United Nations Treaty Series, Vol. 1155, No. 18232, p. 331. Note that Art. 18(1) of the VCLT clarifies that a state that has signed but not yet ratified a treaty is nonetheless obliged to refrain from acts that would defeat its object and purpose, until such state has made its intention clear not to become a party to such treaty.

History of the Convention on the Elimination of All Forms of Discrimination against Women and Pakistan's Role

CEDAW was born out of concerns by governments to address what they saw as customs and practices being inconsistent with the UDHR. Pakistan was one of the countries that requested the Commission on the Status of Women to draft a declaration on eliminating discrimination against women. Out of the 22 countries that did so, the majority were Muslim and countries from Africa and Asia. As such, the argument that CEDAW is a convention imposed on Muslim and Asian countries is inconsistent and without factual basis. Below is the historical timeline of CEDAW's adoption.

- 1954: The UN General Assembly called on governments to abolish laws, customs, and practices "inconsistent with the Universal Declaration of Human Rights."[32] The statement was pivotal to CEDAW.

- 1960s: States, experts, and civil society organizations began to advocate for a global concept of women's human rights under one instrument.

- 1963: Twenty-two countries requested the Commission on the Status of Women to draft a declaration on the elimination of all forms of discrimination against women, namely, Afghanistan, Algeria, Argentina, Austria, Cameroon, Chile, Colombia, Czechoslovakia, Gabon, Guinea, Indonesia, Iran, Mali, Mexico, Mongolia, Morocco, Pakistan, Panama, the Philippines, Poland, Togo, and Venezuela.[33]

- 1967: The UN General Assembly adopted the Declaration on the Elimination of Discrimination against Women on 7 November 1967.[34]

- 1979: The UN General Assembly adopted CEDAW.

State Obligations under the Convention on the Elimination of All Forms of Discrimination against Women

Article 2 of CEDAW specifically obligates the State to adopt a policy to eliminate all forms of discrimination against women by adopting appropriate legislative and other measures prohibiting discrimination against women to modify or abolish existing laws, regulations, customs, and practices which constitute discrimination against women. Article 5 further requires States to modify the social and cultural patterns of conduct of men and women, with a view to achieving the elimination of prejudices and customary and all other practices which are based on the idea of the inferiority or the superiority of either of the sexes or on stereotyped roles for men and women.

---

[32] General Assembly Resolution 843 (IX), *Status of Women in Private Law: Customs, Ancient Laws and Practices Affecting the Human Dignity of Women* (17 December 1954). In UN General Assembly, *Resolutions Adopted by the General Assembly during Its Ninth session from 21 September to 17 December 1954*, A/2890 (1955). p. 23.

[33] UN, General Assembly, Economic and Social Council, Third Committee, *Report of the Third Committee*, A/5606 (15 November 1963). paras. 65–69.

[34] General Assembly Resolution 2263 (XXII), *Declaration on the Elimination of Discrimination against Women*, A/RES/22/2263 (7 November 1967).

Article 2.

States Parties condemn discrimination against women in all its forms, agree to pursue by all appropriate means and without delay a policy of eliminating discrimination against women and, to this end, undertake:

(i)   To embody the principle of the equality of men and women in their national constitutions or other appropriate legislation if not yet incorporated therein and to ensure, through law and other appropriate means, the practical realization of this principle;

(ii)   To adopt appropriate legislative and other measures, including sanctions where appropriate, prohibiting all discrimination against women;

(iii)   To establish legal protection of the rights of women on an equal basis with men and to ensure through competent national tribunals and other public institutions the effective protection of women against any act of discrimination;

(iv)   To refrain from engaging in any act or practice of discrimination against women and to ensure that public authorities and institutions shall act in conformity with this obligation;

(v)   To take all appropriate measures to eliminate discrimination against women by any person, organization or enterprise;

(vi)   To take all appropriate measures, including legislation, to modify or abolish existing laws, regulations, customs and practices which constitute discrimination against women; [and]

(vii) To repeal all national penal provisions which constitute discrimination against women.

Article 5.

States Parties shall take all appropriate measures:

(i)   To modify the social and cultural patterns of conduct of men and women, with a view to achieving the elimination of prejudices and customary and all other practices which are based on the idea of the inferiority or the superiority of either of the sexes or on stereotyped roles for men and women; [and]

(ii)   To ensure that family education includes a proper understanding of maternity as a social function and the recognition of the common responsibility of men and women in the upbringing and development of their children, it being understood that the interest of the children is the primordial consideration in all cases.

CEDAW obligates States to protect women against GBV within the family, at the workplace, in the community or in any other area of social life. Additional specific areas of focus include women in political and public life, women's participation at the international level, nationality, education, employment, healthcare, economic and social benefits, rural women, equality before the law, and marriage and family life.[35]

---

[35]   Gender equality and gender discrimination will be dealt with in Chapter 6.

It is prudent at this juncture to point out that Pakistan's courts have referred favorably to Pakistan's obligation to respect and protect women's human rights as articulated in CEDAW.[36]

III. Cases from Pakistan That Applied International Law

Can Pakistan's courts draw on international law without a legislative instrument? Judicial precedents support accommodating international law even without its domestication through legislation provided they do not conflict with the existing laws.

- *M/s Najib Zarab Ltd v. The Government of Pakistan:* The issue before the Court was whether international law, of its own force and without the aid of municipal/domestic legislation, is applicable in Pakistan. The Court held, "[w]e are of the view that nations must march with the international community and the municipal law must respect rules of international law, even as nations respect international opinion; the community of nations requires that rules of international law may be accommodated in the municipal law even without express legislative sanction provided they do not run into conflict with the Acts of the Parliament."[37]

- *Mst Saima v. The State:* "The question whether petitioners Nos. 1 and 2 were committing an offence within the mischief clause of section 10 of Ordinance VII of 1979 would require a careful understanding of the penal provisions under the said law. [...] In the instant case petitioners Nos. 1 and 2 were of the view that they are validly married. Hence the condition precedent for the offence alleged prima facie does not exist. The Court is also conscious of the protection given to the marriage and the institutions of family under the Constitution of Islamic Republic of Pakistan and the U.N. Convention on Elimination of all Forms of Discrimination against Women. Article 35 of the Constitution enjoins the State to protect the marriage and the family. Article 16 of the Convention on the Elimination of all Forms of Discrimination against Women reads [...] 'States Parties shall take all appropriate measures to eliminate discrimination against women in all matters relating to marriage [...] and in particular shall ensure, on a basis of equality of men and women:-- (a) the same right to enter into marriage, (b) the same right freely to choose a spouse and to enter into marriage only with their free and full consent, (c) the same rights and responsibilities during marriage and at its dissolution.' For what has been discussed above, the prosecution launched against the petitioners prima facie reflects not only malice in fact but also malice in law."[38]

- *Humaira Mehmood v. The State:* In this case of *Zina* (adultery or illicit intercourse) filed by a father against his married daughter, the judge drew attention to CEDAW Article 16 on the right of women to family life on the basis of equality with men.[39]

---

[36] Common law has evolved in most common law countries to not requiring the legislature to promulgate legislation to adopt/domesticate international treaties before its applicability nationally. Cases from several jurisdictions are set out in this chapter.

[37] *M/s Najib Zarab Ltd v. The Government of Pakistan,* PLD 1993 Karachi 93.

[38] *Mst Saima v. The State,* PLD 2003 Lah. 747.

[39] *Humaira Mehmood v. The State,* PLD 1999 Lah 494.

- *Sarwar Jan v. Abdul Rahman:* In a divorce application by a wife on the basis of cruel and inhumane behavior of her husband toward her, the court referred approvingly to CEDAW and the Cairo Declaration of Human Rights.[40]

- *Suo Moto No. 1K of 2006:* In an application by a foreign husband for citizenship, the court drew on the Constitution, Islamic law, and international human rights law (i.e., UDHR, CEDAW, and the Convention on Nationality of Married Women).[41]

IV. Cases from Other Common Law Countries That Applied International Law

Bangladesh

- *Bangladesh National Women's Lawyers Association Vs. Government of Bangladesh & Ors:* "Our courts will not enforce those Covenants as treaties and conventions, even if ratified by the State, are not part of the *corpus juris* of the State unless those are incorporated in the municipal legislation. However, the court can look into these conventions and covenants as an aid to interpretation of the provisions of Part III, particularly to determine the rights implicit in the rights like the right to life and the right to liberty, but not enumerated in the Constitution."[42]

- The provisions of an international convention to which a country is a party, especially the one that declares universal fundamental rights, "may be used by the courts as a legitimate guide in developing the common law. But the courts should act with due circumspection when the Parliament itself has not seen fit to incorporate the provisions of a convention into our domestic law" (footnote 42).

India

- *Vishaka and Ors. v. State of Rajasthan and Ors.:* "Independence of the judiciary forms a part of our constitutional scheme. The international conventions and norms are to be read into them in the absence of enacted domestic law occupying the field when there is no inconsistency between them and there is a void in the domestic law."[43]

- *Mackinnon Mackenzie v. Audrey D'Costa and Another:* The Supreme Court of India interpreted a national legislation in conjunction with the International Labour Organization Convention No. 100 and European jurisprudential practice in the field. It found that Ms. D'Costa had received much lower pay than her male colleagues performing work of equal value. The fact that there was no man employed in the same job

---

[40] *Sarwar Jan v. Abdul Rahman*, NLR 2004 SD 129.

[41] *Suo Moto No. 1K of 2006*, PLD 2008 FSC 1.

[42] *Bangladesh National Women's Lawyers Association Vs. Government of Bangladesh & Ors*, Petition No. 5916 of 2008 (14 May 2009).

[43] *Vishaka and Ors. v. State of Rajasthan and Ors.*, (1997) 6 SCC 241.

in the company was irrelevant, since the principle of equal remuneration presupposed that the same level of pay be guaranteed not only to persons performing identical jobs but also to persons performing work that was different but was considered to be of equal value. The Supreme Court said, "Before dealing with the contentions of the parties, it is necessary to set out the relevant legal provisions governing the case. Article 39(d) of the Constitution of India provides that the State shall, in particular, direct its policy towards securing that there is equal pay for equal work for both men and women. The Convention concerning Equal Remuneration for Men and Women Workers for Work of Equal Value was adopted by the General Conference of the ILO on June 29, 1951. India is one of the parties to the said Convention."[44]

Australia

- *Minister for Immigration and Ethnic Affairs v Teoh:* The obligation under the Convention on the Rights of the Child (CRC) gave rise to the children having a legitimate expectation that their father's application would be treated in accordance with the terms of the CRC. "Where a statute or subordinate legislation is ambiguous, the courts should favour that construction which accords with Australia's obligations under a treaty. […] [T]he fact that the Convention has not been incorporated into Australian law does not mean that its ratification holds no significance for Australian law. Where a statute or subordinate legislation is ambiguous, the courts should favour that construction which accords with Australia's obligations under a treaty or international convention to which Australia is a party, at least in those cases in which the legislation is enacted after, or in contemplation of, entry into, or ratification of, the relevant international instrument. That is because Parliament, prima facie, intends to give effect to Australia's obligations under international law."[45]

Malaysia

- *Lee Lai Ching v Lim Hooi Teik:* In this case, the mother of a child applied to the Court to compel the defendant to undergo a DNA test for purposes of determining paternity, arguing that it was in the best interest of the child to know the identity of his biological father. The Court considered that international conventions and treaties to which Malaysia was signatory had been invoked by courts to resolve disputes when merited. The Court noted that paternity tests had been ordered in the Canada, France, Germany, Israel, the People's Republic of China, the United Kingdom, and the United States (US). The Court found Article 7 of the CRC, which states that a child had the right to know and be cared for by his or her parents, was in conformity with the Federal Constitution, national laws, and national policies of the Government of Malaysia, and therefore was applicable in this case.[46]

---

[44]   *Mackinnon Mackenzie v. Audrey D'Costa and Another,* (1987) 2 SCC 469.

[45]   *Minister for Immigration and Ethnic Affairs v Teoh* (1995) 183 CLR 273.

[46]   *Lee Lai Ching v Lim Hooi Teik,* Civil Suit No. 22-587 of 2004, 8 February 2013.

United Kingdom

- *R v Secretary of State for the Home Department, Ex Parte Daly:* In some of these countries, the courts have developed and proclaimed fundamental human rights to be inherent in the common law, without reference to parliamentary instruments. "[S]ome rights are inherent and fundamental to democratic civilized society. Conventions, constitutions, bills of rights and the like respond by recognising rather than creating them."[47]

V.   Access to Justice

With respect to GBV against women, the court has the following functions:

(i)   Protect the victim

(a)   In most jurisdictions, protection orders may only be issued by courts. In select countries, the police are empowered to order perpetrators to leave their houses and refrain from further violence against victims.[48] This can help diffuse the tension, aggression, or violence. Orders must also have a quick turnaround time.[49]

(b)   This includes allowing victims (and their children) an exclusive use of family assets (e.g., matrimonial home, car). Exclusive use ensures that perpetrators instead of victims (or their children) are punished for violence against women and the lives of other family members remain uninterrupted (e.g., children can stay at home and attend school as usual).

(c)   Address insensitive court procedures that unnecessarily re-traumatize victims during court hearings.

(ii)   Punish the perpetrators

(a)   Holding perpetrators accountable for violence against women is fundamental to the principle of punishment. It creates a level of predictability and certainty, suggesting that perpetrators will have to answer for violence against women (footnote 49).

(b)   Punishment must be commensurate with the severity of the offense and meet international standards. Punishment should be premised on GBV not being justifiable or excusable. Many States also include specific circumstances as aggravating factors for sentencing, such as severity of violence, relationship between perpetrators and victims (*loco parentis*, spouse), capacity of victims (minor), and recidivism of perpetrators.

(c)   Punishment should prevent recidivism, rehabilitate perpetrators, prepare them for reintegration, and deter others from committing similar offenses. Sentences that do not meet the goals of punishment foster recidivism and a sense of impunity, normalizing violence against women in a collective imagination (footnote 49).

---

[47]   *R v Secretary of State for the Home Department, Ex Parte Daly* [2001] UKHL 26.

[48]   For example, Australia and Austria.

[49]   Z. Abdul Aziz and J. Moussa. 2013, reprint 2016. *Due Diligence Framework: State Accountability Framework for Eliminating Violence against Women.* Penang.

(iii)   Provide redress and reparation

While punishment looks at action taken against the perpetrator, redress and reparation focus on the victim, in particular, to allow them to rebuild their lives. Unless the victims are able to rebuild their lives after the violence, they would be reluctant to seek the court's intervention. This is discussed in detail in Chapter 11.

(iv)   Prevent GBV against women

The law and the courts have tremendous, and to a large extent, untapped potential to eliminate GBV against women. In *Muhammad Siddique v. The State*, the Lahore High Court stated, "Law is a dynamic process. It has to be in tune with the ever-changing needs and values of a society. [...] [I]t is this dimension of law that makes it a catalyst of social change. [...] Law, including judge-made law has to play its role in changing the inhuman social mores."[50]

The Role of the Court in Enjoining What Is Good

The role of the law as the arbiter is to ensure that a woman's human rights are protected and that she is guaranteed her fundamental right to a life with dignity without violence.

Furthermore, efficacious implementation of the law sends the message that violence will not be tolerated, and perpetrators will be held accountable. In *Cooper v. Aaron*, a case in the US, the judge emphasized that "educational influences are exerted not only by explicit teaching. They vigorously flow from the fruitful exercise of the responsibility of those charged with political official power and from the almost unconsciously transforming actualities of living under law."[51] This in turn has the potential of deterring others from committing violence. Furthermore, the right to life is widely interpreted not solely as the right to be alive, but the right to live with dignity.

> " Let there arise out of you a band of people inviting to all that is good, enjoining what is right, and forbidding what is wrong: They are the ones to attain felicity.
>
> Al' Imran, verse 3:104, translation Yusuf Ali.

> " [T]hat whosoever killeth a human being for other than manslaughter or corruption in the earth, it shall be as if he had killed all mankind, and whosoever saveth the life of one, it shall be as if he had saved the life of all mankind.
>
> Al-Maidah, verse 5:32, translation Pickthall

---

50   *Muhammad Siddique v. The State*, PLD 2002 Lahore 444.
51   *Cooper v. Aaron*, 358 U.S. 1 (1958), per Frankfurter J. p. 25. This was a case about abolishing slavery in the US.

VI. Conclusory Remarks: Gender-Based Violence Courts

GBV is a complex issue. It has varied causes, its intersections reinforce the risks of violence, and its consequences are far-reaching. Jean Hampton states,

> When all women, regardless of their background, fear the threat of male violence (and modify their behavior so as to avoid it), this violence is not some private affair but a societal practice—with a point. [...] Where violence against women is common, every woman is victimized by the reality of this practice, insofar as where she lives, what she does, what activities she undertakes, and what her family life is like, are all affected either by the threat of such violence, or by the fact of it.[52]

Yet, men and women are partners, one protecting the other. Men and women, according to the Qur'an, are *awliya*. The term *awliya* means alliance, mutual assistance, and mutual reinforcement. This *wilayah* unites men and women, each as a protector of the other.

> " The Believers, men and women, are protectors; One of another: they enjoin what is just, and forbid what is evil: they observe regular prayers, practise regular charity, and obey God and His Apostle. On them will God pour His mercy: for God Is exalted in power, wise.
>
> At-Tauba 9:71, translation Yusuf Ali

This vision of men and women protecting one another fails when one in three women are affected by intimate partner violence (footnote 8). About 58% of all killings of women are committed by their family members. This makes the home the most dangerous place for women and families the most violent of peoples.

The first Gender-Based Violence Court (GBV Court) provides an avenue for discharging the duties as *awliya*, men and women, each protecting one another. The GBV Courts are special courts. The set-up of the GBV Court follows closely the procedures and guidelines set out by the Supreme Court under the *Salman Akram Raja v. Government of Punjab*,[53] as well as the provisions in the Criminal Procedure Code (CrPC), Pakistan Penal Code 1860 (PPC), and Qanun e-Shahadat Order 1984 (QSO).

The GBV Court adopts appropriate court procedures, efficient case management, and a conducive court environment. (The court's guidelines and practice notes, reproduced in the Appendixes, are more particularly discussed in Chapters 8–12.)

These courts are presided by specialized judges who are gender-sensitive and have comprehensive understanding of the various laws and of women's human rights. The GBV Courts also have specialized prosecutors.

---

[52] J. Hampton. 1998. Punishment, Feminism and Political Identity: A Case Study in the Expressive Meaning of the Law. *11 Can. J. L. & Juris*. 23.

[53] 2013 SCMR 203.

Humanitarian aid and women. Social and gender barriers exacerbate discrimination against women in relief camps and other humanitarian situations. Women and girls report a higher incidence of sexual harassment, sexual assault, domestic violence, sexual exploitation, and trafficking (photo by Gerhard Joren/ADB).

Chapter 2

BARRIERS TO WOMEN ACCESSING JUSTICE

I. Introduction

Pakistan ranks 151st out of 153 countries in terms of gender parity, which is the lowest in the South Asia region.[1] Over the last decade, Pakistan has regressed in all categories determining the global gender gap.[2] Access to justice is thus a far cry. Women continue to have little or no say in decision-making and be culturally denied their fair share of inheritance.[3]

Even with recent legislative amendments specifically responding to gender-based violence (GBV), there are still numerous hurdles toward achieving justice for women. Most women are unaware of their rights and those who are aware often lack support or face disapproval from family members in pursuing the justice system. Without family support and financial backing, many victims face serious difficulties in accessing the law. The deep-rooted patriarchal mindsets women have to face at every stage of the legal process are a further obstacle.

This chapter examines some of the obstacles to women reporting GBV and accessing justice. These barriers start at home and exist throughout the entire justice system.

II. Lack of Confidence in the Police and Judicial Process

The motorway rape case is a prime example of unending victim blaming. The head of investigation, the capital city police officer (CCPO) in Lahore, repeatedly blamed the victim, claiming, "She should not think she is in France...she should have checked the petrol. [...] [S]he should have taken GT road instead of [the] motorway."[4] These comments were met with public outcry (in some cities, protests continued for 3 days). Nonetheless, the CCPO demonstrated utter disregard for

---

[1] *Data Stories.* 2019. Gender Gap Index 2020: Pakistan Least Performer in South Asia. 25 December.

[2] World Economic Forum. 2019. *Global Gender Gap Report 2020*. Geneva. p. 277.

[3] S. Shaheen and K. Ali. 2017. *The Justice Prelude: A Socio-Legal Perspective on Women's Access to Justice.* Islamabad.

[4] A. Khan. 2020. Women in France. *Dawn.* 1 October.

the outrage and again blamed the victim during his senate report. He states, "She was travelling late at night without [her] husband's permission."[5] This attitude not only affects the victim, but women in general, demonstrating that reporting a case or approaching the police is likely to be the first hurdle. If a victim doesn't fall within acceptable norms, she is viewed as guilty until proven innocent of the crime of being a victim and deemed responsible for the perpetration of the crime against herself.

The victim initially refused to give evidence or proceed with the case, but she changed her mind after 21 days.[6] Her reluctance can be traced to the trauma of a woman continuously being blamed, her every action dissected and ascribed with guilt. This case grabbed public attention and the victim received rare public support in the midst of her trauma and the continuous criticism she faced from the head of investigation. It is however rare that such a case was picked up by the media. Most cases like this that are not picked up by the media are frequently abandoned.

The pictures below depict how a woman is often treated at the police station (Figure 2.1). She is treated with indifference and uncomfortable stares while she is alone, but when she is accompanied by a man, she generally receives more attentive treatment. Similar discrimination may occur at the judicial level.

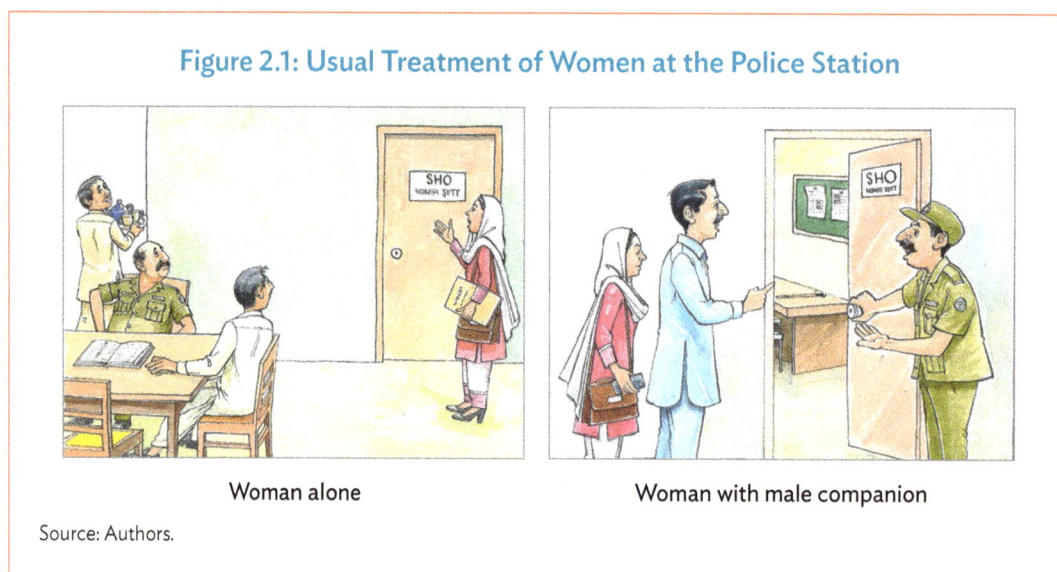

Figure 2.1: Usual Treatment of Women at the Police Station

Woman alone

Woman with male companion

Source: Authors.

Such deep-rooted patriarchal mindsets discourage reporting and deter women from approaching the police due to lack of confidence that they will be taken seriously.[7] According to War Against Rape, a nonprofit advocacy group, only a small proportion of cases are reported to the police due to the stigma surrounding rape and lack of empathy from the police.[8]

---

[5]   W. Satti and Web Desk. 2020. Lahore Motorway Rape CCPO Back in Hot Waters for Remarks in Senate Committee Hearing. *The News*. 28 September.

[6]   *The Express Tribune*. 2020. Gang Rape Victim Agrees to Give Statement. 30 September.

[7]   A. Pasha. 2020. Gendered Response to Policing in Pakistan. *The News*. 28 September.

[8]   S. Childress. 2013. The Stigma of Reporting a Rape in Pakistan. *Frontline*. 28 May.

III. Problematic Interpretation and Implementation of the Law

In the last decade and a half, legislation has been introduced to address GBV. This includes removing rape provisions from the Hudood Ordinance and bringing them under the Pakistan Penal Code (PPC). However, it takes much longer to change almost 3 decades of mindset that equated rape with *Zina* (adultery/illicit intercourse). Under the previous Hudood Ordinance provision, if a rape victim was unable to bring four witnesses to prove that she was raped, she would be accused of and imprisoned for *Zina*. Seldom, if ever, would a woman be raped in front of four righteous men. Consequently, rape victims have become frightened to report rape.

Furthermore, in a rape case, the victim is expected to report without delay, prove that she was conservatively dressed, and show marks and bruises as evidence that she had put up a fight. Though the law does not have similar demands, these social expectations create a mindset that makes it difficult for women to report and allows the perpetrator to escape punishment. Similarly, in honor-related cases, grave and sudden provocation is still being used even after several legal amendments. The perception is that men of the family (husband, father, uncle, brother, cousin, and even underaged male relatives) have the right to control women of the family. If a woman marries a man of her choice, sings at a wedding, texts a boy or takes a selfie, she could be killed by her relatives.[9] In a survey by the Pew Research Center in 2011, four out of 10 Pakistanis justified honor killings.[10] The laws have improved but the thinking has not. From the police to the judiciary, implementation of such laws is difficult and met with resistance and considerable obstacles.

A. Lack of Gender Understanding

Understanding of gender is essential for access to justice to become a reality for women. It is critical that both men and women serving in the legal process are gender-sensitized. More than half of investigation officers quizzed across Pakistan believed women are to blame for the violence perpetrated against them.[11] A news report states, "More than 62% of the investigation officers in the study acknowledged that they were not trained to investigate GBV cases. However, 66% of them recommended that women victims of violence should not visit police stations and resolve their complaints outside the police stations" (footnote 11).

It is similarly important that more women be inducted to bring gender equality in the country's justice system. Between 2014 and 2016, the Punjab Police reported that a crime was committed against a woman on average every 90 minutes.[12] Yet, only 6,899 of the 465,035 officers in the police force are women (less than 2%) (footnote 7). Similarly a very small percentage of the judiciary is female, and no female has ever been a member of the Supreme Court of Pakistan nor

---

9 M. Hanif. 2019. Pakistan: Where the Daily Slaughter of Women Barely Makes News. *The Guardian*. 9 May.

10 S. Thomson. 2016. 5,000 Women a Year are Still being Killed in the Name of 'Honour'. *World Economic Forum*. 22 July.

11 *The Express Tribune*. 2011. Most of Investigation Officers Blame Women for Violence against Them. 19 December.

12 Office of the Inspector General of Police, Punjab, as relayed to the Punjab Commission on the Status of Women (PCSW).

an attorney general of Pakistan. Of a total 113 judges on the high courts, only six are female, and out of 198 members of bar councils, only six are women.[13]

B.   Demystifying Gender and Sex and Gender Stereotyping

Gender sensitization is a process that requires each individual to think about how in their everyday lives they categorize or generalize about people based on whether they are male or female. This categorization is referred to as "gender stereotyping" of people. We tend to ascribe characteristics to people based on their gender due to preconceived beliefs about their gender, instead of who they are.

It is important to note that gender sensitization is not a war between the sexes nor an anti-male campaign. Both women and men can be victims of gender stereotyping which leads to discrimination or inequality. The reality is that both women and men can have difficulty gaining access to justice and both of them can benefit by considering why there are these gender differences and why it is important to redress them.

Gender sensitization requires a personal reflection on why these beliefs, myths, and views about men and women exist, where they come from, how these views are perpetuated, and what we can do to reduce and eventually eliminate gender stereotyping.

Gender sensitization is about the equal valuing of genders and respectful partnerships between genders in society. Gender equality recognizes the similarities and differences between women and men. The clear similarities of men and women are in terms of human features and the clear differences are biological. Research shows that men are more valued in society than women and that women are not treated equally with men.[14] Research also reveals that the overwhelming majority of women are victims of gender inequality and discrimination.[15] Hence, gender sensitization requires the application of a gender lens (Figure 2.2).

Sex of a Person

Sex identifies the biological differences between men and women. It is about the functional differences between women and men and their reproductive potential. It is determined by genes, and the terms men and women or male and female are biological terms. Sex is unchangeable (with rare exceptions).

Gender of a Person

Gender refers to the culturally or socially constructed roles ascribed to men and women. Gender is determined by our awareness and reaction to biological sex combined with cultural and

---

[13]   A.S. Khan. 2020. Feminisation of Law and Judiciary in Pakistan. *The Express Tribune*. 13 September.

[14]   E. Peck. 2016. The Main Reason Women Make Less Money than Men. *Huffpost*. 23 March.

[15]   K. Whiting. 2019. 7 Surprising and Outrageous Stats about Gender Inequality. *World Economic Forum*. 8 March.

Figure 2.2: Application of a Gender Lens

- Think of a gender lens as putting on spectacles.

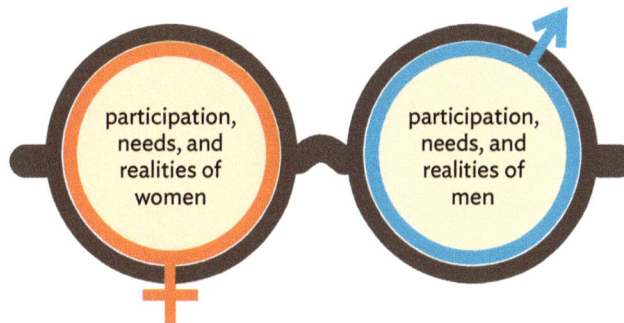

participation, needs, and realities of women

participation, needs, and realities of men

- Our sight or vision is the combination of what each eye sees.

Source: Authors.

sociological factors in society. Gender also identifies social relations between men and women. The terms masculine and feminine refer to gender, and not to the sex of a person. Because gender is a cultural and social construct, it can change over time.

Gender Stereotyping

As mentioned above, we tend to ascribe behaviors or characteristics to persons based on our preconceived beliefs or myths, simply because they are male or female, rather than who they are. This is referred to as gender stereotyping. What do you think about the list of some suggested traditional gender stereotypes in Table 2.1?

Sex and Gender Roles

Sex roles result from a person having certain biological functions depending on whether that person is male or female. For example, pregnancy is a female sex role because only female species may bear children. Sex roles are therefore limited to innate biology.

Gender roles result from learned behaviors that condition us to regard certain activities and responsibilities as being appropriate for male or female. For example, women are regarded as nurturing, and as a result, they are expected to perform the role of looking after the home. Men are regarded as assertive and responsible and told they should be breadwinners. We therefore apply generalized characteristics to women and men which result in women and men taking on certain roles in society. But not all women are nurturing. Even if a particular woman is nurturing, it does not mean that she should stay at home or look after the children. Similarly, not all men are assertive, and even if a particular man is assertive, that does not mean he is capable of certain work. In short, gender roles are very limiting for both men and women. They lock men and women into predetermined life and work roles without any regard of their real aptitudes and qualities (Table 2.2).

Table 2.1: Traditional Gender Stereotypes

Feminine	Masculine
Weak, frail	Strong
Obliging, amiable	Ambitious
Passive	Active, aggressive
Dependent	Independent
Easily influenced, impressionable, susceptible to pressure	Not easily influenced
Submissive, docile, meek	Dominant, forceful
Feeble	Dynamic
Emotional	Logical, analytical
Home-oriented	Worldly
Sensitive, easily hurt	Stoic, not easily hurt emotionally
Indecisive, fickle	Decisive
Talkative, chatty	Reticent
Sensitive to other's feelings	Less attentive to other's feelings
Security conscious, risk-adversed	Not security conscious, risk-taker
Cries easily	Rarely cries
Nurturing, loving, devoted	Not nurturing, tough
Tactful, considerate, accommodating	Blunt, inconsiderate

Source: Authors.

Table 2.2: Gender Stereotypes and Gender Roles

Sex	Gender Stereotype	Gender Role
Woman	Women are home-oriented, caring, passive, and obedient in taking orders.	She will make a good nurse or secretary (female gender role).
Woman	Women are indecisive, emotional, easily influenced, and incapable of leadership.	She will not be suitable to take up training for a managerial role.
Married Woman	Married women are unable to work in a full-time job (as they would have to care and cook for their husband and children).	She would not get promoted to a manager's role based on a gender stereotype, which in fact may not apply to her situation. If she were a man, this would not even be considered as relevant to the job promotion as this assumption does not apply to a man who is married and have children.

Source: Authors.

C. Lack of Sensitivity to Gender-Based Violence

At an institutional level, the same mindset prevails. Generally, there is a lack of gender sensitivity and responsiveness at various levels. An enabling environment where women can access justice is also nonexistent. The motorway rape incident and the police chief response is an example of this mindset. It is a classic example of victim shaming.[16]

In April 2016, a Muzaffargarh woman reportedly claimed that the local police threatened to kill her and implicate her family in forged cases after she filed a gang rape case against her employer and a police officer. This woman threatened to burn herself alive in front of the district police office if she were denied of justice.[17]

In situations where women do reach out for legal recourse, they are faced with several impediments. Social norms and the culturally constructed concept of 'honor' prevent women from getting justice. Recently, a District and Sessions Court granted bail to a suspect after the court allowed the solemnization of the marriage in court between the accused and the victim whom he had allegedly sexually assaulted for months.[18]

There is a lack of trust in the institutions. It is considered taboo to expose private matters to investigation in public spaces. Private matters related to women are supposed to stay within the four walls of a home. Another reason is the lack of sensitivity while responding to crimes related to violence against women. A woman's character and morality are questioned when she seeks legal recourse. It is the victim who ends up being blamed.[19]

Rape victims sometimes resort to suicide, fearing the lifelong stigma of being a rape victim. In Bet Mir Hazar in Punjab's Muzaffargarh district, an 18-year-old girl reportedly set herself on fire outside a police station in 2014. Another woman set herself ablaze in front of the police station a few months later. This was followed by a 35-year-old woman reportedly setting herself on fire in front of a police station in Sheikhupura. In 2016, another woman in Shujabad, Multan tried to commit suicide. All these women were rape victims (footnote 17).

In 2002, the gang rape of Mukhtaran Mai came to light when she reached out for help instead of committing suicide, as is the fate of many rape victims. She fought a lengthy legal battle where in 2011 five of the six men charged with raping her were acquitted because of lack of evidence.[20]

A deep-rooted and highly institutionalized injustice driven by cultural and social norms can be observed when it comes to incidents of violence against women. As seen in Mukhtaran Mai's case, justice is a scarce commodity, especially in the rural areas. The majority of the rural population lacks access to official judicial structures. All male tribal councils—*Jirgas* and *Panchayats*—end

---

[16] *BBC News.* 2020. Pakistan Outcry over Police Victim-Blaming of Gang-Raped Mother. 19 September; and *The Express Tribune.* 2020. Lahore CCPO Apologises for Controversial Remarks Blaming Motorway Gang-Rape Survivor. 14 September.

[17] H. Abbas. 2018. Rape, Murder and Domestic Violence Cases Top List of VAW Crimes Reported in Punjab. *Media for Transparency.* 22 January.

[18] *The Express Tribune.* 2020. Man Granted Bail after Marrying Woman He Sexually Assaulted for Months. 24 September.

[19] *Naya Daur.* 2020. Police Official Called for Help Rapes Girl in Gujranwala. 21 September.

[20] *BBC News.* 2020. Pakistan Outcry over Police Victim-Blaming of Gang-Raped Mother. 19 September.

up deciding the future of women victims of violence. Decisions are based on local traditions, norms, and concepts of honor. For example, Mukhtaran Mai was ordered to be gang raped by the local tribal council in the name of restoring honor and as a form of punishment for her brother's alleged trespass.[21] Mukhtaran Mai's case is a case where the tribal council became a perpetrator, abusing its power and seeking retribution.

D. Understanding Unconscious and Implicit Bias

As humans, we make instinctive decisions about people. Scientific evidence and the work of psychologists reveal that our unconscious preferences or biases affect how we make decisions. Our brains are hardwired to rapidly categorize people instinctively using obvious and visible categories, such as gender, age, size, physical attractiveness, disability, accent, social background, social orientation, nationality, religion, education, and even a job title. As a result, we assign a whole suite of characteristics, both good and bad, to people. For instance, when we see a foreigner, we get surprised if the foreigner speaks fluent Urdu and turns out to love local cuisine. Similarly, we tend to be more confident of someone dressed in a certain way or educated from a certain institution.

Judges perceive themselves as being fair and independent of bias. Yet, judges, like everyone else, may assign people into various categories separated by accessible traits, such as age, gender, and race. Without being conscious of potential blind spots, judges can be vulnerable to making decisions that may be influenced by bias. Research reveals that humans have the instinct to value, support, and defend those who are mostly like ourselves. We cannot process everything about every new person we meet, instead we make rapid judgments about them. This comes from experiences with other people. Judges need to unpack their attitudes about people and cultural values so as to better and more fairly assess what is real and what is biased.

IV. Risk Factors for Judges

A. Emotional States

Certain emotional states such as anger or disgust can increase the risk of implicit bias in making decisions. This may be due to personal matters about domestic issues, arguments, illness, or worry. Or they could arise during a court hearing due to anger or exasperation about counsel, witnesses, staff, or

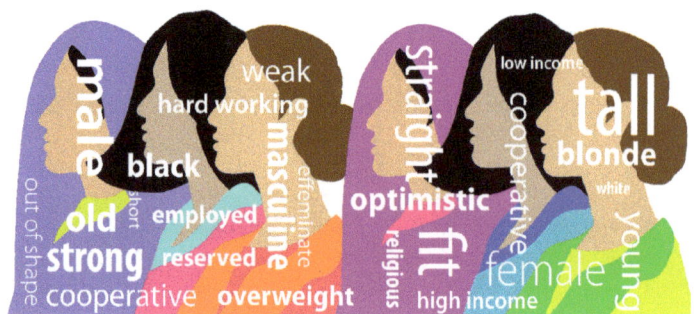

---

[21]   T. Karkera. 2006. The Gang-Rape of Mukhtar Mai and Pakistan's Opportunity to Regain Its Lost Honor. *Journal of Gender, Social Policy & the Law*. 14 (1).

other court matters. We all know, as a matter of our common experience, that thinking and making decisions when we are angry, upset, or in similar high emotional states, does not allow us to think and analyze situations clearly. These emotional states increase the risk that we oversimplify and generalize and fall back on stereotypes and biases.

B.   Ambiguity

When the basis for a judgment is somewhat vague such as the exercise of discretion or when it involves applying new or unfamiliar laws, the risk of unconscious bias is greater. An example is when judges exercise discretion in matters such as deciding on the credibility of consent in rape, or such as when sentencing. Moreover, when judges are required to apply new laws or laws with which they are not familiar, the process can be more difficult and challenging. It is easy to fall back and apply familiar views or experiences, and stay in the comfort zone, which may bring in biases or stereotypes. Judges in Pakistan will need to start applying some of the new pro-women legislation, which will require special attention to these issues.

C.   Distracted or Pressured Decision-Making Circumstances

Judicial work can be tiring with long hours, fatigue, and heavy or diverse caseloads. This is a very common factor in all jurisdictions, but more so in some than others. Jurisdictions with high-pressure and heavy caseloads can result in time pressure that can force a judge into performing complex judgments relatively quickly. Furthermore, hearings are sometimes conducted in busy or noisy conditions. Distractions can result in a judge not being fully attentive to incoming information.

D.   Low-Effort Processing

Pressured circumstances may lead a judge to engage in "low-effort" processing or reasoning. Low-effort processing refers to reasoning that happens when a judge knows they have to reach a decision quickly and get on with the case. They wish to reach a settled view on the witnesses and facts as speedily as possible and this may mean that they do not go through a full evaluation process of conflicts and nuances in the evidence. When this happens, the judge tends to form early views and develop inferences or expectations about a witness early on in the case. If the low-effort reasoning is not addressed, this can affect the approach of the judge to subsequent information and increase the risk of biased assessments and judgments.

E.   How Can Judges Reduce Unconscious Bias

The basic techniques recommended to reduce unconscious bias are as follows:

(i)   Take notes so that you are not forced to rely on memory, particularly if the transcript is not available for you to reflect on what occurred in a court.

(ii)   Set out the reasoning behind your decision as this process gives a chance to review the evidence with a critical eye before giving your decision.

(iii) When you have concerns about matters of interpretation or approaches, seek feedback from other judges for whom you have respect as being fair and independent.

(iv) Regularly engage in training sessions to consider hypothetical cases that raise stereotype issues. This is particularly useful for sentencing remarks.

In summary, judges need to question their own assumptions and beliefs, be aware of the risks of unconscious bias, and slow down their decision-making process as best as they can.

V.   Social Barriers

At the societal level, discrimination based on gender starts the day a girl is born. The preference for sons is so entrenched that it translates into differential treatment of boys and girls by their own parents, resulting in poorer nutritional health and educational care of girls. This leads to disproportionately higher mortality among girls than boys.[22]

> *Day halaq zairey khog wee, dhroon ee Kanree bootee pe khoshalla ee.*
>
> The news of the birth of a boy is sweet. Even nature celebrates it.
>
> A Pushtu proverb

The discrimination leads to extreme forms of violations against girls who are considered a financial and social burden. In 2017, the Edhi Foundation received 14 unwanted babies/children. Twelve out of 14 were girls and the remaining two boys were physically challenged. Under Section 329 of the PPC, burying or disposing of the dead body of a child before, after or during birth, as well as endeavors to conceal the birth, is a punishable offense. However, as with many other crimes, these are rarely reported.[23]

Son preference means that girls end up receiving less nutrition, opportunities, and rights as compared to boys. A girl's basic dignity and status as a human being, irrespective of gender, remains unacknowledged. It is a reflection of the persisting inequality between men and women. Such inequalities and discrimination will continue to prevent women from accessing justice unless it is eliminated.

Social Norms, Culture, and Honor

In the rural areas, it is common to see little girls carrying and cajoling their baby brothers on their tiny bodies, making sure they do not fall on the rugged ground where they themselves stand barefooted. From childhood, girls are expected to hand their brothers the better portion

---

[22]   Z.A. Sathar et al. 2015. *Evidence of Son Preference and Resulting Demographic and Health Outcomes in Pakistan.* Islamabad.

[23]   F. Duranni. 2018. Karachi Becoming a Killing Field for Newborn Girls. *The News.* 26 April.

of meat. As adults, this social conditioning pushes them to waive off her portion of inheritance to a brother. As she grows, she is expected to join the silent band of women, who spend their lives upholding honor by preserving and protecting it through sacrifice, irrespective of the consequences. Women are seen as an embodiment of honor—honor that must be protected and preserved, at any cost.

Avoiding societal scorn and taunts, referred to as *pighore*, is important in Pashtun culture, particularly if it is in relation to transgressions of the unwritten social norms known as *Pakhtu*. These transgressions are considered dishonorable behavior. *Pighore*, says tribal chief Bilal Malak, is like "a slap on the face."[24] Communal decreed *pighore* not only is an attack on one's honor, it can bring about negative economic and social consequences such as loss of economic support and social isolation. These consequences have been known to be so severe, that generations of a family that have transgressed these social norms were unable to return to their village.

Like most cultures, women are expected to be the bearer of family honor. Boys who 'disgrace' their families (for example by acting out) are treated less severely than girls who 'disgrace' their families. Consequently, women and girls pay the heaviest price, including with their lives. Minallah (2013) writes:

> Amidst the graves at an old cemetery of Nawagai is Memunai's grave; she was killed by her husband in the name of 'honor' despite knowing she was innocent. Today, this story of Memunai, who spent her life fighting to restore 'honor' is told as a legend, glorified by poets, and rendered by singers in public vehicles, shops, and *hujras* (traditional meeting area of men) (footnote 24).

> " *Chay nan spak shay, saba ba rowak shee*
>
> Whoever is dishonored today, tomorrow he shall perish.
>
> A famous proverb

Similarly, in the graves of the Jagiranis (Jagiranin jo Kabrustan) in Jummo Aghan, Larkana, men have buried their 'threat to honor' under heaps of mud. Jafri (2008) explains, "*Taana zani* is analogous to the 'buttons' close relatives and friends push to 'drive us up the wall.'"[25] In the local communicative milieu, *taana* is a scorn with sarcasm. These expressions can deny an individual or a community honor. Jafri continues, "[S]ocial pressure on the individual from within the group is the driving force for the act of ['honor'] killing itself."[26] These men have buried their wives, daughters, or sisters in this graveyard in the name of 'honor' to prevent themselves from the being subjected to *taano* or taunts.[27]

---

[24] S. Minallah. 2013. A Threat to Honour. *Newsline Magazine*. June.

[25] A. Jafri. 2008. *Honor Killing: Dilemma, Ritual, Understanding*. Oxford and New York: Oxford University Press. p. 78.

[26] Footnote 25, referencing N. Shah. 1998. Honor Killing. *Dawn*. 19 November.

[27] A. Bhutto. 2019. Graveyard of Honour. *Newsline Magazine*. April.

VI. Types of Culturally Sanctioned Crimes against Women

A. Honor Killings

According to a report compiled by the Sind Police, around 108 women were killed in the name of 'honor' between 31 January 2019 and 30 January 2020.[28] In 'honor' crimes, the police and the entire legal system stand on the sidelines while these crimes are committed on a daily basis. A woman's actions, behavior, and chastity are valued higher than her existence in a society. Any deviance is seen as a crime against a family, clan, or community. Many incidents of murder take place on the basis of mere suspicion. Even if they know that a woman may be innocent, the male members prefer to kill her in order to seek society's approval. Referring to such killings, it is commonly said, "*Zyatee da, kho rawaj dae*" (It is unfair but after all it is our custom).

One such tragic tale is that of Zahida Bibi. Zahida was washing clothes by a stream. A man, Saz Din stopped by and assaulted her, in the process, tearing her dress as she escaped. Despite having escaped, Zahida knew that she would be blamed and made to bear the stigma of having been tainted under *rawaj* (custom). At home, having narrated the incident to her family, she accepted that her life would be forfeited for the dishonor and shame that the incident had brought her family. Minallah (2013) juxtaposes Zahida's killing with the lack of accountability demanded from the culprit:

> Zahida Bibi was led out into the courtyard and there, under a mulberry tree, shot dead by her husband. The actual culprit, Saz Din, who has a certain standing in society, still roams about unharmed (footnote 24).

B. Domestic Violence

Cultural violence against women is considered a private matter and women are expected to remain silent. Around 9% of all 23,189 reported crimes by the Punjab police between January 2014 and June 2017 were beatings in the form of domestic violence (footnote 17). When such crimes end up with the police, officers refrain from filing a proper first information report (FIR). According to Fauzia Viqar, former Chairperson of Punjab Commission on the Status of Women (PCSW), the police resorts to a 'katchi' (incomplete literally 'half-baked') FIR (footnote 17). Incomplete FIRs prevent the police from investigating the case. In 80% of the domestic abuse complaints received on the PCSW helpline, women wanted the husbands only to be warned but not otherwise punished (footnote 17).

---

[28] I. Ali. 2020. 108 Women in Sindh 'Killed for Honour' in 2019 Alone: Police Report. *Dawn*. 31 January.

C. Bride Price, *Sarpaisa, Watta Satta*

Sarpaisa (bride price) is a form of trafficking wherein the groom, "in order to marry, pays a large sum of money to the girl's parents."[29] Minallah (2003) describes how the objectification of the bride is directly tied to her family's honor:

> A bride price transforms a woman into an object of economic value, devoid of emotions or feelings. This living, breathing object of value can actually be sold and resold for a higher price—without a family's 'honor' being at stake. In fact, the higher her value, the more 'honor' her family gains (footnote 29).

A wife can be juggled by her husband to another man for a higher price. In the case of Maimoona, she was first married to her cousin at a bride price of PRs50,000. Her husband received an offer of PRs150,000 for Maimoona, which he unilaterally accepted.

In another case, Niyaz Khela, now in her late fifties, was married to a much older man for PRs5,000 when she was in her teens. Her husband used to beat her mercilessly. Unable to bear the beatings, she eloped with another man. The couple went into hiding for 2 years until her husband had saved enough money to pay the ex-husband PRs10,000. Payment of the bride price allowed him to regain his honor as he had made a financial gain from the loss of his wife.

> In Karak, a married woman has a higher price in the market because her ex-husband, if alive, has to be compensated for his financial loss. Unless he is given a higher price than what he had initially paid for the woman, he is subject to *pighore* (taunt suggesting inability to behave 'honorably') from the community.

> If money is not paid as compensation, the male perpetrator is usually killed and the woman sent back to the parents, who [will] try once again to marry her off. The money they receive from her second marriage [will be] paid to her ex-husband.

> [...] Therefore honour, in this context, is linked more to wealth than to one's moral behaviour.[30]

Bride price is practiced with little variance, as *Addo Bado* in Sindh and *Watta Satta* in Punjab. *Watta Satta* is an exchange marriage where brides are exchanged between two families. This too is considered as a form of strengthening the bond between two families, as it involves mostly endogamous marriages of blood relatives, or persons from the same caste or clan.

D. Compensation and Child Marriages

Very often, whenever there is a murder or a dispute, girls are given as compensation to the aggrieved party as reparation for the crimes committed by their male relatives. This is known

---

[29] S. Minallah. 2003. Brides for Sale. *Newsline Magazine*. November.

[30] Footnote 29. Minallah also underscores the cyclical nature of this practice—at the time the article was published, Niyaz Khela was working as a laborer to pay for the bride of her older son. Her one daughter was given to another family in exchange for their daughter, a bride for Niyaz's younger son.

> *Khowenday chay keenee, Roonra Staee Roonra Chay keenee, Khowenday swaray kay warkaweena*
>
> When sisters come together, they praise their brothers. When brothers meet, they give their sisters away as Swara!
>
> A verse from a Pushtu wedding song

as *Swara*. The murderer gets away with his crime and one or more girls have to pay the price of the crime for the rest of their lives.

Likewise, child marriage is still prevalent in Pakistan. Estimates vary—while the United Nations Children's Fund (UNICEF) estimates that that one in five girls are married before the age of 18, the United Nations Population Fund has that figure as one in three.[31] In any event, both are perceived as conservative estimates (footnote 31).

Compensation and child marriages are discussed in detail in Chapter 5.

VII. Delayed Reporting or Non-Reporting

It is believed that like all other crimes, rape and other gender-based violence (GBV) cases are reported immediately. Realistically, this is not so, as victims of GBV crimes, and especially rape, are afraid of facing stigma. The victim, instead of receiving support or empathy, generally faces victim blaming which only deters them from reporting. This phenomenon takes place across cultures and classes. It is easy to report a dacoity or a murder case, but not a sexual assault or rape case. Nazish Brohi, an eminent lawyer, very aptly stated at the Women's Action Forum conference that most of the women who are raped or assaulted were afraid to disclose even to friends or family due to the stigma attached to rape, let alone reporting to police.[32]

Reporting also depends on who the rapist is—whether it is an enemy, stranger, or someone the woman knows. It is difficult to report when the rapist is someone known to the family or part of the family, or when the rapist is politically connected or powerful. Consequently, the victim feels threatened and will not report the incident (footnote 32). In case a woman and her family find the courage to report the case, the case may continue for years. All this will deter reporting or pursuing the case (footnote 32). For a large number of women, the cost of reporting and following a case is very high and majority of them are financially dependent on the men of the family and are not the decision makers. Reporting and pursuing a case will be dependent on male family members deciding the matter.

Another reason why the victim and the family are discouraged from reporting is the low conviction rate. Conviction rate for rape cases is less than 3%, according to Karachi-based organization War Against Rape.[33] The low conviction rate discourages most of the victims from reporting knowing very well that there is a 97% chance that the perpetrator will go scot-free and might take revenge

---

[31] Society for the Protection of the Rights of the Child. 2018. *The State of Pakistan's Children: Introduction and Overview of Child Rights*. p. 13.

[32] M. Maher. 2019. This is Why Women Won't Report Rape in Pakistan. *SAMAA*. 16 June.

[33] *Global Village Space*. 2020. Conviction Rate in Rape Cases under 3% in Pakistan: Report. 15 September.

against the victim filing the case. With no actual protection given to a victim, their families often pressure them to keep it under cover. According to Brohi, the rich usually do not report and do not rely on the existing investigative and judicial system; instead they simply take the law in their own hands, and the institutions and systems are bypassed (footnote 32). The "onus to change the state," according to Brohi, falls entirely on the lower-middle class which is not capable of bringing the required change (footnote 32).

Many women are also hesitant to report because they are uncomfortable and embarrassed of the insensitive treatment they anticipate by doctors or law enforcement personnel, and of the cross-examination by defense lawyers. In general, stereotyping exists during evidence collection. For instance, the victim will get more sympathetic favorable response if "she arrived promptly, in a wretched state, confused and not normal, [and] bruised;" the lack of bruises and marks would go against her.[34] In reality, women will usually not be prompt in reporting and would come when they are a bit stable. To encourage victims to report, it is important to change the mindset and attitude of the police and the judiciary.

A. Coercion and Resiling and Fear of Retribution

In a large number of cases, the victim resiles from the case due to coercion and threat by the accused, or compromise between the victim's family and the accused (see Chapter 12 on Resiling and Attrition). These compromises take place even in cases where such compromises are forbidden under the law (such as rape and crimes committed under the pretext of honor).

B. A Horrific Example of Coercion in a Rape Case

In 2013, a 2-year old daughter of a rape victim was axed to death by an alleged rapist in revenge for filing a case against him. The husband of the victim refused to withdraw the case and the rapist along with five accomplices killed the rape victim's daughter.[35]

There is absolutely no protection of the victim, and in the above case, of her family. The system has failed women at all stages; even when she and her family had been courageous enough to file the case and carry it forward, no support was provided to protect her and her family.

C. Autonomy, Mobility, Financial Resources, Shelter, Interim Maintenance, and Housing

Women comprise approximately half of the population in Pakistan but make up only 9%–26% of the formal labor force.[36] Women who do work are mostly underpaid and in the informal sector and vulnerable employments (footnote 36). "Ownership of house or land is an essential

---

[34] M.B. Langrial. Laws against Rape in Pakistan. *Human Rights Review.*

[35] *Pakistan Press Foundation.* 2013. Infant Murdered for Father's Refusal to Withdraw Rape Case. 9 February.

[36] Y. Zaidi and S. Farooq. 2016. *Women's Economic Participation and Empowerment in Pakistan: Status Report 2016.* Islamabad: UN Women. p. 18.

component of economic empowerment of women, however, only 2% of women in Pakistan own a land or a house."[37] "Only 13% of women have access to loans as compared to 87% of men."[38]

Under these circumstances, women have very little financial resources and autonomy of decision-making. Reliance is on male family members to decide whether to report a case or not. Due to the stigma attached to such incidents culturally, most male members are hesitant to report cases and spend money, and women have no or little access to legal aid to report and follow up the case.

Similarly, there are a few women shelters in the cities and hardly any in rural and remote areas of Pakistan where the prevalence of GBV is high but not reported due to lack of resources and protection. There is a need to set up safe and adequate shelter homes and women hostels, especially for women who face domestic violence or other issues, which would require a victim to separate herself from her family.

VIII. Conclusory Remarks

There are certain actions and steps that can be taken immediately, and other short-term, medium-term, and long-term measures that can be implemented subsequently. The GBV Courts are set up to make the complainant feel protected and able to speak the truth without fear. Similarly, police stations should provide an environment where the complainant is able to access justice on their own. In the short to medium term, the existing amendments to the PPC and Criminal Procedure Code (CrPC) must be implemented to provide protection for witnesses and shelter for the complainant. In the long run, it is expected that the judicial and prosecutorial training curriculum is reviewed and amended to make it more gender-friendly. The concerned authorities should also be trained regularly.

---

[37]   Footnote 36, pp. 42, 47.
[38]   Footnote 36, p. 43.

Mother and children in Sindh, Pakistan. Sindh was the first province in Pakistan to pass a domestic violence law, the Sindh Domestic Violence (Prevention and Protection) Act, 2013 (photo by Syed Muhammad Rafiq/ADB).

Establishing safe public spaces. Gender-based violence in public spaces—such as rape, sexual remarks, and touching—restricts the freedom of movement of women and girls and their right to participate in their community (photo by Madiha Aijaz/ADB).

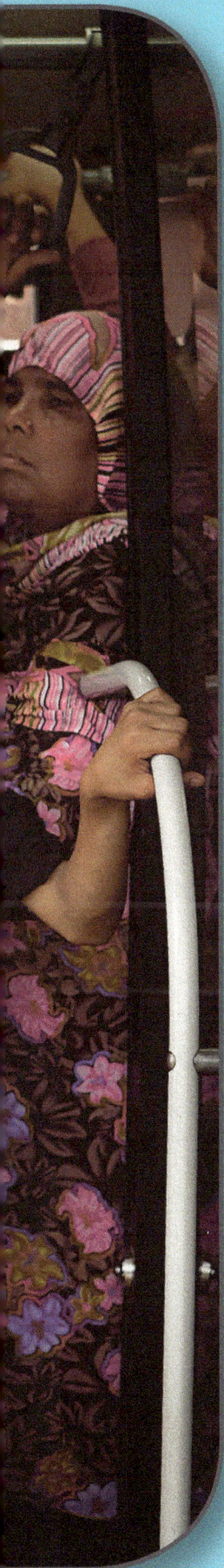

Chapter 3

UNDERSTANDING GENDER-BASED VIOLENCE AGAINST WOMEN

I. Introduction

While both men and women suffer violence, the way they experience violence is vastly different, as is the way violence is experienced by transgender individuals. World Health Organization (WHO) data reveals that **31% of women (or one in every three women) aged 15–49 have been subjected to physical and/or sexual violence from a current or former husband or intimate partner, or sexual violence from a non-partner, or both in their lifetime.**[1] Twenty-seven percent of women aged 15–49 who have been in a relationship report that they have experienced violence by their intimate partner.[2] In South Asia, this figure has risen to 35%.[3] Another study in Asia and the Pacific shows that 58% of all killings of women were committed by family members.[4] This makes the home the most dangerous place for women.

Similarly, both men and women are killed in the name of *ghairat* (honor). The Pakistan Human Rights Commission recorded 1,096 female victims and 88 male victims of honor crimes in 2015.[5] The female victims vastly outnumber the male victims. Similarly, victims of domestic violence, sexual harassment, *Swara* (giving of girls in marriage to settle disputes), and sexual assault are predominantly women.

---

[1] WHO, on behalf of the United Nations Inter-Agency Working Group on Violence against Women Estimation and Data (VAW-IAWGED). 2021. *Violence against Women Prevalence Estimates, 2018: Global, Regional and National Prevalence Estimates for Intimate Partner Violence against Women and Global and Regional Prevalence Estimates for Non-Partner Sexual Violence against Women.* Geneva.

[2] Footnote 1, p. 37.

[3] Footnote 1, p. 76.

[4] E. Fulu et al. 2013. *Why Do Some Men Use Violence against Women and How Can We Prevent It: Quantitative Findings from a United Nations Multi-Country Study on Men and Violence in Asia and the Pacific.* Bangkok: UNDP, et al.

[5] M.S. Rafique. 2017. Gender-Based Violence in Pakistan. *International Development Journal.* 29 January.

II.   What Is Gender-Based Violence?

Gender-based violence (GBV) against women is violence directed at a woman because she is a woman or that affects women disproportionately. Violence against women is an act of GBV "that results in, or is likely to result in, physical, sexual, psychological or economic harm or suffering to women, including threats of such acts, coercion or arbitrary deprivation of liberty, whether occurring in public or in private life."[6]

Violence against women has evolved over time to reflect discourses on structural violence and understanding of gender inequality and gendered power imbalances within cultures and society. A broad and nuanced definition of violence against women is necessary to address the causes. Generally, GBV can be divided into three categories (with overlaps) (Figure 3.1):

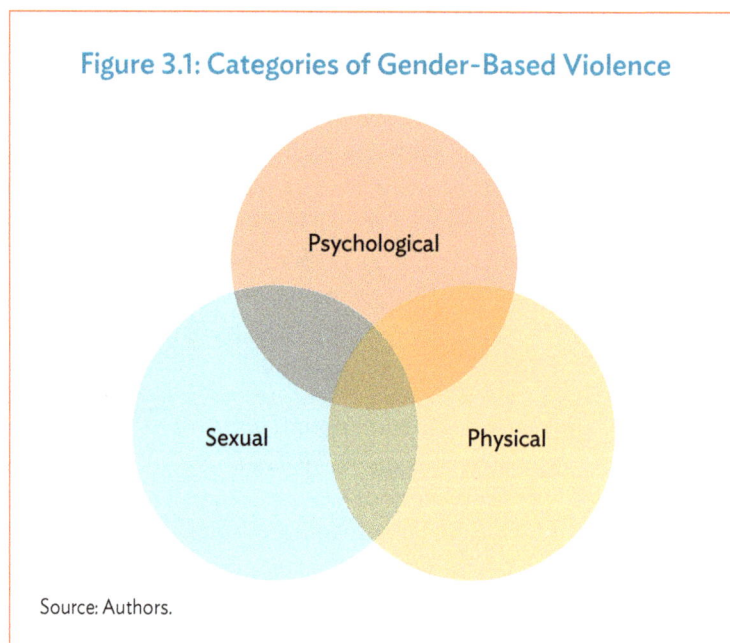

Figure 3.1: Categories of Gender-Based Violence

Psychological

Sexual

Physical

Source: Authors.

(i)   Physical violence involves intimate partner violence; domestic violence, rape, and sexual assault; femicide/feminicide occurring in various settings within the family and the community whether during times of peace or conflict (including "honor killing" and dowry-related killing);[7] acid attacks; trafficking; sexual exploitation and sexual harassment; forced or early marriage; harmful practices such as female genital mutilation; and forced sterilization and forced pregnancy.

(ii)   Psychological/emotional violence is a sophistication of the use of violence that is not evidenced by physical injury. For instance, constant verbal abuse is as harmful

---

[6]   General Assembly Resolution 48/104, *Declaration on the Elimination of Discrimination against Women*, A/RES/48/104 (20 December 1993). Art. 1.

[7]   Tehseen Saeed. 2016. Dowry Murder (Letter to the Editor). *The Express Tribune*. 25 March.

and injurious as any form of physical violence, and sometimes even more harmful. Psychological/emotional violence includes verbal abuse, shaming, isolation, intimidation, controlling behavior, online violence or technology-based violence, and harassment. Other examples can also be seen during conflict, such as solitary confinement and putting someone in perpetual fear of physical violence.

(iii) Economic violence involves denial of or exclusion from health care, employment, education,[8] property including inheritance and agricultural resources, financial resources, decision-making and right to livelihood.

III. Causes and Impact of Gender-Based Violence

The underlying causes of GBV are complex, but there is general agreement that the main features are gender inequality, power imbalance, and controlling behavior within relationships.

Community attitudes toward gender roles, sexuality, family violence, and sexual assault can strongly influence the prevalence of violence and reporting rates. Cultural attitudes that support male authority over women stigmatize victims of violence.[9] The language used in the community adds to the normalization of GBV and trivializes its seriousness (e.g., "It was only a slap"). For example, both males and females believe that violence can be excused and that rape results from men not being able to control their need for sex or from women "asking" to be raped.

The culture and the law provide excusatory loopholes that take the form of justifications, defense, and mitigations for acts of violence against women. Crimes of honor, victim blaming, crimes of passion, and defense of provocation all exemplify this.[10] Furthermore, society also has different standards in excusing 'bad behavior' and placing the blame on someone. Table 3.1 shows the common stereotypical reactions to men's behavior and women's behavior.

---

[8] Islam made the quest for education and knowledge the duty of every Muslim, male and female:
> Say (unto them, Muhammad), Are those equal, those who know And those who do not know?
> Qur'an (translation by Yusuf Ali, 39:9).
Indeed, the first verse revealed to Muhammad is the command to read in the name of God.

[9] Globally, violence against women is acknowledged to have derived essentially from cultural practices. Para. 118 of the Beijing Declaration and Platform for Action states, "Violence against women throughout the life cycle derives essentially from cultural patterns, in particular the harmful effects of certain traditional or customary practices and all acts of extremism linked to race, sex, language or religion that perpetuate the lower status accorded to women in the family, the workplace, the community and society." United Nations (UN), *Report of the Fourth World Conference on Women, Beijing, 4–15 September 1995*, A/CONF.177/20/Rev.1 (1996). p. 49.

[10] It is important to note that a defense of provocation must be premised on an absence of opportunity to avert violence, in the sense that the provocation must have been grave and sudden. 'Honor' crimes, however, are often premeditated punishment for alleged moral transgressions against family, and more particularly, against male honor. Therefore, acknowledging that honor crimes are crimes of revenge reflects more correctly the nature of the crime and the responsibility the law can expect of the perpetrator.

The following are NOT the causes of, or justifications for, GBV:

- Refuses to obey father/husband
- Insufficient dower/bridal gifts
- Insists on going out at night
- Wearing inappropriate clothes
- Spends too much time chatting on Facebook
- Cannot control children, children too noisy
- Turns down interest/marriage proposal.

Table 3.1: Common Reactions to the Behavior of a Man and a Woman

Male	Female
He had such a bad day. He was grumpy and tired. His family should understand.	She was rude. And she refused to obey me.
He wants a son. God has only blessed him with daughters.	She cannot even give her husband a son.
He dresses well. He is handsome.	She is showing off her beauty. She is shameless.
It is important for him to socialize with his office colleagues after work.	She often goes out in the evenings. It is unacceptable.
He is knowledgeable and informative, and he likes to share.	She is irritating and talks too much.
She likes him but he does not like her. She must be sad.	How dare she refused his proposal. She deserves to be punished.
They divided the inheritance fairly. All the sons got equal shares.	A daughter will only marry into another family. She should give up her share.
She respects and loves her husband. She would never hurt him.	As a husband, he has the right to beat his wife.

Source: Authors.

It is important to understand that the underlying causes of GBV can usually be traced to gender inequality and the (cultural) perception of women. Culture is thus formalized into perceiving violence against women as a socially sanctioned punishment when women are deemed to transgress cultural values (e.g., she is rude, she is shameless, she talks too much). This allows victims (and not perpetrators) to be held responsible for their own injury (e.g., "she deserves to be raped" instead of "no one deserves to be raped" or even speculating "she must have deserved the beating"). Consequently, sanctions in regard to violence occurring among men are enforced, but perpetrators of violence against women are rarely punished (Figure 3.2).[11]

---

[11]   Z. Abdul Aziz. 2013. Culture, Power and Violence in Domestic Violence Narrative. In M. Mohamad and Anor, eds. *Family Ambiguity and Domestic Violence in Asia: Concept, Law and Process.* London: Sussex Academic Press. pp. 53–77. This understanding of violence against women is underlined (i) in General Recommendation 19 on Violence against Women by the Convention on the Elimination of All Forms of Discrimination against Women (CEDAW) Committee, and (ii) the Council of Europe Convention on Preventing and Combating Violence against Women and Domestic Violence.

Figure 3.2: Violence against Women vs. Violence among Men

Source: Authors.

It is critical for the court to examine and understand how cultural narratives are created and reproduced to deny women of human rights (footnote 11). The high incidences of GBV against women, lack of reporting, isolation of the victim, and complicity of family members and communities are all indicative of the high tolerance of GBV against women.

IV. Gender-Based Violence Offenses

In October 2019, the Law and Justice Commission of Pakistan, under the direction of the chairman of the National Judicial (Policy Making) Committee/Law and Justice Commission of Pakistan, issued a circular on a list of cases referred to the Gender-based Violence Courts (Table 3.2).

Table 3.2: List of Cases Referred to Gender-Based Violence Courts

No.	Common description of offenses in the Penal Code and Prevention of Electronic Crimes Act (All crimes constitute domestic violence if committed by the accused related to the victim or living in same household)	PPC and PECA Sections
Sexual violence (PPC)		
1	Rape	375 and 376 (1)
2	Gang rape	376 (2)
3	Rape of a minor	376 (3)
4	Rape by police or other official[s]	376 (4)
5	Sodomy (male or female and children)	377
6	Outrage of modesty and stripping	354 and 354A
7	Insulting modesty of women or sexual harassment	509
Abduction, kidnapping, and selling of persons (PPC)		
8	Gender-based abduction and kidnapping	362–374
9	Kidnapping of women to compel marriage	365B
10	Gender-based kidnapping of children under 14	364A
11	Gender-based kidnapping of a child under 10	369
12	Selling a person for prostitution	371A
Gender-based killing (PPC)		
13	Honor killing	300–302
14	Murder (femicide) and attempted murder	300–301, 324
15	Hurt resulting in death	315
Gender-based hurt		
16	All hurt cases	332, 337A to 337Z
17	Acid and corrosive substance attack	336B
Offenses relation to marriage (PPC)		
18	*Swara/Wanni/Sangchatti* (the customary practice of giving of a woman or girl in marriage or otherwise compelling her to enter into marriage in consideration of settling a civil dispute or a criminal liability)	310A
19	Forced marriage	498B
20	Prohibition of marriage with the Holy Qur'an	498C
Economic violence (PPC)		
21	Depriving women of inheritance	498A

continued on next page

Table 3.2 *continued*

No.	Common description of offenses in the Penal Code and Prevention of Electronic Crimes Act (All crimes constitute domestic violence if committed by the accused related to the victim or living in same household)	PPC and PECA Sections
Gender-based intimidation (PPC)		
22	Criminal intimidation	506
Gender-based electronic crimes (PECA)[a]		
23	Unauthorized access to, copying, or transmission of system/data	3, 4
24	Electronic fraud or forgery	11, 12
25	Unauthorized use of identity	14
26	Unauthorized interception	17
27	Offenses against dignity or modesty of natural person/minor	18, 19
28	Child pornography	19A
29	Transmission of malicious codes	20
30	Cyber stalking	21
31	Spamming	22
32	Spoofing	23

PECA = Prevention of Electronic Crimes Act, 2016; PPC = Pakistan Penal Code 1860.

Note: The above list is not necessarily a closed list.

[a] The federal government, in consultation with the respective chief justices, is required to designate gender-based violence judges to try PECA offenses.

Source: Law and Justice Commission of Pakistan.

V. Gender-Based Violence: Violation of Constitutional Rights

GBV against women is a violation of their right to life and the prohibition against torture (see Chapter 5). In the case of *Opuz v Turkey*, the European Court of Human Rights found that further violence against the applicant and her mother was foreseeable given the applicant's ex-husband's past behavior.[12] Prior to killing his mother-in-law, he ran over the two women with a car and stabbed the applicant seven times with a knife. The State's failure to take action in the face of numerous complaints violates:

- right to life (the applicant's mother who was killed);
- prohibition of torture and of inhumane and degrading treatment; and
- prohibition of gender-based discrimination bearing in mind the general passivity of the judicial system and impunity enjoyed by aggressors of GBV in Turkey.

---

[12] *Opuz v Turkey*, Application No. 33401/02, [2009] ECHR 870.

States (and State organs) are accountable for complicity in violence against women, whenever they fail to provide protection against GBV against women or whenever they create or implement discriminatory laws that may trap women in abusive circumstances. This includes laws that restrict women's right to divorce or to inheritance, or laws that prevent them from gaining custody of their children, receiving financial compensation, or owning a property. They all serve to make women dependent upon men and limit their ability to leave a violent situation.[13]

In summary, GBV impairs women's and girls' human constitutional rights including the following:

- Right to life (interpreted as not merely alive but living with dignity)
- Right not to be subjected to torture or cruel, inhuman or degrading treatment or punishment
- Right to liberty and security
- Right to equal protection under law
- Right not to be discriminated on the basis of sex
- Right to equality within family
- Right to highest standard attainable in physical and mental health
- Right to education
- Right to just and favorable conditions of work.[14]

It is incumbent on the Court to uphold these constitutional rights.

Furthermore, under Article 4 of the Constitution of Pakistan, every person has the inalienable right to enjoy the protection of the law wherever he or she may be. In particular, the Constitution mandates that no action detrimental to the life, liberty, body, reputation, or property of any person shall be taken except in accordance with the law. Article 14, on the other hand, declares that the dignity of a person is inviolable. The Supreme Court in dealing with the joint effect of Articles 4 and 14 declared:

> [A woman's] right to dignity under Article 14 of the Constitution is an absolute right and not subject to law. Dignity means human worth: simply put, every person matters. No life is dispensable, disposable or demeanable. Every person has the right to live, and the right to live means right to live with dignity. A person should live as "person" and no less. Human dignity hovers over our laws like a guardian angel; it underlies every norm of a just legal system and provides an ultimate justification for every legal rule. Therefore, [the] right to dignity is the crown of fundamental rights under our Constitution and stands at the top, drawing its strength from all the fundamental rights under our Constitution and yet standing alone and tall, making human worth and humanness of a person a far more fundamental a right than the others, a right that is absolutely non-negotiable.[15]

---

13   UN Committee on the Elimination of Discrimination against Women, *General Recommendation No. 19: Violence against Women*, Eleventh Session (1992). para. 23.

14   Footnote 13, para. 7.

15   *Atif Zareef v. The State*, Criminal Appeal No. 251/2020 and Criminal Petition No. 667/2020, 4 January 2021. para. 11.

Informal justice system. A *Jirga* (traditional village council) in Sindh, Pakistan. ADB trainer and expert Samar Minallah Khan attended this *Jirga* meeting to understand how the informal justice system works in the area (photo by Samar Minallah Khan).

Culturally appropriate women empowerment campaigns. A local theater group in Multan, Punjab holds a puppet show about legal prohibitions against compensation marriages (photo by Samar Minallah Khan).

میں اپنی بیٹی کو
اُسکے قانونی اور دینی
حق سے محروم نہیں کروں گا۔
اور آپ ؟

Chapter 4

MANIFESTATIONS OF GENDER-BASED VIOLENCE: SEXUAL ASSAULT, ACID ATTACKS, AND ONLINE GENDER-BASED VIOLENCE

I. Rape and Sexual Assault

According to data obtained from the Punjab police, over 8,000 rape cases and 646 gang rape cases were reported to the police between 2014 and 2016.[1] Further, in the first 6 months of 2017, 1,365 rape and 84 gang rape cases were reported to the police (footnote 1). The data also shows that rapes constituted 41% of all reported violence against women cases between January 2014 and July 2017 (footnote 1).

A study by the United Nations Development Programme (UNDP) and UN Women on why men rape found that the most common motivation for rape (70%–80%) is related to sexual entitlement—men's belief that they have a right to sex, regardless of consent.[2] The second most frequently reported motivation is related to entertainment-seeking followed by anger or punishment (footnote 2). The motivation of anger and punishment accords with the use of violence to resolve conflict. The research also confirms that rape and sexual assault are not crimes of passion but expressions of power.

The offense of sexual assault should be defined so as to include all forms of nonconsensual touching that are sexual in nature; the primary interest of the law must respect the victims' sexual integrity and autonomy.

Rape is premised on the nonconsent of the victim. This makes it different from *zina* (illicit intercourse, or fornication/adultery) where consent is central. For this reason, rape should never be conflated with *zina* and failure to prove rape does not equate to confession of *zina*. This distinction was also made in the 2006 amendments prohibiting the conversion of a rape case into a case of fornication or *zina*.

---

[1]   H. Abbas. 2018. Rape, Murder and Domestic Violence Cases Top List of VAW Crimes Reported in Punjab. *Media for Transparency*. 22 January.

[2]   E. Fulu et al. 2013. *Why Do Some Men Use Violence against Women and How Can We Prevent It: Quantitative Findings from a United Nations Multi-Country Study on Men and Violence in Asia and the Pacific*. Bangkok: UNDP, et al.

It is also important to recognize that a rape or an attempted rape of a minor is no less a rape or an attempted rape and as such, where appropriate, charges should be brought under the rape provisions and not under the child sexual abuse provisions (Section 377A of the Pakistan Penal Code 1860 [PPC]). Another pertinent provision is Section 366A of the PPC which prohibits procuring a girl under 18 for the purposes of forced sexual intercourse. Furthermore, Section 366B of the PPC is applicable if a girl is under 21 and brought from a foreign country with the intent that she may be or is likely to be forced into sexual intercourse. In the aforementioned provisions, there is no requirement to prove lack of consent.

Article 375 of the PPC provides

> A man is said to commit rape who has sexual intercourse with a woman under circumstances falling under any of the five following descriptions:
>
> (i)   against her will;
>
> (ii) without her consent;
>
> (iii) with her consent, when the consent has been obtained by putting her in fear of death or hurt;
>
> (iv) with her consent, when the man knows that he is not married to her and that the consent is given because she believes that the man is another person to whom she is or believes herself to be married; or
>
> (v)   with or without her consent when she is under sixteen years of age (generally referred to as 'statutory rape').

The article establishes two main tracks of proving rape:

> (i)   Against her will means the woman resisted and there was opposition. This is generally abandoned (or recommended to be abandoned) in light of emphasis on consent.[3]
>
> (ii) 'Without her consent' requires positive consent to deny rape. The absence of consent is pivotal in rape.

Proving rape is different from proving sodomy. Sodomy is constituted irrespective of consent. In other jurisdictions, similar provisions have been interpreted to apply to nonconsensual sodomy.[4]

A.   Ascertaining Consent

Ascertaining consent is critical. Consent must be unequivocal and voluntary agreement to participate in the specific act in question (footnote 3). Consent pertains only to the exact act to which the consent was given. For example, a woman may consent to kissing, patting or even intimate touching, but consent to these acts is not sufficient to prove consent in rape. As such, defining consent (and the factors that vitiate "consent") is crucial in gender-based violence (GBV) and must be addressed in all relevant laws and cases.

---

3   See J.S. Verma, L. Seth, and G. Subramanium. 2013. *Report of the Committee on Amendments to Criminal Law.*

4   See *Navtej Singh Johar v. Union of India,* (2018) 10 SCC 1.

Furthermore, consent also cannot be presumed on the basis that the victim does not offer physical resistance to the act of penetration (footnote 3). The accused cannot argue that he believed that there was consent, rather, he must demonstrate that he took reasonable steps to ascertain consent to the specific sexual activity. A person consents if he or she agrees by choice and has the freedom and capacity to make that choice.

B. Vitiating Consent

Under the law consent is deemed vitiated/legally impaired in instances of rape if the consent was obtained through fraud, impersonation, fear, coercion, or if the victim is below 16 years of age.[5]

The notion of fear may include fear of injury or death of the victim or those the victim loves (e.g., her children, siblings, parents, and husband). Similar to other crimes, when a victim is compelled to submit (e.g., to hand over her jewelry or cash) due to threats made to her loved ones, such submission is not considered consent, and the crime is no less a robbery due to such submission.

For instance, under Malaysian law, consent can be vitiated if such consent was obtained by putting the victim in fear of death or hurt to herself or any other person, or obtained under a misconception of fact that

(i)   she was lawfully married to the accused;

(ii)   the accused was someone to whom she would consent;

(iii) she was unable to understand the nature and consequences of that to which she gives consent to; or

(iv)   her consent was obtained by using the accused's position of authority over her, or because of professional relationship or other relationship of trust in relation to her.[6]

Caution must be exercised in differentiating the legal requirements of rape from the many legal myths and misconceptions attached to rape. For example, in *Vertido v. Philippines*, the Committee on the Elimination of Discrimination against Women was asked to decide if Judge Hofileña-Europa relied on gender-based myths and misconceptions about rape and rape victims in her decision.[7]

The Committee held that there was a failure in investigating, prosecuting, and punishing the perpetrator and providing redress to Vertido, due in part to the stereotypes and gender-based myths relied upon in the judgment.

In this regard, the Committee stressed that stereotyping negatively affects a woman's right to a fair trial and that the judiciary must not create or perpetuate inflexible standards of what someone should or should not have done when confronted with a rape situation.

---

[5]   Section 376 of the PPC.

[6]   Section 375 of the Malaysian Penal Code.

[7]   United Nations, Committee on the Elimination of Discrimination against Women, *Views of the Committee on the Elimination of Discrimination against Women under Article 7, Paragraph 3, of the Optional Protocol to the Convention on the Elimination of All Forms of Discrimination against Women, Concerning Communication No. 18/2008 [Vertido v. Philippines]*, CEDAW/C/46/D/18/2008 (16 July 2010).

It is clear from the judgment that the assessment of the credibility of the author's [victim's] version of events was influenced by a number of stereotypes, the author [victim] in this situation not having followed what was expected from a rational and 'ideal victim' or what the judge considered to be the rational and ideal response of a woman in a rape situation. [...] [T]he Committee finds that to expect the author [victim] to have resisted in the situation at stake reinforces in a particular manner the myth that women must physically resist the sexual assault. In this regard, the Committee stresses that there should be no assumption in law or in practice that a woman gives her consent because she has not physically resisted the unwanted sexual conduct, regardless of whether the perpetrator threatened to use or used physical violence.

[...] In this regard, the Committee views with concern the findings of the judge according to which it is unbelievable that a man in his sixties would be able to proceed to ejaculation with the author resisting the sexual attack. Other factors taken into account in the judgment, such as the weight given to the fact that the author and the accused knew each other, constitute a further example of 'gender-based myths and misconceptions.'[8]

Traditionally, a rape victim was held to a higher burden of proof than victims of other crimes due to the myths and misconceptions surrounding rape. For example:

(i)   One of the most common myths is that women lie when they are raped. This resulted in laws allowing the character of the victim to be attacked at trial. This is dealt with under 'victim blaming' (see Chapters 2 and 9).

(ii)   The need for rape evidence to be corroborated (see Chapter 9).

(iii) The centrality of virginity testing (two-finger test) in proving rape, or the habituality of the rape victim to sexual intercourse (see Chapter 9).

(iv)   Rape can be settled by the rapist marrying the rape victim (see Chapter 11).

Gradually, the law evolved to apply the general rules of evidence, instead of demanding a higher scrutiny, for rape. The following should be applied when investigating and deciding on a rape case:

(i)   Corroborative evidence is not necessary (Chapter 9).

(ii)   Evidence of victim's sexual history is irrelevant and therefore prohibiting character attacks on the victim (Chapter 9)

(iii) Penetration, no matter how slight, is sufficient to prove rape. Evidence of tearing of the hymen is not required and has no probative value (Chapter 9).

(iv)   Victims are to be examined by registered medical practitioner for medical evidence. Medical-legal protocols have been set up for this purpose, including rape medical kits (Chapter 9).

---

8   Footnote 7, pp. 15–16.

The following rights are provided under the law:

- The victim of crimes under Sections 354A, 376, 377, and 377B of the PPC has a right to legal representation

- The police officer is obligated to advise her of this right

- If the victim requires legal aid, the police officer shall provide her with a list of lawyers maintained by the Bar Council (Section 161A, Criminal Procedure Code [CrPC] [2016 Am])

- Presence of female police officer or female family member or other person of her choice (Sections 154 and 161, CrPC)

- Nondisclosure of the victim's identity (Section 376A, PPC)

- That her/his case shall be decided within 3 months (Section 344A, CrPC)

- Appeal shall be decided within 6 months (Section 417[5], CrPC)

- That her/his case shall be conducted in camera (court closed to the public) (Section 352[2], CrPC)

- Special measures including holding the trial via video link or using screens to protect the victim and witnesses (Section 352[3], CrPC)

- Nonpublication or nonbroadcast of proceedings (Section 352[4], CrPC)

- See also Punjab Witness Protection Act, 2018 which provides protection in court (e.g., special measures) and out of court (e.g., shelter, nondisclosure).

II. *Zina*

It is extremely important to ensure that victims of sexual crimes are not punished in order to encourage victims to come forward to report. It was for this reason that the previous legal provisions that allowed rape victims to be prosecuted for *zina* has now been repealed.

Rape cannot be conflated with *zina*. However, it used to be that if a woman's rape complaint was dismissed, she would then be liable to be charged for *zina* due to the incorrect assumption that a woman's complaint is evidence that she had consensual sexual intercourse with someone. The State's ability to convert a rape complaint into a *zina* charge resulted in reluctance by rape victims to lodge rape complaints and constitutes yet another example of converting a sexual assault victim into a transgressor of moral values.

Zina is defined as an act involving a man and a woman, who are not married to each other, having sexual relations consensually and the act is consummated by penetration. Central to the offense of *zina* is that unless prosecution is based on confession, *zina* must be proven by the testimony of four adult and upright Muslims who have witnessed the act of penetration or *ilaj*.[9]

---

[9]   Al-Qur'an (An-Nur verse 24:4).

Zina, by definition, is an offense that can only be committed by a man and a woman simultaneously. What makes *zina* a GBV against women is that while *Zina* is an act that is committed by two persons, a man and a woman, the persons accused and sentenced for *zina* are predominantly women. As noted by Justice Haziqul Khairi in a speech he delivered in 2017, while 1,600 women had been accused of adultery, not a single man was accused, even though men were just as much involved in the act.[10]

In *Safia Bibi v. State*,[11] an acutely myopic domestic helper reported that she was raped (*zina bil-jabr*). She gave birth. Under Section 10(2) of the *Zina* Ordinance, the lower court sentenced her to 3 years of imprisonment, 15 stripes, and a fine of PRs100. She was acquitted upon appeal.

In *Zafran Bibi v. State*,[12] the lower court had held that "in accusing her brother-in-law of raping her, Ms. Zafran had confessed to her crime." Furthermore, "[t]he illegitimate child is not disowned by her and therefore is proof of *zina*." Zafran Bibi's conviction was overturned upon appeal.

Charging a rape victim with *zina* is now prohibited under the provisions of Offence of *Zina* (Enforcement of Hudood) Ordinance 1979:

(i)   Section 5A states that no case is to be converted, lodged, or registered under certain conditions

(ii)   No complaint of *zina* under Section 5 is to be read with Section 203A, CrPC. No case where an allegation of rape made shall at any stage be converted into a complaint of fornication under Section 496B of the PPC. No complaint of fornication shall at any stage be converted into a complaint of *zina* under Section 5 or an offense of similar nature under any other law for the time being in force.

The CrPC too was similarly amended to prohibit charging rape victims for *zina*. Section 203C(6) of the CrPC provides that, "Notwithstanding the foregoing provisions or anything contained in any other law for the time being in force no complaint under this section shall be entertained against any person who is accused of *zina* under section 5 of the Offence of *Zina* (Enforcement of Hudood) Ordinance, 1979 (Ordinance No. VII of 1979) and against whom a complaint under section 203A of this Code is pending or has been dismissed or who has been acquitted or against any person who is a complainant or a victim in a case of rape, under any circumstances whatsoever."

In the case of *Amir Razzaq v. The State*,[13] the Lahore High Court held that, the prosecutrix in a rape case is "constitutionally protected against self incrimination and, thus, cannot be exposed to corporal consequences in the face of rejection of her narrative." Added the Court, Section 203(c) of the CrPC 1898 also created a procedural impediment for any suggested prosecution of a rape complainant.

---

[10]   Justice Haziqul Khairi (retired), former chief justice of the Federal Shariat Court and a former justice of the Sindh High Court, speaking on "Iqbal's concept of a state" at a contest sponsored by the Pakistan Women's Foundation for Peace. See A. Datta. 2017. Iqbal's Dream of a State with Social and Economic Justice has been Shattered. *The News*. 23 November.

[11]   PLD 1985 FSC 120.

[12]   PLD 2002 FSC 1.

[13]   2019 LHC 298.

Zina or adultery is provided under both the PPC and the Offence of *Zina* (Hudood Offences) Act, 1979, as well as other laws:

- **PPC**

  Section 496B. Fornication. A man or a woman not married to each other are said to commit fornication if they wilfully have sexual intercourse with each other. Whoever commits fornication shall be punished with imprisonment for a term which may extend to five years and shall also be liable to fine not exceeding ten thousand rupees.

  Section 496C. Whoever brings or levels or gives evidence of false charge of fornication against any person, shall be punished with imprisonment for a term which may extend to five years and shall also be liable to fine not exceeding ten thousand rupees.

- **Offence of *Zina* (Enforcement of Hudood) Ordinance 1979**

  Section 4. A man and a woman are said to commit *zina* if they wilfully have sexual intercourse without being married to each other.

- **Criminal Procedure Code (CrPC)**

  Section 203A (1). No court shall take cognizance of the offense under Section 5 of the *Zina* Ordinance except on complaint lodged in the court of competent jurisdiction. Subsection 2 requires that proving the offence shall be by way of the testimony of four adult male Muslim witnesses.

  Section 203B. No court shall take cognizance of the offense under Section 6 of the Qazf Ordinance except for the complaint lodged in the court of competent jurisdiction

- **Offence of Qazf (Enforcement of Hudood) Ordinance 1979**

  Section 3 provides that false accusation of *zina* shall be punishable with 80 stripes.

According to *Zina* Ordinance, only adults may be charged. An "adult" is defined as a man 18 years and above and a girl/woman 16 years and above. The discrepancy in the ages is indicative of systemic discrimination against girls who are burdened with higher accountability at a younger age than the boys.

Given the heavy burden of proof (of four adult witnesses), some argue that *zina* was meant to regulate the permissible sexual conduct in public [why else would four adult, upright Muslims be available to witness a sexual act] rather than in private. A jurist opined, "[I]t is a condition that the witnesses are four [...] because God the Exalted likes [the vices of] his servants to remain

Avoid suspicion as much (as possible): for suspicion in some cases is a sin: And spy not on each other, Nor speak ill of each other behind their backs.
Al Qur'an, Hujarat, verse 49:12

concealed, and this is realised by demanding four witnesses, since it is very rare for four people to observe this vice."[14]

The fact that *zina* requires such stringent proof is warning enough of the seriousness of making accusations of *zina*. Further, the Qur'anic admonishment of those who slandered against Aisha (ra) underlines the gravity of this accusation.[15]

Both the Qur'an and the Prophet (PBUH) warned against spying, suspicion, and bearing false witness.[16] The Qur'an also regards privacy as a fundamental right and protects the sanctity and privacy of the home. No person is to enter another's home without issuing salam (greetings).

III. Acid Attacks

More than 3,400 cases of acid burning were reported between 1999 and 2019.[17] Chemical burns are among the most painful experiences—like being burned by hot water with unbearable pain going deeper into bones, teeth, and eyes. Women are attacked to teach them a lesson or cripple or deface them for life (e.g., for wanting a divorce or refusing a marriage proposal).[18] Section 336B provides for a minimum punishment of 14 years and a fine of PRs1 million, but due to loopholes in the law, many go free.[19]

Below are some examples where the perpetrators of acid attacks have been punished:

> Asmatullah threw acid on his ex-fiancée at her refusal to marry him. According to doctors, the attack disfigured the face of the 24-year-old and damaged her eyes. The court sentenced the accused to 25 years in jail on two counts under Anti-Terrorism Act, 1997, another 10 years under Section 324 of the PPC, and a fine of PRs3.9 million to be paid to the victim as compensation.[20]

> An antiterrorism court sentenced a man to 14 years for attacking a flight attendant with acid and causing her critical injuries in July 2015 for turning down a marriage proposal. The court also directed the convict to pay *diyat* (compensation) of over PRs800,000 to the victim and ordered that he remain in prison even after completing his sentence in case of non-payment.[21]

---

[14] Ali Al-Qari Al-Harawi. Quoted in K. El-Rouayheb. 2009. *Before Homosexuality in the Arab-Islamic World, 1500–1800*. Chicago: University of Chicago Press. p. 123.

[15] Al-Qur'an, An Nur 24:12-13.

[16] "Shall I not tell you of the most serious of the major sins?" We said: "Of course, O Messenger of Allah." He said: "Associating anything with Allah (SWT), and disobeying parents." He was reclining, but then he sat up and said: "And bearing false witness," and he kept repeating this until we wished that he would stop (i.e., so that he would not exhaust himself with his fervour)."

[17] M. Shahzad. 2019. Woman Falls Victim to Acid Attack in Lahore. *The Express Tribune*. 21 September.

[18] S. Azam et al. 2014. *Causes and Consequences of Acid Attacks on Women: A Case Study of District Lahore, Pakistan*. Presentation at The European Conference on Cultural Studies 2014. The International Academic Forum.

[19] *BBC News*. 2012. Pakistani Women's Lives Destroyed by Acid Attacks. 19 April.

[20] *Dawn*. 2017. Acid Attack Convict Sentenced to 60 Years in Jail. 16 November.

[21] *Dawn*. 2019. Man Sent to Jail for 14 years in Acid-Throwing Case. 22 March.

Still, two cases recorded in a documentary *Against All Odds: Acid Crimes and Dowry* show that not every perpetrator is punished.[22] In one case, Zainab Bibi (17 years old) slapped her neighbor for making advances and harassing her. Three nights later, while Zainab was asleep, her neighbor climbed over the wall into her family home and splashed two doses of acid on her. His motive was to ensure that no one would marry her. Zainab's family could not afford a lawyer. A tribal *Panchayat* (village council) was called where the neighbor swore upon the Holy Qur'an that he had not harmed her. Zainab and her family were forced to accept his word.

In another case, Tahira Bibi (22 years old) experienced an acid attack by her abusive and jealous husband while visiting her parents. It happened so suddenly that her mother could not help. Tahira recalls, "He did threaten me once saying that he would leave me in such a state that no one would ever lay eyes upon me again. Little did I know that his means of achieving this would be through the use of acid."

IV. Online Gender-Based Violence

While both men and women may be subject to online harassment, women are disproportionately targeted by online violence and suffer serious consequences.[23] Threats issued online are often meant to intimidate.

Online or information and communication technology (ICT) related GBV includes the following:

- cyber stalking (unwanted surveillance or monitoring of a person by using ICT, namely the internet or other electronic applications and platforms. It is a pattern of behavior that causes harm or distress;

- cyber bullying (use of ICT to bully);

- online threats and blackmail. It is more challenging to investigate and more likely to be trivialized;

- online sexual harassment. Victims are often told to 'just ignore it.' This response ignores the reality we live in and the fact that, in an increasingly digital world, the victim often doesn't have the luxury of turning off their computer to avoid the behavior;

- assessing or uploading/disseminating intimate photos, videos, or audio clips without consent;

- accessing or disseminating private data and images without consent; morphing photos or videos (e.g., "deep fake") and uploading them to pornographic websites;

- creating fake profiles (where the perpetrator then poses as the victim and acts in the victims' name, often in manner that is humiliating or harmful). For example, a perpetrator

---

[22] S. Minallah. 2010. *Against All Odds: Acid Crimes and Dowry*. Documentary.

[23] United Nations, Human Rights Council, *Report of the Special Rapporteur on Violence against Women, Its Causes and Consequences on Online Violence against Women and Girls from a Human Rights Perspective,* A/HRC/38/47 (18 June 2018).

may pretend to be their female target, advertise sexual services online, and provide the actual contact information of the unwitting victim);

- mob attacks (e.g., "shaming mobs");

- sextortion (extorting sex/sexual favors by threatening to disseminate intimate images and rape footage);

- digital voyeurism (placing hidden digital cameras and streaming footage online);

- cyber-flashing (receiving unsolicited images of male genitalia often with the purpose of silencing women);

- grooming predation (befriending and developing trust of a child to facilitate child sexual abuse);

- doxing (searching and publicizing someone's personal data);

- multiple platform harassment (harassing someone across different online or digital media, such that there is no relief from the harassment). Given the importance of digital connections, this can be a profoundly isolating experience for the victim;

- dog piling (vicious mob attack of a person over a comment); and

- exploitation of women and girls.[24]

In a five-country research project/undertaking involving India, Malaysia, Pakistan, the Philippines, and the Republic of Korea, all respondents (civil society advocates) reported that the most commonly occurring form of ICT violence against women is misogynist comments or gender hate speech.[25]

It is worth noting that the easy and rapid dissemination of information and content across multiple platforms provides the optimal space to amplify harm because of the ease with which information and images can be shared, liked, reposted, stored, and downloaded. ICT GBV happens not merely on the first upload by the primary perpetrator, but every time it is liked, shared, downloaded, or forwarded (these can be considered secondary perpetrators). The aggregated harm is the result of hundreds or even millions of people who wittingly or unwittingly participate in the violence.

Consent is pivotal in determining whether the sharing of intimate data and images constitute ICT GBV. Consent must be specific to the act in question (e.g., sharing of intimate photos). When and how the images came to be in the perpetrator's possession is not relevant to whether consent was obtained for disseminating the images.

Content uploaded onto the digital space remains accessible for years. This can jeopardize an individual's job search and credit score decades after the online GBV.

---

24 Z. Abdul Aziz. 2017. *Due Diligence and Accountability for Online Violence against Women.*
25 Z. Abdul Aziz. 2020. *Online Violence against Women: A Multicountry Study.* Bangkok: UN Women.

Perpetrators may also hide their identity through encryption. This may pose a challenge to investigators. However, it should be remembered that encryption, anonymity, and the concept of security also creates a zone of privacy that protects opinion and belief.[26]

The internet has the effect of disinhibiting us. Many users tend to disclose more and act out more (including committing violent acts), lulled by the fact that they are speaking to a box rather than a live audience.

Below are what victims and advocates say about online GBV:[27]

- An advocate explained that only 12 out of 70 girls she spoke to had their own Facebook profiles with their names and pictures. Due to hacking and harassment, the girls had anonymous accounts, used accounts belonging to their male relatives or even stopped using Facebook completely.

- Another advocate shared that she started getting a lot of Skype calls/WhatsApp calls and flashing of private parts (cyber-flashing), including unsolicited pictures of male genitals. It was one way to harass and silence women. The advocate said, "I experienced psychological trauma. There were also direct threats sent via messaging to my number."

- Blackmailing is very common and that is why women do not come forward. Women are often intimidated to report cases due to blackmails (i.e., threats to release the material online, whether genuine or fake).

- Families do not want to disclose that their female family members were being harassed; they would rather register a gender-neutral crime. This caused underreporting of harassment cases and widespread impunity.

- Investigating officers still question the victim's responsibility in instigating the violence instead of focusing on the perpetration of the online violence.

Online GBV is another manifestation of GBV; it is used not merely to intimidate but also to silence women. Yet, where GBV does not involve physical violence, it tends to be trivialized, and thus receives inappropriate responses.

In *Yasir Lateef v. The State*, the accused hacked into the victim's Facebook account and uploaded her personal pictures without her consent. The court condemned the actions as "obnoxious and filthy in nature."[28]

---

[26] Footnote 25. See also United Nations, Human Rights Council, Special Rapporteur on the Promotion and Protection of the Right to Freedom of Opinion and Expression, *Report on Encryption, Anonymity, and the Human Rights Framework*, A/HRC/29/32 (22 May 2015).

[27] Focus group discussions by Zarizana Abdul Aziz with advocates and experts. Lahore, Pakistan. August 2019. See footnote 25.

[28] *Yasir Lateef v. The State*, 2016 P Cr. LJ 1916.

In 2016, perpetrators hacked into several women's Facebook accounts and transposed their photos over naked bodies of women which were uploaded to a Facebook page. Each picture included the woman's name, her phone number, and a lewd message: "I am available for sex. Call me for a quickie."[29]

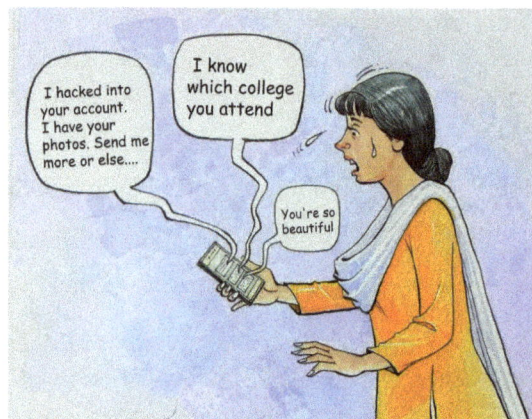

Furthermore, nonphysical harassment can evolve into physical violence, and perpetrators of technology related GBV often employ a continuum of violence both offline and online. Users also 'go live' showing footage of rapes, killings, and torture.[30] About 12% of reported sexual violence victims reported being filmed by their perpetrators.[31] The recordings were used to further harass the victims (footnote 31).

The impact is severe. A total of 70% of surveyed women in Pakistan suggested they were afraid of their pictures being posted online and 40% of them reported they had been harassed through messaging apps.[32]

Women are also attacked for alleged transgressions of cultural/social norms including inappropriate dressing or behavior on the internet. The first case of honor killing and digital technology was reported in Kohistan, Pakistan, where four women were killed for clapping and singing in a video. The whistleblower and three of his brothers were similarly killed.[33] In another case, a model, Qandeel Baloch, was killed by her brother because, according to him, "[s]he was doing videos on Facebook."[34] In 2013, a group of men murdered two teenage girls and their mother after a video was posted online that showed them dancing in the rain.[35]

Like offline violence, most perpetrators are known to the victims. In Pakistan, 70% of survey respondents said the perpetrators were friends and acquaintances of the victims. Sharing this same sentiment were 65.7% of respondents in Malaysia and 80.5% in the Philippines.[36]

Internet intermediaries have taken action to curb online GBV, albeit often after their platforms are used to perpetrate the violence.[37]

---

29 S. Parkin. 2016. Pakistan's Troll Problem. *The New Yorker*. 28 June. See also B. Shah. 2015. How Social Media is Failing Pakistan's Women. *Aljazeera*. 18 October.

30 O. Solon. 2017. Why an Increasing Number of Criminals are Using Facebook Live to Film Their Acts. *The Guardian*. 27 January; and *BBC News*. 2015. How a Rape was Filmed and Shared in Pakistan. 26 February.

31 Human Rights Commission of Pakistan. 2015. *Annual Report: State of Human Rights in 2015*. Islamabad. p. 11.

32 Digital Rights Foundation. 2017. *Measuring Pakistani Women's Experiences of Online Violence: A Quantitative Research Study on Online Gender-Based Harassment in Pakistan*.

33 *BBC News*. 2019. Kohistan Video Murders: Three Guilty in 'Honour Killing' Blood Feud. 5 September.

34 *The Guardian*. 2016. Model Qandeel Baloch was Killed by Her After Friends' Taunts—Mother. 27 July.

35 S. Parkin. 2016. Pakistan's Troll Problem. *The New Yorker*. 28 June.

36 Z. Abdul Aziz. Questionnaire on Information Communication Technology Related Violence against Women. Unpublished (Survey administered to civil society organizations in Malaysia, Pakistan, and the Philippines).

37 J. Kiss. 2016. Twitter Planning 'Regular and Consistent Action' to Curb Harassment and Abuse. *The Guardian*. 9 February.

COVID-19 gender impacts. United Nations data show that all types of violence against women and girls intensified during the COVID-19 pandemic. There has been an uptick in calls to domestic violence hotlines, while resources to address gender-based violence were realigned to COVID-19 response (photo by Rahim Mirza/ADB).
Source: UN Women. The Shadow Pandemic: Violence against Women during COVID-19.

Right to marry and found a family. A groom holds his bride's hand during a wedding ceremony in Islamabad, Pakistan. Pakistani law and international law both guarantee that men and women have the same right to freely choose a spouse and to enter into marriage only with their free and full consent (photo by Iqra Zaib).

Chapter 5

MANIFESTATIONS OF GENDER-BASED VIOLENCE: FAMILY-RELATED GENDER-BASED VIOLENCE

I. Introduction

This chapter deals specifically with gender-based violence (GBV) committed by family members: (i) domestic violence; (ii) economic violence, including denial of women's inheritance rights; (iii) femicide (killing of women) on the pretext of honor; and (iv) offenses related to forced marriage of women and girls and what passes off as "marriage" of women and girls.

II. Domestic Violence (Intimate Partner Violence)

In 2017 and 2018, the National Institute of Population Studies conducted a survey covering population, maternal, and child health issues in Pakistan.[1] In total, more than 4,000 women were successfully interviewed about domestic violence in accordance with World Health Organization (WHO) guidelines on ethical collection of information on domestic violence. Nationally, the survey found that

- 28% of women from age 15 to 49 experienced physical violence since age 15, around 6% experienced sexual violence, and 7% of women who have been pregnant have experienced violence during pregnancy;

- 8% of ever-married women report that their husbands display three or more specific types of controlling behavior;

- 34% of ever-married women have experienced spousal physical, sexual, or emotional violence. The most common type of spousal violence is emotional violence (26%), followed by physical violence (23%). Around 5% of women experienced spousal sexual violence; and

---

[1] National Institute of Population Studies and ICF International. 2019. *Pakistan Demographic and Health Survey 2017–18*. Islamabad, Pakistan, and Rockville, Maryland, United States.

- 26% of ever-married women who have experienced spousal physical or sexual violence have sustained injuries. Cuts and bruises are the most common types of injuries reported.

The survey also indicates the following:

- Ever-married women age 15–19 are most likely to have experienced physical violence since age 15 (32%), whereas women age 20–24 are least likely to have experienced such violence (21%).

- By region, the percentage of women who have experienced physical violence is highest in the Federally Administered Tribal Area (56%), followed by Balochistan (48%) and Khyber Pakhtunkhwa (43%). Women in Sindh are least likely to have experienced physical violence (15%).

- Divorced, separated, and widowed women are more likely to have experienced physical violence (41%) than currently married women (27%).

- Around 78% of ever-married women who have experienced sexual violence since age 15 report their current husband as the perpetrator, while 18% report a former husband as the perpetrator. Around 2% each report other relatives and police/soldiers as perpetrators.

The figures accord with the WHO data that 35% of women in South Asia who have ever been in relationships had experienced violence by their intimate partners.[2] That makes one in three women who have ever been in a relationship has experienced violence by someone close to them (footnote 2). WHO data also shows that intimate partner violence starts early, with one in four ever married adolescent girls (aged 15–19 years) having been subjected to physical or sexual violence at least once in their lifetime (footnote 2).

Physical, psychological, or sexual violence does not occur in isolation. Women may experience a combination of all three forms, which can have long-lasting negative effects on women's lives, health, and well-being. Women victims of intimate partner violence are more likely to have a low-birth-weight baby. They are also more likely to have an abortion, and experience depression as compared to women who have not experienced partner violence (footnote 2).

Critically, 56% of women who have experienced any type of physical or sexual violence have not sought any help or talked with anyone about stopping the violence.[3] Among those who sought help, 76% did so from their family; 36% from their husband's family; and 2% from their husbands, former husbands, and neighbors. Very few women went to lawyers, the police, or social work organizations (1% each). Those who experience physical violence and sought help reported that they sought help because they were afraid of more violence or could not endure more violence (77%). Twenty-four percent of women said they were encouraged by friends and family to seek help.

---

[2] WHO, on behalf of the United Nations Inter-Agency Working Group on Violence against Women Estimation and Data (VAW-IAWGED). 2021. *Violence against Women Prevalence Estimates, 2018: Global, Regional and National Prevalence Estimates for Intimate Partner Violence against Women and Global and Regional Prevalence Estimates for Non-Partner Sexual Violence against Women.* Geneva.

[3] World Health Organization, London School of Hygiene and Tropical Medicine, and South African Medical Research Council. 2013. *Global and Regional Estimates of Violence against Women: Prevalence and Health Effects of Intimate Partner Violence and Non-Partner Sexual Violence.* Geneva.

Islam urges Muslims to eschew domestic violence. The Prophet held himself as the best example of treating his wives.[4] The Qur'an also urges husbands to treat their wives with love and kindness.[5]

Domestic violence also tends to be viewed as a private matter, as the home is argued to be under the stewardship of its male members. Domestic violence is NOT a private matter. Violence is always a public matter. Violence that approximates or constitutes torture definitely lies within the ambit of State mandate. Violence at all times, and wherever occurring, triggers State intervention.

In domestic violence cases, the perpetrators' rights could not supersede the victims' rights to life and physical and mental integrity.[6] The authorities also could not rely on the victims' attitude or failure to take adequate measures which could have prevented the likelihood of an aggressor carrying out his threats.

Domestic violence cannot be trivialized. An international expert on torture equates domestic violence to torture:

> Domestic violence, as well as torture, tends to escalate over time, sometimes resulting in death or leaving women's bodies mutilated or permanently disfigured. Women who experience such violence, whether in their homes or in a prison, suffer depression, anxiety, loss of self-esteem, and a feeling of isolation. Indeed, battered women may suffer from the same intense symptoms that comprise the post-traumatic stress disorder identified in victims of official torture as well as by victims of rape. Another parallel between privately battering women and torture, which refers back to the element of powerlessness, is the intention to keep the victim in a permanent state of fear based on unpredictable violence by seeking to reduce the person to submission and destroy his/her capacity for resistance and autonomy with the ultimate aim of achieving total control.[7]

Categorizing domestic violence and other forms of GBV against women—such as female genital mutilation, human trafficking, traditional practices (e.g., dowry-related violence, widow burning), sexual violence, and harassment—as torture or cruel, inhuman, and degrading treatment is supported by international human rights experts.[8] States and their organs should be held accountable for complicity in violence against women whenever they fail to provide protection or implement discriminatory laws that trap women in abusive circumstances. This includes laws

---

4   "The best of you are those who are the best to their wives, and I am the best of you to my wives." Narrated by al-Tirmidhi, 3895; Ibn Maajah, 1977; classed as *saheeh* by al-Albaani in Saheeh al-Tirmidhi; "How does anyone of you beat his wife as he beats the stallion camel and then embrace (sleep with) her?" Al-Bukhari, English Translation. Vol. 8. Hadith 68. pp. 42–43.

5   "And of His signs is this: He created for you helpmates from yourselves that ye might find rest in them, and He ordained between you love and mercy. Lo! herein indeed are portents for folk who reflect." (Ar-Rum verse 30: 21.) The Meaning of the Glorious Qur'an (Translation by M.M. Pickthall).

6   *Opuz v Turkey*, Application No. 33401/02, [2009] ECHR 870.

7   United Nations (UN), Human Rights Council, *Promotion and Protection of All Human Rights, Civil, Political, Economic, Social and Cultural Rights, Including the Right to Development: Report of the UN Special Rapporteur on Torture and Other Cruel, Inhuman or Degrading Treatment or Punishment, Manfred Nowak*, A/HRC/7/3 (15 January 2008).

8   UN Committee against Torture, *General Comment No. 2: Implementation of Article 2 by States Parties*, CAT/C/GC/2 (24 January 2008). para. 19.

that restrict women's right to divorce or inheritance, or that prevent them from gaining custody of their children, receiving financial compensation or owning property. These laws serve to make women dependent upon men and limit their ability to leave a violent situation.

Any legal treatment of domestic violence must understand the nature of domestic violence and capture its repetitive nature (Figure 5.1). Often, domestic violence consists of a series of non-grievous harms committed over a long period of time. This converts what is non-grievous hurt (if viewed individually) into grievous hurt when taken together. It is not possible to isolate each incident and deal with it separately.

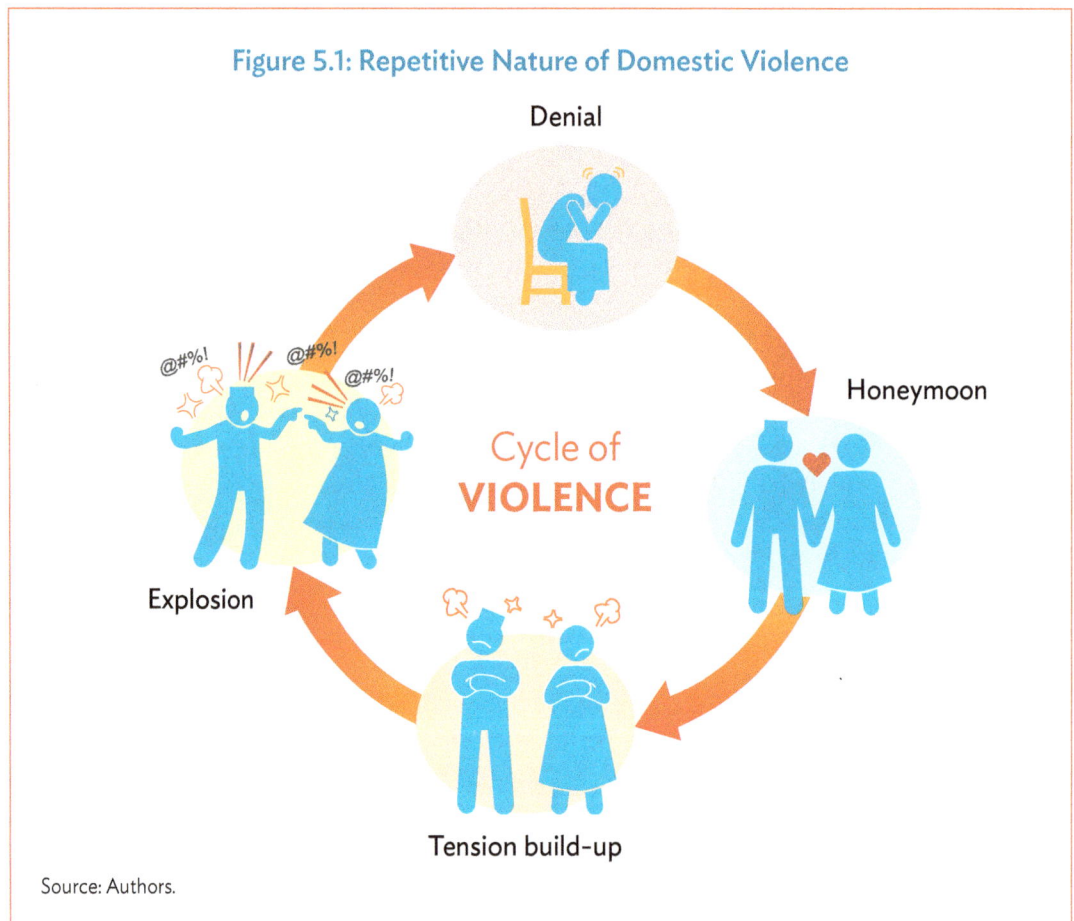

Figure 5.1: Repetitive Nature of Domestic Violence

Denial

Honeymoon

Cycle of **VIOLENCE**

Explosion

Tension build-up

Source: Authors.

In such circumstances, women may experience a battered women syndrome, a psychological disorder of women subjected to long-term abuse. In battered women syndrome, a woman may believe that she deserves to be abused or that she is unable to escape the violence. This is a learned behavior due to the repetitive violence. It is a form of post-traumatic stress disorder.

In the case of *Adnan Zar v. Mst Khadeeja Khanum*, the Islamabad High Court interpreted Section 5 of Family Courts Act to mean that it is mandatory for Family Court judges to initiate criminal proceedings if there was evidence of violence by one spouse against the other in any family petition before them.[9] The Court also held that, "The Family Court, while deciding the issue of cruelty, may frame specific charge for the offence, consider the evidence on the touchstone and requirement of ingredients of offences referred in Part-II of the Schedule and pass a sentence simultaneously in the same judgment or may proceed separately in accordance with procedure provided under the CrPC." Justice Moshin Akhtar Kayani, speaking for the Court, also warned that failure so to do constitutes judicial misconduct and shall be dealt with.

III. Economic Violence

The Pakistan Constitution guarantees every citizen the right to acquire, hold, and dispose of property in any part of Pakistan, subject to the Constitution and reasonable restrictions imposed by law. It also guarantees freedom of trade, business, and movement and a right to education. Yet 66.6% of women in Pakistan have no choice in selecting their profession.[10] Of all the provinces in Pakistan, Balochistan is the most restrictive, with 96% of women in the province not having the choice to select their profession (footnote 10). Around 66.1% of women in Pakistan lack the independence to travel; meanwhile in Balochistan, 100% of women lack that freedom (footnote 10). While women comprise approximately half of the population of Pakistan, they make up only 9% to 26% of the formal labor force.[11] Women are mostly underpaid and in vulnerable employments (footnote 11).

Ownership of property is an essential component of economic empowerment. Figure 5.2 shows the percentage of women and men age 15 to 49 by ownership of specific assets. Only 2% of women own land and 3% own a house.[12] Only 6% use a bank account, and 39% own a mobile phone (footnote 12). Only 13% of women have access to loans as compared to 87% men.[13] The Office of the High Commissioner notes that, "[r]ights to land, housing and property are essential to women's equality and wellbeing. Women's rights in access to and control over land, housing and property is a determining factor in women's living conditions, especially in rural economies. Despite the importance of these rights for women, they still disproportionally lack security of tenure."[14]

The Universal Declaration of Human Rights (UDHR) similarly provides the right to own a property; the right to a standard of living for health and well-being; and the right to security in the event of unemployment, sickness, disability, widowhood, old age or other lack of livelihood in circumstances beyond one's control.[15]

The Punjab Protection of Women Against Violence Act, 2016 defines economic abuse in a domestic relationship as denial of food, clothing, and shelter to the aggrieved person by the defendant in accordance with the defendant's income. The Balochistan Domestic Violence

[9]   *Adnan Zar v. Mst Khadeeja Khanum*, 2020 MLD 1147.

[10] National Commission on the Status of Women. 2008. *Women's Right of Inheritance and its Implementation.* p. 78.

[11] Y. Zaidi and S. Farooq. 2016. *Women's Economic Participation and Empowerment in Pakistan: Status Report 2016.* Islamabad: UN Women. p. 18.

[12] Footnote 1, p. 273.

[13] Footnote 11, p. 43.

[14] United Nations Office of the High Commissioner for Human Rights. Women and Housing, Land and Property.

[15] General Assembly Resolution 217 A (III), *Universal Declaration of Human Rights*, A/RES/217(III) (10 December 1948).

Figure 5.2: Ownership of Assets by Women and Men Age 15–49
(%)

Asset	Women	Men
Own house (alone or jointly)	3	72
Own land (alone or jointly)	2	27
Use bank account	6	32
Own mobile phone	39	93

■ Women   ■ Men

Source: National Institute of Population Studies and ICF International. 2019. *Pakistan Demographic and Health Survey 2017–18.* Islamabad, Pakistan, and Rockville, Maryland, United States.

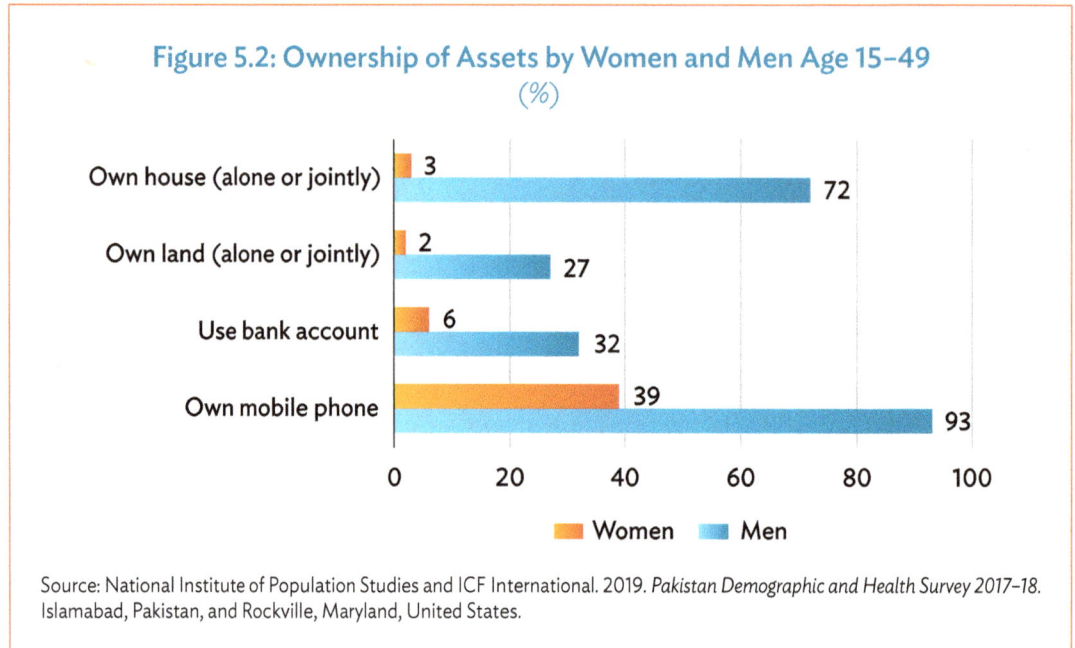

(Prevention and Protection) Act, 2014 and the Sindh Domestic Violence (Prevention and Protection) Act, 2013 define economic abuse as deprivation of financial resources or restriction to access to such resources to which the aggrieved person is entitled.

Where ownership in property is vested in a woman, no one is entitled to prevent her from exercising control over the property. The Dissolution of Muslim Marriages Act, 1939 provides that cruelty for purposes of divorce include disposing of a woman's property or preventing her exercise of her legal rights over it.[16] In the Supreme Court case of *Fawad Ishaq and Mst. Khurshida Ishaq v. Mst. Mehreen Mansoor,* the husband of a woman attempted to dispose of her house as their son's dower to the bride (their daughter-in-law) at the son's wedding.[17] The Supreme Court held that the property could not be gifted as dower as the woman was not a signatory to the *nikahnama* (marriage contract); and the husband, not having been granted a power of attorney by the woman, could not effect transactions over her property.

A.   Denial of Women's Inheritance Rights

Islam provides inheritance rights to women and makes deprivation of inheritance a major sin.[18] The Prophet (pbuh) in his farewell sermon (Khutbatul Wada', 632 A.D.) called on his followers to "regard the life and property of every Muslim as a sacred trust. Return the goods entrusted to you to their rightful owners. Hurt no one so that no one may hurt you."[19] Depriving rights to property is a violation of this trust.

---

[16]   Dissolution of Muslim Marriages Act, 1939, sec. 2 (viii) (d).
[17]   *Fawad Ishaq and Mst. Khurshida Ishaq v. Mst. Mehreen Mansoor,* PLD 2020 269.
[18]   Surah Nisa 4:7, 4:13, 4:14, 4:19, 4:33, and 4:34.
[19]   Sahih Muslim, Book 15 (The Book of Pilgrimage), hadith 159.

Cultural traditions continue to deprive women of their rights. Women are encouraged, bullied or coerced into relinquishing their rights to inheritance out of "natural love and affection" for their brothers. Women are also married to the Qur'an, or within the family to retain property within the family.[20] According to a survey by the National Commission of Women, 40.81% of women "succeeded in acquiring inheritance," (45% with moveable and 34.5% with immovable).[21] Realistically though, while women may inherit property, the right to manage the property remains with the men of the family (footnote 21).

In *Ghulam Ali v. Ghulam Sarwar Naqvi*, the Supreme Court of Pakistan held that "relinquishment" by a female of her inheritance is contrary to public policy as understood in the Islamic sense.

Islam provides that women inherit from their parents' and relatives' estate.[22] The hallmark of property in Islamic jurisprudence is underlined by the notion of dual ownership. Islamic legal theory insists ownership of everything belongs to God. The Qur'an states, "Unto Allah belongeth whatsoever is in the heavens and whatsoever is in the earth."[23]

Women relinquishing their rights to inheritance is not recognized under Islamic and Pakistani law. The 2010 amendment to the Pakistan Penal Code (PPC) (Section 498A) made denying inheritance rights to women a criminal offense.[24] Box 5.1 highlights jurisprudence from various courts in Pakistan upholding women's inheritance rights.

The Punjab Land Revenue Act, 1967 (Section 135A) was amended in 2012 and 2015 to facilitate the speedy transfer of inheritance shares. The Punjab Partition of Immoveable Property Act, 2012 likewise facilitated speedy partition of urban immoveable property in cases of inheritance. Both laws specifically provided safeguards to ensure women access to their inheritance.

In the case of *Mst. Kausar Bibi vs. Mst. Ayesha Bibi and 6 Others*, the Lahore High Court castigated the judicial officer who denied the deceased's daughters their rightful shares of the estate in favor of the deceased's son.[25] The court said the judicial officer "should not be tolerated in the system" and that the beneficiaries and the judicial officer should be made answerable. The High Court directed the registrar of the Court to trace the judicial officer and, if he was still in service, the matter should be reported to the administrative judge for further proceedings.

---

20 S.K. Pakistan. 2017. The Taboo of *Haq Bakshish* in Pakistan where Women are Forced to Marry the Quran. *Parhlo*. 29 April.

21 Footnote 10, p. 82.

22 Surah Al Nisa: verse 33 (Translation Yusuf Ali).

23 Surah An Nisa'a 4: verse 131.

24 Section 498A of the Pakistan Penal Code (PPC) on prohibition of depriving a woman from inheriting property provides, "Whoever by deceitful or illegal means deprives any woman from inheriting any movable or immovable property at the time of opening of succession shall be punished with imprisonment for either description for a term which may extend to ten years but not be less than five years or with a fine of one million rupees or both."

25 *Mst. Kausar Bibi vs. Mst. Ayesha Bibi and 6 Others*, 2017 CLC 1601.

Box 5.1: Pakistani Case Law on Women's Inheritance Rights

Ghulam Ali v. Ghulam Sarwar Naqvi, PLD 1990 SC 1

The Supreme Court of Pakistan held that the brothers had no moral grounds to oust their sister from inheriting their fathers' property. "Relinquishment" by a female of her inheritance is undoubtedly opposed to "public policy" as understood in the Islamic sense. Accordingly, the relinquishment, though denied by the sister, was against public policy. Therefore, female heirs cannot opt or contract out of this protection.

Mst Halima v. Muhammad Alam and Others, 1999 MLD 2934

On the inequality between the shares of male and female children in Islamic law, the Sindh High Court ruled:

[...] [T]he law of inheritance in Islam is exceedingly strict and the shares of male and female children are well-defined. The inequality between the shares of male and female children in Islamic law of inheritance, as it is being practiced in an essentially male-dominated society of ours, is by no means a declaration of a female's inferiority in status and thereby lending sanction to the practice as depriving of females of their right of inheritance. Indeed the provisions regarding a female child being entitled to half the share of the male child is being subjected to wrong interpretations by attributing immutability to it and is being perpetuated only because of male chauvinistic attitudes in society. Islam by giving half a share to females only lays down the lowest limit and not the highest. It is, however, possible for an Islamic state, through exercise of ijtihad [independent reasoning], to increase the female's share. At least in one Muslim country, i.e., Turkey, male and female children have equal rights to inheritance. It is a paradox of today that because Islam has given full right to a woman over her property as enshrined in Married Women's Property Act 1874 (Act No.111 of 1874), ironically enforced in British India by non-Muslim colonial rules, that such practices as mentioned above have arisen with regard to deprivation of the women of the shares they are rightfully entitled to.

Mst Mahar Angiza v. Bakhti Raja, 2014 MLD 962

In this case, the applicant instituted a suit against her brothers for a declaration to the effect that she is the legal sharer of a piece of land, as she is the legal heir of her father. As such, the defendants had no right to deny or interfere in the property. The defendants contested the suit, claiming that their sister had already received her hereditary share in the form of cash from one of her brothers. The Peshawar High Court ruled that (i) the allegation that the applicant was paid must be proven, but (ii) the alleged sale was not proved through cogent and reliable evidence.

M Akbar v. Mst Suraya Begum, 2014 MLD 1080

The Peshawar High Court placed a heavy onus on the person claiming greater inheritance proportions.

Islam-Ud-Din v. Noor Jehan, 2016 SCMR 986

The Supreme Court of Pakistan held in favor of the female heir 25 years after her father's death, despite the fact that both appellant and respondent had died.

Source: Authors.

Another common claim made by male heirs to deny female heirs' shares is to challenge the paternity of the female heirs. In the case of *Mst. Rubina Kausar v. Additional Sessions Judge*, the Lahore High Court noted that the paternity of the petitioner was only challenged when she claimed her share of inheritance.[26] The High Court also disapproved parties resorting to DNA testing as a matter of routine and held that the paternity issue could be proved by oral and documentary evidence already recorded by the trial court.

The Supreme Court, in another case, delivered a similar judgment and disapproved of DNA testing for the purpose of denying the deceased's daughter her share of the inheritance. Such DNA testing cannot be ordered without the permission of a person. In the case of *Laila Qayyum v. Fawad Qayyum*, the plaintiff sought to deprive his sister of her inheritance.[27] The Court held that it could not legally make the declarations the plaintiff sought nor could it order the cancellation of the documents. "To keep such a suit pending only harasses the petitioner further and may deprive her of her inheritance" (footnote 27).

IV. Femicide on the Pretext of "Honor"

Femicide is a gender-related killing of women. A research study by the United Nations Office on Drugs and Crime found that globally, although only 20% of all homicides are by an intimate partner or family member, 82% of victims of intimate partner killings are women and girls.[28] Sixty-four percent of all murdered women and girls are killed by family members or intimate partners, making family members and intimate partners the most dangerous people in women's lives (footnote 28).

Femicide is never honorable. It is abhorred and cannot be justified. Yet, gruesome murders are colored as honorable and are justified because men of the family are dishonored by certain acts of (generally) women in the family (e.g., marriage of her choice, talking to a man, singing at a wedding, sending a text message, not making a proper *roti* [bread]).[29] Four out of 10 people in Pakistan justify honor killings of women.[30]

Condemning the brutal killing of a 16-year old girl on the orders of a *Jirga* (an all-male tribal council), the Human Rights Commission of Pakistan warned that "rulers past and present [...] have a lot to answer for. Not least because of their failure to confront or push back strongly enough against abhorrent crimes in the name of honour, and indeed addressing the perceptions or place of women in society."[31]

It is estimated that 5,000 women are murdered globally each year in the name of honor. In Pakistan, the figure is close to 1,100.[32] The Pakistan Supreme Court noted that "Pakistan has one

---

[26] *Mst. Rubina Kausar v. Additional Sessions Judge*, PLD 2017 Lahore 604.

[27] *Laila Qayyum v. Fawad Qayyum*, L D 2019 Supreme Court 449.

[28] United Nations Office on Drugs and Crime. 2018. *Global Study on Homicide: Gender-Related Killing of Women and Girls*. Vienna. p. 18.

[29] M. Hanif. 2019. Pakistan: Where the Daily Slaughter of Women Barely Makes the News. *The Guardian*. 9 May.

[30] N. Sahgal and T. Townsend. 2014. Four-in-Ten Pakistanis say Honor Killing of Women Can Be At Least Sometimes Justified. *Pew Research Center*. 30 May.

[31] Pakistan Human Rights Commission. 2016. HRCP Aghast at Girl's Jirga-Ordained Murder. News release. 6 May.

[32] D. Selby. 2016. Everything You Should Know About Honor-Based Violence. *Global Citizen*. 22 July.

of the highest, if not the highest per capita honour killings in the world and predominantly the victims are women. By stating that murder was committed on the pretext of *ghairat* (honour) the murderer hopes to provide some justification for the crime. It may also elevate the murderer's social status with those not familiar with what Almighty Allah Commands in the Holy Qur'an. This is unfortunate, more so because there is no honour in such killings."[33]

Until recently, perpetrators of femicide on the pretext of honor had claimed provocation; the killing was due to a loss of self-control by grave and sudden provocation. Provocation requires the response to be immediate, but many femicides on the pretext of honor appear to have been planned.

What if the accused maintained that the killing was not planned and committed through a response that is immediate? In *Ali Muhammad v. The State,* the Supreme Court held that "whether the provocation was grave and sudden enough to prevent the offence from amounting to murder is a question of fact."[34] However, the latest Supreme Court decision in the *Muhammad Abbas* case held that excuses—such as seeing one's wife with a stranger—do not amount to grave and sudden provocation.[35]

One example is the murder of Naghma, a 13-year-old who was reportedly killed by her uncles on the order of a *Jirga* because she had allegedly attempted to run away with two men.[36] Naghma's murder, like many killings on the pretext of honor, was retribution carefully planned and executed. It is critical to emphatically reject retribution and revenge as defenses under the law.

Another tragic incident was the killing of Samia Sarwar who was seeking a divorce from her husband who was abusing her. Samia fled her home, seeking refuge in Lahore. Samia eventually agreed to meet her mother at her lawyer's office to discuss the divorce that her family opposed. Samia was shot at point blank by the assistant at her lawyer's office. Thereafter, the family escaped from Lahore after a chase through the city.[37] The killing was clearly premeditated, complete with an escape plan. It must be defined as vengeful retribution, not provocation. The latter requires sudden and grave response, rather than premeditation.

Currently, Section 302(c) of the PPC has removed the defense based on the pretext of honor due to the State designating these murders as falling under the category of *fasad-fil-arz,* which refers to the State's interest in prohibiting and eliminating rottenness, depravation, and corruption of society.[38]

In the *Muhammad Siddique* case, the Supreme Court castigated those who commit murder on the pretext of honor.

---

[33] *Muhammad Abbas v. The State,* Jail Petition No. 499 of 2015. para. 16.

[34] PLD 1996 SC 274.

[35] Footnote 33, para. 15.

[36] A. Malik. 2017. Relatives Kill Teenage Girl for 'Honour' on Tribal Jirga's Orders in Khyber Agency. *Dawn.* 30 June.

[37] R. Galpin. 1999. Woman's 'Honour' Killing Draws Protests in Pakistan. *The Guardian.* 8 April. See also *Dawn.* 2010. Relatives with Blood on Their Hands. 10 September.

[38] Section 299(ee) of the PPC defines "*fasad-fil-arz*" as including the past conduct of the offender, or whether he has any previous conviction, or the brutal or shocking manner in which the offense has been committed which is outrageous to the public conscience, or if the offender is considered a potential danger to the community, or if the offense has been committed in the name or on the pretext of honor.

These killings are carried out with evangelistic spirit. Little do these zealots know that there is nothing religious about it and nothing honourable either. It is male chauvinism and gender bias at their worst. These prejudices are not country specific [...] or people specific.[39]

Similarly, in *M. Akram Khan v. The State*, the Supreme Court held that nobody has the right to take the law in his own hands and take a life in the name of *ghairat* (in the name of 'honor').[40]

Neither the law of the land nor religion permits so-called honor killing, which amounts to murder (*Qatl-i-Amd*) simpliciter. Such iniquitous and vile act is violative of fundamental right as enshrined in Article 9 of the Constitution of Islamic Republic of Pakistan, which provides that no person, would be deprived of life or liberty except in accordance with law. Thus, any custom or usage in that respect is void under Article 8(1) of the Constitution.[41]

The 2020 case of *Muhammad Abbas v. The State* is the latest Supreme Court decision to consider the several conflicting decisions on the defense of provocation in a murder where the accused claims *ghairat*.

It may be clarified that we have relied on the law with regard to statement of the accused recorded under section 342 as expounded by this Court in the *Faiz* case, which was a judgment by a five-member Bench, and not on the *Muhammad Qasim* case, a judgment which was by a three-member Bench. We have also not relied on the obiter observations of another three-member Bench in *Muhammad Ameer* case. In the *Muhammad Qasim* case, the mandatory requirement to seek guidance from the Holy Qur'an and Sunnah, stipulated in 338F PPC, was not done, therefore, *Muhammad Qasim* cannot be categorized as having decided a question of law or is based upon or enunciates a principle of law.[42]

The Supreme Court went on to say unreservedly that killing is never honorable.

For Muslims the Holy Qur'an is the word of God. Killing a person is abhorrent and a grave sin. The Holy Qur'an also does not mandate the punishment of death for the offence of adultery. If the petitioner suspected his wife of infidelity, he should have followed the path prescribed by the Holy Qur'an and the law of Pakistan to resolve the matter. [...]

[...] The petitioner then couched his criminal and un-Islamic conduct by stating he became enraged to see his wife in the company of a man and on account of his *ghairat* he killed her. Almighty Allah loves those who amongst others restrain their anger. To become enraged is not an admirable trait nor is *ghairat*. The word *ghairat* nor the Arabic *ghairatun* is not used in the Holy Qur'an. The Holy Qur'an also does

---

39   *Muhammad Siddique v. The State*, PLD 2002 Lahore 444.
40   *M. Akram Khan v. The State*, PLD 2001 SC 96.
41   Footnote 40, p. 100.
42   Footnote 33, para. 17.

not permit killing on the ground of adultery, let alone on the ground of *ghairat* (*ghairatun* in Arabic), nor prescribes a lesser punishment for such killings. The law of Pakistan also does not permit this. [...]

It needs restating that killing is never honourable. And, a murder should not be categorized as such. It will help deter such killings if the term *ghairat* is not used to describe them. It is also inaccurate to translate *ghairat* into English as honour. The word *ghairat* does not have an exact English equivalent. A more accurate translation of the trait of *ghairat* would be 'arrogance' and the one with such trait is an 'arrogant' person. Almighty Allah tells us that Hell is the abode of the arrogant (*mutakabirina*). 'Those who disdained to worship Him (Allah) and were proud (*takbaru*) He (Allah) will punish them with a painful torment'. And, 'those who reject Our verses and treat them with arrogance, they are companions of the Fire, to dwell therein forever.'[43]

V. Forced and Early Marriage of Women and Girls

Forced marriage is when at least one party is forced to consent to marriage. It is a violation of human rights.[44]

An overwhelming majority of marriages in Pakistan are endogamous. Guardians—mostly fathers, brothers, and uncles—traditionally exercise the exclusive right to select marriage partners for their children, particularly girls, and their decisions are final. Around 76.1% of women do not have the freedom to choose their spouse; in Balochistan, this figure rises to 96% (footnote 10). Where a marriage is registered, guardians may deliberately omit the bride's rights. Girls and women who defy their family's wishes are at risk of being killed.

Section 365B of the PPC criminalizes the abduction or kidnapping of a woman when it is likely she will be compelled to marry or seduced to illicit intercourse. PPC Section 496A refers to detaining a woman with criminal intent for illicit intercourse. In practice, the police seem to prefer the charges under Sections 365B and 496A. Still, criminal law cannot be the sole tool to eliminate forced marriages. The State must address cultural, economic, and social norms that interact to place girls and women at risk of early and forced marriage.

A. Child Marriages

Child marriage is a form of forced marriage because children cannot give consent. Most provinces allow girls as young as 16 years to marry but maintain the minimum age for boys at 18 years

---

[43] Footnote 33, paras. 13, 15, and 18.

[44] *Convention on the Elimination of All Forms of Discrimination against Women*, New York, 18 December 1979, *United Nations Treaty Series*, Vol. 1249, No. 20378, p. 13. Art. 16. See also United Nations Office of the High Commissioner for Human Rights. Child and Forced Marriage, Including in Humanitarian Settings.

(except in Sindh where the minimum age for both man and woman is 18 years).[45] Art. 16(2) of the Convention on the Elimination of All Forms of Discrimination against Women (CEDAW) declares that the "betrothal and the marriage of a child shall have no legal effect." Child marriages also deny girls the opportunity to healthy development and education. They also expose girls to increased risk of health complications due to early pregnancy and domestic violence.[46]

Implementation of child marriage laws remains difficult due to various reasons, including "traditional norms, low rates of birth and marriage registration, and weaknesses in the police investigations and the judicial process."[47] "Data compiled by the Society for the Protection of the Rights of the Child from 20 newspapers reveal that girls suffer the most when compared to boys from harmful traditional practices."[48] Obtaining data on this is challenging because a high proportion of marriages are unregistered.[49]

B. *Watta Satta*

Another form of forced marriage is *Watta Satta*. It is a form of an exchange marriage, wherein a girl or woman from family A is married to a boy or man from family B, and a girl or woman from family B is married to a boy or man from family A. At times, there might be no suitable match, but due to the requirement of exchange marriage, they are married under duress. This is common in both rural and urban families of all strata. The prevalence is highest in one of the federally administered northern areas at 17.5%, followed by Punjab at 13.5%, Balochistan at 12.5%, North West Frontier Province/Federally Administered Tribal Area at 12%, and Azad Jammu and Kashmir at 8.5%.[50]

In addition to bad matches, if one marriage fails, pressure is placed on the other spouses to dissolve their marriage as well. The same goes for domestic violence.

C. *Ghag*

Ghag or *avaaz lagana* means to make something known. It is a Pashtun custom where a man declares that a girl is engaged to him without her or her family's consent.[51] The custom still exists although it is un-Islamic and against the Constitution and the Khyber Pakhtunkhwa Elimination of Custom of *Ghag* Act, 2013.

---

[45] The Child Marriage Restraint Act, 1929; and Sindh Child Marriages Restraint Act, 2013.

[46] UNICEF. Child Marriage is a Violation of Human Rights, But is All Too Common.

[47] S. Malkani. 2021. Why Ending Child Marriage Has Not Been Easy in Pakistan. *Scroll.in*. 15 January.

[48] G. Zahid. 2011. *Legislation and its Implementation to Protect Girl Children under 18 from Harmful Traditional Practices: Importance of the Holistic Approach.* Submission to Joint CEDAW-CRC General Recommendation on Harmful Practices.

[49] M. Ahamad Zia, et al. 2018. Child Marriages in Pakistan: Issues of Sampling, Representativeness and Generalization. *The Pakistan Journal of Social Issues*. IX. p. 163.

[50] Footnote 10, p. 79.

[51] M. Kari. 2016. Do You Know What Ghah Is? *The Express Tribune*. 10 September.

D.   Marriage to the Holy Qur'an

Marriage of girls and women with the Holy Qur'an is morally and religiously reprehensible and forbidden under Section 498C of the PPC (footnote 20). As stated earlier in the section on inheritance, these marriages occur to deprive women of their share of inheritance and from owning a property. In 2000, there were more than 5,000 women in Sindh married to the Holy Qur'an.[52]

E.   *Badla-e-Sulha, Swarra, Wanni, Sung Chatti*

Marriages that are prohibited under Section 310A of the PPC—*Badla-e-sulha* or *Wanni* or *Swara* marriages—constitute another appalling category of forced marriage. These are compensation marriages, i.e., forced marriages where girls are given as compensation to the aggrieved party as reparation for crimes committed by their male relatives. Box 5.2 contains a Punjabi poem from the perspective of a compensation marriage victim.

Box 5.2: Perspective of a Compensation Marriage Bride
(Saraiki Poem from South Punjab)

نياڑي نا توار

فاطمہ زہری مریم رابعہ بصری اریت
نے نتخاٹ زندہ جہان اٹ نسل ءنائستی دریت
ستی وسوری تابو جھ ءکو پہ غاتیا ای ہفیٹ
مسوٹ سوداای اکثر ڈ ہن مریک میٹل ہیٹ

پر کناحق آتے اتنے پاکٹے کس پُہہ متو
ای اریٹ اخداہم داباروٹ کس سوچتو

I represent Fatima, Zehra, Maryam, Rabia Basri,

I ensured your survival and your race's continuity

Bore the burdens and hardships throughout.

Yet I was treated as a merchandise, without doubt.

O! Why weren't my rights recognized by others?

O! Why wasn't I given the rights I deserved?

Source: Tahira Ehsas

Compensation marriages are widely accepted as a way of keeping the peace. "However, [underaged] girls torn from their homes in this manner often end up systematically abused and forced into a life of virtual slavery."[53] "The price of this dispute settlement is paid by women and girls by way of unceremonious wedlock, to remind the aggressors of the injustice their men bestowed upon the bereaved family."[54] Even the rituals of legal marriage are not conducted— there is no consent, no *mehr* (dower), and no public announcement. More than linkages to a specific cultural or geographic region, lack of development, illiteracy, and poverty are the common factors in areas where this is practiced.

---

[52]   Human Rights Commission of Pakistan. 2000. *Annual Report.* Islamabad.

[53]   United Nations Population Fund. 2007. *Virtual Slavery: The Practice of Compensation Marriages.*

[54]   S. Minallah. 2007. Judiciary as a Catalyst for Social Change. *Pakistan Journal of Women's Studies: Alam-e-Niswan.* 14(2).

An example is the 2005 case of three sisters in Mianwali who refused to be handed over in *Wanni*. Abda, Amna, and Sajda, then all in their teens, were promised in *Wanni* marriages 14 years before. The decision, decreed by the local *jirga*, was to save their paternal uncle who committed a murder and wanted to escape a death sentence. The sisters filed a complaint in the Supreme Court of Pakistan and were lucky to get justice and escape the marriages.[55]

After an amendment was made in the PPC criminalizing such marriages, another high-profile case from Kashmore, Sindh came to light. A parliamentarian, Mir Hazar Khan Bijarani, was allegedly involved in a *Jirga* decision where five minor girls were handed over in marriage to resolve a dispute. In 2006, the Supreme Court ordered his arrest.[56]

Similarly, in 2008, 15 minor girls were pledged in marriage to end a tribal dispute that started with the killing of a dog in Balochistan.[57]

Compensation marriages are clearly against Islam. These are heinous violations of the Holy Qur'an, which states

> And no bearer of burdens will bear the burden of another. And if a heavily laden soul calls [another] to [carry some of] its load, nothing of it will be carried, even if he should be a close relative. You can only warn those who fear their Lord unseen and have established prayer. And whoever purifies himself only purifies himself for [the benefit of] his soul. And to Allah is the [final] destination.[58]

They also violate fundamental rights under the Constitution, and penal laws of the country. Yet, compensation marriages continue.

VI. Conclusory Remarks

The ideal family, which serves as a sanctuary for men and women, where they can be safe and cared for, is sometimes wrecked with violence. This must be considered an abberation, and not a norm to be tolerated. It is the aggressors and perpetrators that commit violence who shatters the family, and not the victim of violence. Judges need to heed that stopping violence in the family is necessary to preserve a family's integrity.

It is incumbent on society to protect the weakest among us. Whether shrouded in the name of culture, erroneously justified in the name of religion or lapses in temper, the law is often the last resort to which victims appeal for violence to stop.

---

[55] *The New Humanitarian.* 2006. Focus on 'Vani'—The Practice of Giving Away Young Women to Settle Feuds. 16 March.

[56] N. Iqbal. 2007. SC Orders Arrest of Jirga Members: Handing Over of Minor Girls to Victim's Family. *Dawn.* 16 August.

[57] D. Walsh. 2008. 15 Child Brides Used to Settle Pakistan Feud. *The Guardian.* 5 June; and S. Shah. 2008. Daughters Bear the Cost of Pakistan's Family Feuds. *The Globe and Mail.* 10 June.

[58] Surah-i-Fatir 35:18.

Right to education. A father reads with his daughter in Mohmand Agency, Peshawar. Article 10 of the Convention on the Elimination of All Forms of Discrimination against Women obliges States Parties to "take all appropriate measures to eliminate discrimination against women in order to ensure them equal rights with men in the field of education" (photo by Samar Minallah Khan).

Chapter 6

UNDERSTANDING GENDER DISCRIMINATION AND GENDER EQUALITY

I.   Introduction

In order to understand gender-based violence (GBV), it is critical to be cognizant of gender discrimination and gender equality. This chapter unpacks the concepts of gender discrimination and gender equality. As mentioned in the previous chapters, GBV is a manifestation of gender discrimination and its underlying cause is rooted in gender inequality. Special provisions are required to address GBV.

II.   Gender Discrimination

A.   General Principles

The victims of GBV are predominantly women; therefore, this violence constitutes discrimination against women. It is violence perpetrated against women because they are women, or where the disproportionate impact of the violence is on women.

Discrimination against women is

(i)   any distinction, exclusion, or restriction made on the basis of sex;

(ii)   has the **effect or purpose** of impairing or nullifying the **recognition, enjoyment, or exercise** by women irrespective of their marital status;

(iii) on the basis of equality of men and women, of human rights and fundamental freedoms; and

(iv)   in the political, economic, social, cultural, civil or any other field.[1]

Discrimination against women is often sustained and perpetuated by laws, policies, cultural norms or customary practices. These policies and practices entrench gender stereotypes in society and in the law (see Chapter 2 on gender stereotyping and implicit bias). Such systemic discrimination has become

---

[1]   General Assembly Resolution 48/104, *Declaration on the Elimination of Discrimination against Women*, A/RES/48/104 (20 December 1993).

accepted and has morphed into unquestioned social norms and standards. This is referred to as **structural discrimination** or **systemic discrimination**. Structural or systemic discrimination requires a change in mindset and re-assessment of common sociocultural and legal notions of gender.

There are two other kinds of discrimination:

(i)   **Direct discrimination.** Direct discrimination occurs when someone is treated less favorably than another for prohibited reasons or due to protected characteristics. Direct discrimination is usually easily identifiable. An example is a bank that denies a woman financing facilities because she is a woman.

(ii) **Indirect discrimination.** At times what appears to be a neutral position, law, policy, or measure, actually results in discrimination of women. Sometimes, women and girls are unable to access certain facilities or take advantage of opportunities, not due to direct or intended discrimination, but, rather, because certain rules or policies are difficult or, if not impossible, for women to comply with, or because such laws inadvertently disadvantage women.

For example, an advertisement for a bank manager position requires that the bank manager be at least 5-foot, 7-inch tall, so the first question one must ask is whether this requirement can be more easily met by men than by women. In this case, the impact of the height requirement is that less women can apply as most women are generally shorter than men, and few women are 5-foot, 7-inch in height. The next question that must be considered is whether being 5-foot, 7-inch is an inherent requirement of the job. It is not discriminatory if a person can only carry out the job if he or she fulfills the requirement. Can a bank manager only carry out his duties if he is 5-foot, 7-inch in height? In this case, it is not an inherent requirement and therefore this requirement constitutes gender discrimination.

In *Israt Batool v. Government of Punjab,* the High Court was asked to decide on a recruitment policy for educators who did not allow females to apply for appointment in boys' schools.[2] The female petitioners contended that they possessed the requisite qualifications and were in a position to compete with male candidates. The Court found that the respondents were unable to prove how female candidates were unfit to perform the function of the advertised positions as educators in the boys' school. The Court reasoned that gender stereotyping, classification based on stereotype roles, or social expectations tantamount to discrimination are not permissible under the Constitution. This stereotyping goes against the constitutional mandate of equality and safeguard against discrimination in service.

Let's assume that a specific requirement included in a job advertisement is an inherent requirement. The question that remains is: can reasonable adjustments be made to help a person fulfill the inherent requirements of the job? Adjustments are reasonable if they would not be too expensive, difficult or time consuming, or would not cause some other hardship to the employer. For example, if an employer can modify the workplace to accommodate a person in a wheelchair, then the employer must make such reasonable adjustments. It is a violation of human rights to dismiss a person if reasonable adjustments can be made to help a person fulfill the inherent requirements of the job.

---

[2]   *Israt Batool v. Government of Punjab,* 2018 PLC (C.S.) Note 165.

B.   Who Is the Comparator?

In order to determine whether a person has been discriminated against, we need to identify a comparator. A comparator is a person against whom we compare the victim to assess whether there has been discrimination. If the task is to compare whether a person is discriminated because of her/his gender, then we must compare this person to another person of a different gender.

To better understand the role of the comparator, consider a situation where a flight attendant was dismissed because she was pregnant. Pregnancy is a challenging argument because only women can become pregnant. One argument put forward was that the dismissal was discriminatory on the basis of gender because of the differential treatment between a female flight attendant and a female ground staff or female chief flight attendant. This was because a female ground staff or chief flight attendant would not be dismissed if she were to become pregnant, but a flight attendant would be dismissed.

The Federal Court of Malaysia before whom this argument was made in *Beatrice Fernandez v Malaysian Airlines* held, "The applicant cannot compare herself with the ground staff or with the senior chief stewardesses or chief stewardesses as they were not employed in the same category of work."[3] The Court also said

> The equal protection guarantee [in the Constitution], therefore extends only to persons in the same class. It recognizes that all persons by nature, attainment, circumstances and the varying needs of different classes of persons often require separate treatment. Regardless of how we try to interpret [...] the Federal Constitution, we could only come to the conclusion that there was obviously no contravention (footnote 3).

Respectfully, it was incorrect to compare the flight attendant to the female ground staff or chief stewardess.[4] In a case of gender discrimination, the comparison should be between a woman and a man working in the same position. Here, the comparator to determine whether there was gender discrimination cannot be between a woman and another woman. By necessity, it must be between a woman (the plaintiff who was a female flight attendant) and a person of a different gender, in this case, a man (a male flight attendant). The plaintiff and the comparator need to be in the same class but different genders.

Was there discrimination between a man and a woman in this case? Firstly, we can try to locate a comparator as was done by the court. Obviously, a man cannot become pregnant biologically. So how do we compare them? The answer is in the fact that both men and women can have children and become parents. Here there was discrimination because a woman could not have a family and held her job as flight attendant, but a man could have a family and continued his job as flight attendant.

---

[3]   *Beatrice Fernandez v Malaysian Airlines* [2005] 2 CLJ 713.

[4]   For an analysis of the *Beatrice Fernandez* case, see Z. Abdul Aziz. 2008. Mechanisms to Promote Gender Equality: The Need for Legislation. In R. Manjoo, ed. 2008. *Women Living Under Muslim Laws*. Dossier No. 29. pp. 79–94.

Alternatively, we can also argue that in pregnancy discrimination, a comparator is not needed at all if we accept that pregnancy is a protected characteristic.

C. Protected Characteristics

Admittedly, pregnancy discrimination is one of the more complicated arguments to make as pregnancy is only experienced by one sex. Also in this category are childbirth and breastfeeding that are specific to only one sex.[5] This discussion will focus only on pregnancy and maternity.

In most cases of pregnancy discrimination, it is best to start by determining whether the discrimination is direct or indirect. For example, if a pregnant woman is dismissed because she is pregnant as in the case of Beatrice Fernandez, then it is direct discrimination.

However, oftentimes, pregnancy is not overtly stated as the reason for the dismissal. A case in point was the dismissal of a pregnant postal service employee who was medically advised to limit her lifting to 20 pounds (lb), equivalent to 9 kilograms (kg), instead of the employer-mandated 70 lb (31.7 kg). Upon closer scrutiny, the dismissal could be said to have been indirectly due to the pregnancy. If it is indirect discrimination, then reasonable accommodation could have been made. For this reason, some scholars and jurists argue that pregnant women should be compared to a temporarily disabled person. The Supreme Court of the United States, in finding that the dismissed postal service employee could bring a case of pregnancy discrimination, cautioned that the reason for such dismissal cannot be that it was "more expensive or less convenient to add pregnant women to the category of those (similar in their ability or inability to work) whom the employer accommodates."[6] She was unavailable for work for a certain period and therefore should be provided leave.

On the other hand, pregnancy protection and maternity leave can be uncommonly long (upward of 12 weeks). Comparing a pregnant woman to any other person who is unable to work for health reasons does not address the characteristic that pregnancy is attributable to only one sex, namely women.

As the Canadian Supreme Court puts it, "[i]n retrospect, one can only ask -- how could pregnancy discrimination be anything other than sex discrimination? [...] It is only women who bear children; no man can become pregnant. It is unfair to impose all of the costs of pregnancy upon one half of the population. Discrimination against some women must be taken to be discrimination against all women."[7] In the example of sexual harassment, an employer who sexually harasses only some of his female employees and leaves other female employees alone cannot be said not to discriminate by reason of sex because the harassment affects only one group of women adversely.[8] Similarly, discriminating against only pregnant female employees alone cannot be said not to discriminate by reason of sex because the discrimination affects only one group of women adversely.

---

5   Other prohibited grounds include but are not limited to marital status, parenthood, family responsibilities, expressions or characteristics, and prejudices that are generally identified or not identified to a person of that gender.

6   *Young v. United Parcel Service*, Inc., 575 U.S. 206 (2015).

7   *Brooks v Canada Safeway Ltd* [1989] 1 SCR 1219.

8   Footnote 7, citing *Zarankin v Johnstone* [1984] 5 C.H.R.R. D/2274.

Maternity (including pregnancy) is protected under both the Constitution and international law. Violation of this protection constitutes discrimination. Article 25 of the Constitution guarantees equality and prohibits gender discrimination. Article 25(3) further allows the State to make special provisions for women and children. In most provinces, maternity leave benefits legislation mandates 12 weeks of paid leave (16 weeks in Sindh). Similarly, Article 4 of the Convention on the Elimination of All Forms of Discrimination against Women (CEDAW) provides that special measures aimed at protecting maternity shall not be considered discriminatory.[9] Maternity protection constitutes a separate and distinct claim under discrimination law. In other words, these are positive rights provided for pregnant women and nursing mothers (special measures on protecting maternity are discussed below).

D. Intersectional Discrimination

Gender discrimination may not be the only form of discrimination encountered by a person who comes to court. For example, a woman who is poor may face two downward pressures. She may be discriminated against because she is a woman and because she is poor. Another instance is that female victims often do not have autonomy to decide whether to file or withdraw a complaint as such decisions are often made by their male relatives. A female victim from a poor family is more vulnerable to coercion and threats not to testify in court against her rapist or to lie that she had 'misidentified' the accused. This is because she faces two forms of discrimination, firstly, because she is a woman and secondly, because she is poor.[10]

Justice is blind, so the saying goes. Unfortunately being blind does not mean that justice is equally accessible to all. It is important to remember that access to justice is often more challenging for certain groups or communities, and women from these groups or communities face multiple obstacles and intersectional forms of discrimination.

E. Gender Discrimination Violates the Right to Life

Gender discrimination is a grave issue impacting the right to life. The Constitution protects fundamental rights and freedoms, including the rights to life, security, information, property, and education; freedom from slavery; freedom of movement, speech, and association; equality of citizens; and freedom from gender discrimination. The right to life has been defined to include the inherent right to live with dignity.

The Supreme Court of India's definition of the "right to life" is instructive:

> Equality, dignity of person and right to development are inherent rights in every human being. Life in its expanded horizon includes all that give meaning to a person's life including culture, heritage and tradition with dignity of person. The fulfilment of that heritage in full measure would encompass the right to life. For its

---

9   *Convention on the Elimination of All Forms of Discrimination against Women*, New York, 18 December 1979, *United Nations Treaty Series*, Vol. 1249, No. 20378, p. 13.

10   K. Crenshaw. 1989. *Demarginalising the Intersection of Race and Sex*. Chicago: University of Chicago Legal Forum. pp. 139, 151.

meaningfulness and purpose every woman is entitled to elimination of obstacles and discrimination based on gender for human development. Women are entitled to enjoy economic, social, cultural and political rights without discrimination and on a footing of equality. Equally in order to effectuate fundamental duty to develop scientific temper, humanism and the spirit of enquiry and to strive towards excellence in all spheres of individual and collective activities [...] facilities and opportunities not only are to be provided for, but also all forms of gender-based discrimination should be eliminated. It is a mandate to the State to do these acts. Property is one of the important endowments or natural assets to accord opportunity, source to develop personality, to be independent, right to equal status and dignity of person. Therefore, the State should create conditions and facilities conducive for women to realise the right to economic development including social and cultural rights.[11]

III. Gender Equality

A. General Principles

Gender equality is rooted in the principle that men and women should be valued equally because of their similarities and despite their differences. We need equal, respectful partnerships between men and women in the same way that we need both eyes to see best.

Generally, there are three principles of equality. All three are practiced but only one is accepted as the correct and applicable principle. CEDAW adopts the correct substantive equality principle.

(i) Formal equality

The principle of formal equality does not recognize differences. It treats men and women the same and requires equal treatment of men and women. It assumes equality is achieved so long as the law does not expressly treat men and women differently. Formal equality is premised on the fact that women are "like" men, and therefore women and men are to be treated the same. This notion requires similarly situated persons to be treated alike.

Formal equality does not recognize nor account for legitimate differences between men and women. Neither does it look at inequality between men and women as to opportunity or effect. It also uses male standards, and puts the burden on women to measure to the male standard.

What if equal treatment yields disparate results? Sometimes treating women and men the same is discriminatory and sometimes treating them differently is discriminatory. Much like how sometimes treating persons without disabilities and persons with disabilities as the same is discriminatory and, at other times, treating

---

[11] *C. Masilamani Mudaliar v. Idol of Sri Swaminathaswami Swaminathaswami Thirukoil*, (1996) 8 SCC 525.

them differently is discriminatory.[12] Formal equality cannot resolve this and does not consider nuance or shades of gray when examining discrimination.

(ii) Protectionist equality

Protectionist equality recognizes differences and considers women's weakness as the rationale for different treatment. This is based on the misconceived notion that women's weakness requires women to be protected from, or makes them unsuitable for, certain activities otherwise available to men. The protectionist equality principle considers women's weakness as justification for unequal treatment between men and women.

Consequently, the protectionist equality principle drives and justifies inequality in the name of protectionism. Under this principle, women may be banned or dissuaded from holding certain jobs or offices that are considered too dangerous, too demanding, or just plainly unsuitable for women. For example, the protectionist equality principle may be used to prohibit women from running for electoral office on the false argument that being a politician is too demanding for a woman. Consequently, women lose the chance to obtain a varied range of opportunities due to exclusion.

In *Government of Punjab v. Qanoot Fatima*, the Court noted that although female corporals were appointed, they were not assigned field work because they were considered vulnerable and weak, hence they were given office jobs and not field work.[13] This justification, said the Court, could not be appreciated or given legal sanctity as women must be trained along with their male counterparts and allowed to participate in the field. The Court further stated that "Gender stereotyping or classification based on stereotype roles or social expectations is tantamount to discrimination which is not permissible under the Constitution and goes against the constitutional mandate of equality" (footnote 13).

(iii) Substantive equality

The principle of substantive equality recognizes differences and affirms equality between men and women. It places an obligation on the State to correct the environment that disadvantages women and considers equality to have been achieved only when there is

(i)   equality of opportunity,

(ii) equality of access; and

(iii) equality of results or outcomes.

For example, in Figure 6.1, the illustration on the left is based on the formal equality model and the one on the right is based on the substantive equality model. The illustration on the right ensures equality of opportunity, access, and results/outcomes.

---

[12]   A glaring example of how formal equality should not be applicable is in relation to persons with disabilities. Equal treatment between persons with disabilities and persons without disabilities may result in exclusion of persons with disabilities.

[13]   *Government of Punjab v. Qanoot Fatima*, 2018 PLC (C.S.) 22.

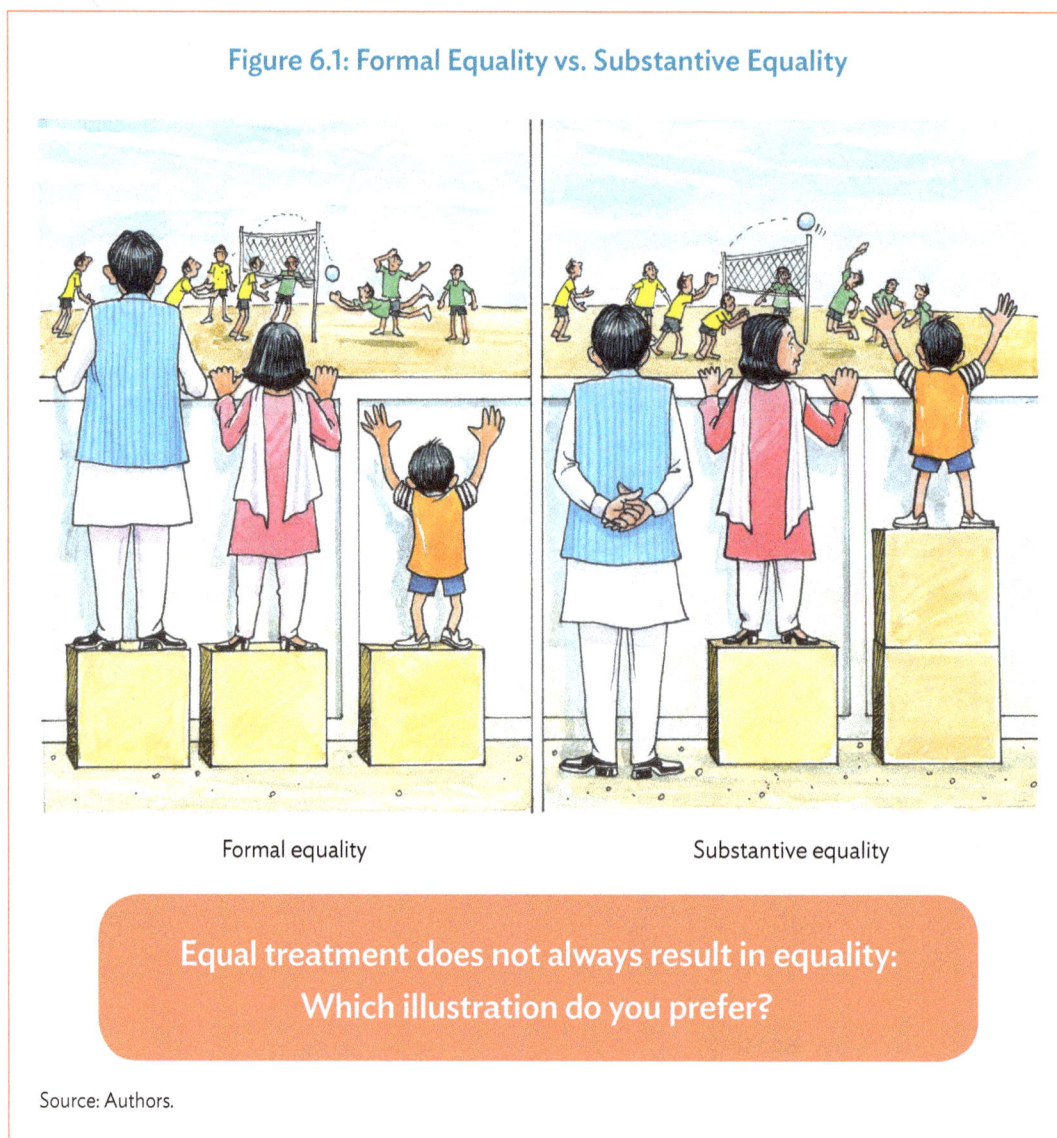

Figure 6.1: Formal Equality vs. Substantive Equality

Formal equality   Substantive equality

Equal treatment does not always result in equality: Which illustration do you prefer?

Source: Authors.

The doctrine of equality has evolved from the requirement that women be treated equally with men to the requirement that women not be subjected to detrimental treatment due to their gender. This is the principle adopted under CEDAW. Under this principle, if it is safe for a boy, but not for a girl, to travel to school and back home each day, then the answer is the authorities must make sure it is safe for both boys and girls to travel to school. It is discriminatory on the basis of gender for the State not to ensure that travelling to school each day is safe for both girls and boys.

B.   Special Measures

Another important principle is special measures. Special measures are equivalent to the constitutional exception under Article 25(3) of the Pakistan Constitution which states, "[n]othing in this Article shall prevent the State from making any special provision for the protection of women and children." Similarly, Article 4 of CEDAW provides for adoption by State Parties of special measures, including those measures contained in the present Convention, aimed at protecting maternity which shall not be considered discriminatory.

The constitutional special provisions relate to two categories of special provisions. The first of these are nonidentical treatment of women and men due to their biological differences. They are considered of a permanent nature, and refer to the provision of general conditions or the adoption of general social policies to improve the situation of women and girls. Clear examples are protection of maternity or women's reproductive rights. Biological differences dictate that only women can become pregnant and nurse babies. Therefore, special provisions relating to maternity benefits and crèches to enable nursing mothers to breastfeed are not discriminatory. In international law (CEDAW) parlance, these are called special measures. These special measures are permanent.

Constitutional special provisions under Article 25(3) may also relate to provisions that are not due to biological differences but historical disadvantage. Under CEDAW, these are called temporary special measures. Temporary special measures aim to address past (historical) and current discrimination and accelerate the achievement of de facto or substantive equality between men and women. An example is the imposition of gender quotas for tertiary education or candidates put up by political parties for election. These quotas are not discriminatory because they are intended to address past and current discrimination—that is to neutralize the effect of some of the barriers to girl's education and women's political participation and accelerate the achievement of equality between genders.

Temporary special measures cannot just be the imposition of quotas but must also include adequate training to imbue women with the knowledge and skills to fill quotas. For example, women who have not had opportunities to be involved in the political process, because of social and cultural barriers, need special training to develop knowledge of the electoral process and skills on how to run for elections, including raising funds and establishing a constituency, to effectively fulfill the quotas.

Temporary special measures are not discriminatory. On the contrary, they are measures to address discrimination and, as such, as soon as equality is achieved and when there are no more past discriminatory practices or bias to be addressed, these measures should be removed.

For example, in Figure 6.1, the woman is given a special measure (one box). This special measure is permanent (the woman's height is permanent). The boy is given a temporary special measure (two boxes). It is temporary because the boxes will be removed one after another as the boy grows up, and as soon as he is tall enough, he won't need any more boxes.

It is important to remember that temporary special measures are meant to accelerate the achievement of substantive equality. For this reason, measures such as quotas and reserved seats represent the "very minimum number" and NOT the maximum number of designated persons to be appointed. If there are more women who are qualified than the minimum requisite number under the quota, the qualified women should all be equally able to compete in the recruitment process. Implementing a gender quota to limit the number of women appointees to the very minimum runs contrary to the Constitution; the quota is used not to limit the number of women appointed but is instead meant to guarantee that the maximum number of women are given the opportunity to be appointed (footnote 13). For example if the parliamentary quota for women is 30%, it does not mean that women can only run for 30% of the parliamentary seats. It means that women can run for as many seats as they wish, but at least 30% of those seats must be occupied by women.

IV. Culture and Gender Ideology

Gender ideology is the complex set of ideas related to beliefs about roles and behaviors associated with women and men. Each society comes with their own unique gender ideology. It is this gender ideology that plays a vital role in determining the status relegated to genders in a given society.

Culture is the site of many of our good values and judgments. It is also the site of many of our prejudices and social practices. In some cultures, men believe they are spiritually superior to women and that women are dangerous, polluting, weak, and untrustworthy.[14] These beliefs allow for the oppression of women in all aspects of life and cause a serious impediment in the growth and prosperity of an entire gender. The cultural assumption that girls are inferior to boys permeates many aspects of a female child's life.

The manifestations of gender ideology, such as the belief that infant girls are inferior or expressing grief and shame at the birth of a female child, are exhibited in everyday cultural practice. The practice also serves as a constant reminder that the female child is a guest in her home, soon will marry and leave her family, tribe, and *Biradari* (patrilineal clan or paternal lineage), and that she is living on borrowed time in her nuclear family.[15] As a result of this cultural belief, preference is given to males during distribution of wealth and resources, denying girls and women of their rights to inheritance, painting girls and women as the bearer of misfortune, and even sacrificing them for the sake of male 'honor.' What is more egregious is the conversion of women to chattels that can be used to pay debts to other males and groups in society, denying women their humanity and condemning them to lives of suffering.

Each country is entitled to practice and preserve its culture. Indeed the defense of cultural diversity is an ethical imperative, inseparable from respect for human dignity. This is protected under international instruments such as the United Nations Educational, Scientific and Cultural Organization (UNESCO) Universal Declaration on Cultural Diversity.[16]

Preserving culture, however, does not mean preserving every societal or customary practice. Culture is dynamic and continuously changing. Detrimental practices need not be preserved. Other practices, even those that privileged powerful members of society defend in the name of culture, have been delegitimized or abandoned due to changing values and ethos.[17] Practices

---

[14] M. Harris. 2007. *Cultural Anthropology*. Seventh Edition. Los Angeles: University of California.

[15] A person who marries outside his *Biradari* is considered to have accepted an inferior status. Preferential marriages are cousin marriages from the father's family.

[16] *UNESCO Universal Declaration on Cultural Diversity*, Paris, 2 November 2001.

[17] Z. Abdul Aziz. 2013. Culture, Power and Violence in Domestic Violence Narrative. In M. Mohamad and Anor, eds. *Family Ambiguity and Domestic Violence in Asia: Concept, Law and Process*. London: Sussex Academic Press. pp. 53–77.

like slavery and torture have evolved over time from acceptable practices to prohibited norms internationally.[18] After all, as eloquently said by the Supreme Court of Pakistan in the *Muhammad Siddique* case, "[n]o tradition is sacred, no convention indispensable, and no precedent worth emulation if it does not stand the test of the fundamentals of a civil society generally expressed through the law and the Constitution."[19]

The Supreme Court of the United States, in a case on discriminatory racial segregation, reasoned that

> Local customs, however hardened by time, are not decreed in heaven. Habits and feelings they engender may be counteracted and moderated. Experience attests that such local habits and feelings will yield, gradually though this be, to law and education. And educational influences are exerted not only by explicit teaching. They vigorously flow from the fruitful exercise of the responsibility of those charged with political official power and from the almost unconsciously transforming actualities of living under law.[20]

Let's take the example of women and education. Islam places great emphasis on seeking knowledge. However, a massive number of girls are prohibited from studying beyond primary school due to orthodox and conservative cultural mindsets erroneously passed off as religious practices. The dwindling number of female students in the student body as it progresses from primary to university level is a case in point.

In Pakistan, while 96.47% of the population is Muslim and Islam is declared in Article 2 of the Constitution as the State religion, most of the cultural aspects dominating the lives and relationships between genders are interpreted with notions stemming from the local subcontinental customary or traditional practices.[21] Examples include denying women inheritance, the practice of dowry, discouraging widowed women from remarrying, and various forms of forced marriages justified in the name of culture, such as *Watta Satta, Walwar, Sar Paisa, Addo Baddo, Sang Chatti, Swara, Wanni, Pait Likhi* (betrothals of girls at birth to a male member of the family), and marriage to the Qur'an. A research in 2017 involving 4,385 ever-married women, aged 18–83 years, from six rural districts, found 12% marriages were the result of *Wanni, Swara, Sang Chatti, Badal, Bazo* (i.e., to settle blood feuds) and 58.7% were *Watta Satta/Pait Likhai* (i.e., exchange marriages and pledging a fetus).[22] In 7.9% marriages, the bride was bought; 1.0% marriages were *Badal-i-Sulh* (i.e., to settle disputes other than murder); and 0.1% women were married to Qur'an (footnote 22). The traditional marriages, where wishes of both families and consent of the couple to be married are considered, constituted 20.3% (footnote 22).

---

[18] Z. Abdul Aziz. 2013. *Slavery has been Declared a Crime against Humanity*. See also (i) *Slavery Convention*, Geneva, 25 September 1926; (ii) *Supplementary Convention on the Abolition of Slavery, the Slave Trade, and Institutions and Practices Similar to Slavery*, Geneva, 30 April 1957, *United Nations Treaty Series*, Vol. 266, No. 3822, p. 3; and (iii) *Convention against Torture and Other Cruel, Inhuman or Degrading Treatment or Punishment*, New York, 10 December 1984, *United Nations Treaty Series*, Vol. 1465, No. 24841, p. 85.

[19] *Muhammad Siddique v. The State*, PLD 2002 Lahore 444.

[20] *Cooper v. Aaron*, 358 U.S. 1 (1958), per Frankfurter J. p. 25. This was a case about abolishing slavery in the United States.

[21] Pakistan Bureau of Statistics. 2021. Final Results of Sixth Population & Housing Census-2017: Population by Sex, Religion and Rural/Urban.

[22] N. Rehan and K. Qayyum. 2017. Customary Marriages in Rural Pakistan. *Med J Malaysia*. 72 (3).

These are all customs which are not part of Islam and, in fact, are fundamentally against the basic principles of Islam. These detrimental and harmful cultural practices are not protected under international law, nor should they be. No one may invoke cultural diversity to infringe upon or limit the scope of human or fundamental rights guaranteed by law.[23] The idea of achieving cohesion of a cultural community by denying women their rights is prohibited by CEDAW. CEDAW obligates State Parties to take all appropriate measures to modify the social and cultural patterns of conduct of men and women, with a view to achieving the elimination of prejudices, customs, and all other practices that are based on gender stereotypes or the idea of the inferiority or superiority of either of the genders.[24]

A cursory look at the life of Prophet Muhammad (PBUH) shows that far from considering women dangerous, polluting, weak and untrustworthy, the Prophet (PBUH) held women in high esteem. These traditions however were muffled in the formal and informal enculturation of generations of Muslims which has ignored the role religion positively played in empowering women. Yet, examples from his life show time and again how much the Prophet (PBUH) trusted the advice, help, and support coming from the women in his life.

During many of the most critical turning points in the Prophet's (PBUH) life, it was a woman that stood by him. On the night of the first revelation, a time when the Prophet had the most astounding experience of his life, he hastened to tell his wife Khadija. He flung himself, shivering, into Khadija's arms and exclaimed, "Cover me! Cover me!" (Sahih Bukhari 1:3). Of all the people he could go to, he went to his wife and not to his uncle Talib, or friend Abu Bakr, or cousin Ali.

The role played by Asma bint Abu Bakr in the Prophetic journey called Hijra, which is a watershed moment in Islamic history, is another example. At a juncture when the Prophet's enemies were searching for him, the Prophet (PBUH) only trusted a few people with his secret refuge at Saur cave—among them was the 27-year-old Asma who served as the Prophet's supply line. Asma narrates, "I prepared the journey-food for Allah's Apostle in Abu Bakr's house when he intended to emigrate to Medina. I could not find anything to tie the food container and the water skin with. So, I said to Abu Bakr, 'By Allah, I do not find anything to tie (these things) with except my waist belt.' He said, 'Cut it into two pieces and tie the water skin with one piece and the food container with the other.'" The sub-narrator added, "She did accordingly and that was the reason for calling her *Dhatun-Nitaqain* (i.e., two-belted woman, in reference to Asma who took food and water to the Prophet (PBUH) when he was hiding in Saur cave)."[25]

Whether in the Mosque or in the battlefield, the Prophetic conduct regarding gender roles had always been revolutionary. Nusaiba bint e Kaab, also known as Umm e Ammara, was one of those privileged to have gone down in history as part of a small band which defended the Prophet in the battle of Uhud. At the battle of Uhud, the Prophet was quoted as saying, wherever he looked he saw Umm e Ammara. This should have served as proof of the high regard for women and a beacon of light and shining example of the vital role women could and should play in society.[26]

---

[23]   Footnote 16, Article 4.

[24]   Footnote 9, Article 5.

[25]   Sahih Bukhari Book 52, Hadith 222.

[26]   A. Husain. 2020. Appreciating Nusaybah Bint Ka`b: The Humanitarian and Warrior. *About Islam*. 13 October.

Combating detrimental cultural practices does not jeopardize the existence and cohesion of a specific cultural community. According to Farida Shaheed, former UN Special Rapporteur in the Field of Cultural Rights, it is critical to address "the primary hold of custom. [...] Legal and institutional reform must therefore be accompanied with advocacy to modify behaviour and attitudes including campaigns to change mindset, provision of legal, financial and other support to women so as to enable them to claim their rights safely without endangering their lives and the lives of those who support them."[27]

V. Discrimination Based on Gender Identity

Discrimination based on gender identity is another form of gender discrimination. Gender identity is the intrinsic sense of being female, male, or transgender. The Supreme Court of India, in affirming the fundamental rights of transgenders, said, "Seldom, our society realizes or cares to realize the trauma, agony and pain which the members of Transgender community undergo, nor appreciates the innate feelings of the members of the Transgender community, especially of those whose mind and body disown their biological sex."[28]

Even simple applications to recognize the gender of a transgender person is fraught with legal obstacles. In the Malaysian case of *JG v Jabatan Pendaftaran Negara*, the High Court of Kuala Lumpur granted the applicant's application that the requisite amendments be made in the national registry to reflect the applicant's gender identity.[29] The Court held that of the four determinants of gender—namely, chromosomal factor, gonadal factor (presence of testes or ovaries), genital factor (including internal sex organs), and psychological factor—psychological factor had received insufficient prominence in the determination of the gender of a person. That presumption needs to be corrected because the psychological factor could not be considered at birth, as it is not yet manifested, but it may become an overriding consideration subsequently as the individual develops.

In a Pakistan High Court decision, the court directed that the petitioner be allowed to get treatment for Gender Dysphoria, including a sexual reassignment surgery.[30] In *Mian Asia v. The Federation of Pakistan*, the Lahore High Court held that everyone has the right to recognition and is entitled to enjoy all human rights without discrimination on the basis of gender identity.[31] No one can be denied the right to obtain a computerized national identity card (CNIC) or citizenship because the person does not know the whereabouts of her parents (which is required when applying for a CNIC).

The scope of the principle of equal treatment for men and women cannot be confined to the prohibition of discrimination based on the fact that a person is of one or the other sex but must also seek to safeguard discrimination arising from the gender reassignment of a person.[32]

---

[27] S. Farida. 1998. *Engagements of Culture, Customs and Law: Women's Lives and Activism*. Lahore: Shirkat Gah. See also United Nations, Human Rights Council, *Report of the Special Rapporteur in the Field of Cultural Rights*, A/67/287 (10 August 2012).

[28] *National Legal Services Authority v. Union of India*, (2014) AIR 2014 SC 1863.

[29] *JG v Jabatan Pendaftaran Negara* [2005] 4 CLJ 710.

[30] [citation intentionally omitted]

[31] *Mian Asia v. The Federation of Pakistan*, PLD 2018 Lahore 54.

[32] Directive 2006/54/EC of European Parliament and of the Council (5 July 2006).

Truck art. A man paints the caption on a truck art in Multan, Punjab: "*Vanni* (compensation marriages) are illegal and un-Islamic." The placard the girl is holding says, "Education is light" (photo by Samar Minallah Khan).

Chapter 7

UNDERSTANDING AND INTERACTING WITH VICTIMS DURING THE CRIMINAL PROCESS

I.   Introduction

This chapter builds upon the previous chapters, notably Chapter 2, on the barriers to women accessing justice. The focus is on three issues: (i) what victims experience before the court in their communications with the police and medical personnel (first responders); (ii) victims' need for protection and support; and (iii) availability of legal aid.

The chapter explores the practices in Pakistan and international good practices of first responders, and how judicial officials may improve justice outcomes for victims, particularly through timely and effective protection orders.

II.   Before Coming to Court

It takes courage for women to lay a complaint for gender-based violence (GBV) crimes committed against them. Frequently women do not report GBV at all.

A 2017 report by the Overseas Development Institute noted that in Bangladesh, Nepal, and Pakistan, domestic violence was underreported and the formal justice system was a major challenge.[1] The study reveals that the view "intimate partner violence is a private matter" was widely held. It reports that in Pakistan, formal services are often not accessed until "women's lives are in danger" and there is a strong desire to keep intimate partner violence a private matter. Further, additional violence is often inflicted by the in-laws when the woman seeks justice.

First responders need to adopt a mindset that prioritizes assisting the victims without judgment and treating them with dignity. This also means recognizing that while human dignity is the autonomy of the individual will and freedom of

---

[1]   F. Samuels, et al. 2017. *Men and Intimate Partner Violence: From Research to Action in Bangladesh, Nepal and Pakistan*. London: Overseas Development Institute (ODI). ODI is an independent global think tank that undertakes cutting-edge research and analysis.

> "The way in which victims are treated by first responders when they first report a crime against them, particularly sexual assault, is key to their ability to pursue their case through the justice system and their ability to recover from the trauma of the crime.
>
> Source: College of Policing (United Kingdom). Briefing Note for Police First Responders to a Report of Rape or Sexual Assault.

choice, "human dignity is infringed if a person's life or physical or mental welfare is harmed."[2]

A. Police

Social barriers such as victim blaming, lack of support from family members, fear of rejection by family and/or community, fear of retribution, and feelings of shame and self-blame, all work together to cause nontypical responses from police first responders.[3] Women may appear calm, but first responders should ensure they do not interpret composure or even apparent cheerfulness as indications that an assault did not occur.

First responders need to understand the psychological effects on victims as well as the relationships between victims and the criminal justice system. The guidelines from the United Kingdom's College of Policing may serve as good practice. The guidelines provide the following critical protocol in responding to victims of GBV:

- Where possible, allow victims to choose whether they [want to] speak to [a] female police officer;

- Remain calm and actively listen (concentrating on what the victim is saying and using an appropriate tone of voice in response);

- Acknowledge the victims' ordeal;

- Work toward gaining the victim's trust;

- Make appropriate referrals to other service providers; and

- Under no circumstances should [the] police engage in victim blaming.[4]

The police need to ask questions of the victim and understand that victims may struggle to remember precise details of the violence, or they may experience emotional numbness. If interviews are conducted by male police and prosecutors, this might create a gender dynamic that may be especially uncomfortable for a woman or girl who has suffered violence at the hands of a man. Victims often need to feel safe and supported before reporting and trauma can result in delayed reporting.[5]

---

[2] *Asfandyar Khan Tareen v. Government of Punjab*, PLJ 2018 Lahore 508.

[3] A.R. Klein. 2008. *Practical Implications of Current Domestic Violence Research, Part II: Prosecution.* Report submitted to the National Institute of Justice, United States.

[4] College of Policing (United Kingdom). Briefing Note for Police First Responders to a Report of Rape or Sexual Assault.

[5] United Nations Office on Drugs and Crime. 2014. *Handbook on Effective Prosecution Responses to Violence Against Women and Girls.* Vienna. pp. 50–51.

Pakistan Police Practice

In October 2016, the Criminal Law (Amendment) (Offences Relating to Rape) Act, 2016 introduced many changes to the Criminal Procedure Code (CrPC) and the Pakistan Penal Code (PPC), including with regard to police contact. On many occasions throughout reporting and trial, the victim may come into police contact. Contact occasions can be

(i)   at the place of the incidence;

(ii) at the time of case registration or when the police take or record the victim's statement;

(iii) when taken by the police for medical examination, including contact when obtaining judicial permission for the examination;[6]

(iv) when attending the laboratory for DNA testing after the initial medical examination for DNA;[7] and

(v)   when the victim is taken before a magistrate to have a statement recorded.

Additional statutory provisions include the following:

- The police shall register all cases if the information given by the woman relates to a cognizable offense. If the offense is one in which a woman is hurt by a corrosive substance (PPC Section 336B); or a woman's modesty is outraged (PPC Section 354); or a woman is stripped naked in public (PPC Section 354A); or a woman is raped (PPC Section 376); or sexual harassment (PPC Section 509) is committed in the presence of a witness, it is mandatory to note this information while recording the case (PPC Sections 376 and 509, respectively). Presence of a female police officer or a family member or any other person with her consent is mandatory.

- If a woman complainant of any of the offenses mentioned above is distressed, the case shall be recorded by an officer at a place the victim chooses in the presence of a female police officer or a family member or another person with the victim's consent.

Police Standard Operating Procedures. Police conduct is, or should be, guided by standard operating procedures (SOPs). In Punjab, the Inspector General of Police issued SOPs on 20 August 2013, primarily in relation to rape cases. They refer to good practices, such as treating a victim courteously and with utmost sympathy, and not asking embarrassing or indecent questions. The incident must be recorded as early as possible in the informant's own words. After the formation of GBV Court in Lahore, the SOP established in October 2017 provides that the arrangements for taking the Section 164 statement of the victim should enable the statement to be recorded during the first half of the day and no unrelated person should be present in the court room. Regrettably, these measures may not be known or implemented in practice. The relevance of this information for judges and prosecutors is that if the police do not follow their

---

6   See discussion on the need for consent of the female victim and the need for a female police officer in Chapter 9.

7   See Chapter 9 on the need for consent where practicable.

SOP with victims, the conduct should not be ignored; it should be called out in court judgments or formal complaints should be made to the relevant authority.

Female Police Officers

Pakistan's 2018 periodic report to the Committee on the Elimination of Discrimination against Women states that 20 "Women Police Stations" (i.e., staffed with female officers) have been established in different cities all over Pakistan.[8] Meanwhile, women help desks and complaint cells have been established in 696 police stations in Punjab to facilitate female victims accessing police stations (footnote 8). By contrast, the Human Rights Commission of Pakistan 2018 report notes that there were only three women police stations in Punjab province that were staffed with female police officers (Lahore, Rawalpindi, and Faisalabad).[9] It would therefore appear that relatively few women police officers are in fact employed. In 2017, women accounted for less than 2% of the police force in spite of the 10% quota, and they are under resourced (footnote 9).

It is critical to not only have female officers at help desks, but also to have female officers investigating the crimes. Research indicates that female police officers tend to be more supportive than male police officers.[10] If a female victim does not receive attention from a female police officer, judges should call attention to this in their judgments.

Women Attending Police Stations

In making a complaint, it is common for women to come to the police accompanied by a man. A 2017 research report states that "in Pakistan's male-dominated culture, women are suppressed and therefore vulnerable to exploitation and violence. Even after an incident, they must depend on their male relatives to seek justice."[11]

A needs assessment undertaken by the Asian Development Bank (ADB) found that even if the male member was supportive of a woman making a complaint, he may be persuaded to abandon the formal complaint even by the police due to sociocultural views about domestic violence.[12] The 2017 National Commission on the Status of Women report indicates that it is not uncommon for the police to refuse to register rape cases.[13]

These accord with the United States Department of State Human Rights Report 2018, which indicates that the police and judges were sometimes reluctant to act on domestic violence

---

[8]   Government of Pakistan. 2018. *Fifth Periodic Report Submitted by Pakistan under Article 18 of the Convention, Due in 2017.* Islamabad. para. 73.

[9]   Human Rights Commission of Pakistan. 2019. *State of Human Rights in 2018.* Lahore. p. 78.

[10]   J. Hirschel and D.J. Dawson. 2000. *Violence against Women: Synthesis of Research for Law Enforcement Officials.* Report submitted to the United States Department of Justice.

[11]   S.B. Khan and S. Gul. 2017. The Criminalisation of Rape in Pakistan. *Chr. Michelsen Institute Working Paper Series.* No. 8. Bergen: Chr. Michelsen Institute. p. 18.

[12]   Asian Development Bank (Office of the General Counsel). 2017. Consultation Mission to Punjab, Pakistan: Legal Literacy for Women Technical Assistance. Needs Assessment Report (internal).

[13]   S. Warraich et al. 2017. *Access to Justice for Survivors of Sexual Assault: A Pilot Study.* Islamabad: National Commission on the Status of Women in Pakistan. p. 34. Cited in United Kingdom Home Office. 2020. *Country Policy and Information Note, Pakistan: Women Fearing Gender-Based Violence.* p. 48.

cases, viewing them as a family problem; and they typically respond by encouraging the parties to reconcile.[14]

Additional views elicited during the ADB needs assessment survey reveal further complications:

- Often a male relative who is not a witness is the complainant and not the victim resulting in the complaint containing hearsay information.

- Often police officers fail to use the words of the victim.

- Male complainants sometimes make false allegations. They would claim, for example, that their daughter was abducted, when it was a runaway marriage, forcing the daughter, if found, to similarly make a false allegation.

In summary, it is imperative for police officers to

- take a full statement in the victim's own words and read it to her if she cannot read;

- ensure she is treated and spoken to sensitively;

- ensure the victim is not under pressure to make the allegation (allowing the victim to make her complaint in the absence of the male who accompanies her); and

- ensure a proper investigation is conducted.

Such an approach by the police will go a considerable way to help increase conviction rates and reduce resiling and attrition (see Chapter 12).

B. Medical Personnel

Medical personnel are also frequently first responders.[15] The World Health Organization (WHO) provides good practice recommendations for healthcare providers on how to identify and treat domestic violence or sexual assault.[16] Summarizing these recommendations, first-line support should include

- consultation conducted in private;

- questions about history of violence, without pressuring her to talk;

- providing nonjudgmental support and validation;

- offering comfort and help to alleviate anxiety;

- providing practical support that responds to her concerns; and

- helping her access information about resources, including coping strategies, legal, and other services that might be helpful.

---

[14] Government of the United States, Department of State, Bureau of Democracy, Human Rights, and Labor. 2019. *Country Reports on Human Rights Practices for 2018: Pakistan.* p. 39.

[15] West Virginia Foundation for Rape Information and Services, Inc. *First Response to Sexual Assault.*

[16] WHO. 2013. *Responding to Intimate Partner Violence and Sexual Violence Against Women: WHO Clinical and Policy Guidelines.* Geneva.

Pakistan Medical Examination Practice

Section 164A of the CrPC has particular requirements about a medical examination for offenses under Sections 376, 377, and 377B of the PPC:

- Where possible, female victims must be escorted by a female police officer or family member.

- The medical examination must be done without delay.

- The victim must be examined by a registered medical practitioner, and in cases of rape or where a victim is female, by a female registered medical practitioner (see Chapter 9).

- The medical examination is mandatory unless an adult victim or the guardian of the victim does not consent.

- Section 164B CrPC requires that where practicable, DNA samples be collected from the victim with consent.

Section 164A CrPC does not require permission from a magistrate for medical examination of the victim. However, Police Rules, 1934 (rule 25.22) erroneously requires a written order from a magistrate; and the Police SOPs in Punjab issued on 10 November 2020 prohibit medical examination without a judicial order, which can cause delay when time is important. SOPs state that if the case is reported for medical examination within 96 hours of alleged occurrence of the crime, all evidence must be collected, but after that time, only clothing or items outside the body can be collected.

Reports about medical examinations in Pakistan have raised various issues:

- Victims of sexual assault lack awareness that they should not change clothes or wash their bodies before a medical examination.[17]

- Delays in the medical examination of victims affect the timing of the collection of materials for DNA testing and integrity of DNA evidence.[18]

- Improper collection and preservation of evidentiary material.

- Insufficient familiarity of lawyers and judicial officers with DNA evidence (footnote 18).

- Lack of sufficient training or equipment for medical personnel (footnote 14).

- Lack of an integrated victim service center ("one-stop shop") that will facilitate medical examination.

Section 13 of the Punjab Protection of Women Against Violence Act, 2016 provides for the setting up of one-stop centers, but currently there is only one in Multan. This center does not have all

---

[17]   Q. Hassan et al. 2007. Medico–Legal Assessment of Sexual Assault Victims in Lahore. *Journal of the Pakistan Medical Association.* 57 (11). pp. 539–542.

[18]   N. Rasool and M. Rasool. 2020. DNA Evidence in Sexual Assault Cases in Pakistan. *Medicine, Science and the Law.* October. 60 (4). pp. 270–277.

the facilities mentioned in Section 13. However, it has a police station, two public prosecutors posted for cases of women needing court assistance, services of a psychologist, mediation and counselling facilities, and initial medical examination services.[19] Civil society organizations have expressed that there are insufficient expert medico legal officers, and existing ones are not adequately trained to deal with rape cases.[20] It is an important start, but more centers with complete facilities are required under the Act.

In summary, there is much to be done to improve the processes of medical examination. If deficiencies exist in court cases, it should be mentioned in a judgment. Similarly, prosecutors who are impeded by delayed or deficient medical examination should formally complain to the relevant authority.

III. Protection Orders and Restraining Orders

Restraining and protection orders are crucial in stopping the violence and dissipating the fear that victims have in coming forward with complaints of GBV. A combination of laws is required to facilitate the orders and practically implement them. Practical implementation is sometimes the hardest part as the police can be reluctant to take action and as resources are stretched.

Studies show that victims fear repercussions from the perpetrator or his family and the loss of housing.[21] Figure 7.1 shows the findings of a survey conducted with 300 civil society respondents on obstacles to women reporting.

Too frequently, women victims are forced to leave their homes and go to shelters. Laws providing for protection orders should include the criteria for their issuance, how they are to be served by the police, and how best to allow victims to continue to stay in their homes safely. Protection orders can be issued by the courts, police, and other authorities.

For protection orders to be issued immediately, the police must respond to the crime promptly, coordinate with other agencies, and evaluate how to best protect the victim and avoid further violence.

A. Protection Orders under Pakistan Law

There are two types of protection orders: general protection orders and specific protection orders.

---

[19] S. Warraich. 2019. *Special Mechanisms to Address Violence Against Women in Punjab: A Study of Model Gender-Based Violence Court in Lahore and Violence Against Women Centre in Multan.* Lahore: Punjab Commission on the Status of Women (PCSW).

[20] Z. Ali. 2019. 'Hardly 2% of Domestic Violence, Rape Cases End Up in Conviction.' *Express Tribune.* 17 June.

[21] Z. Abdul Aziz and J. Moussa. 2013, reprint 2016. *Due Diligence Framework: State Accountability Framework for Eliminating Violence against Women.* Penang; and United Nations Office of the High Commissioner for Human Rights. 2012. *Women and the Right to Adequate Housing.* New York and Geneva.

Figure 7.1: Obstacles to Women Reporting
(%)

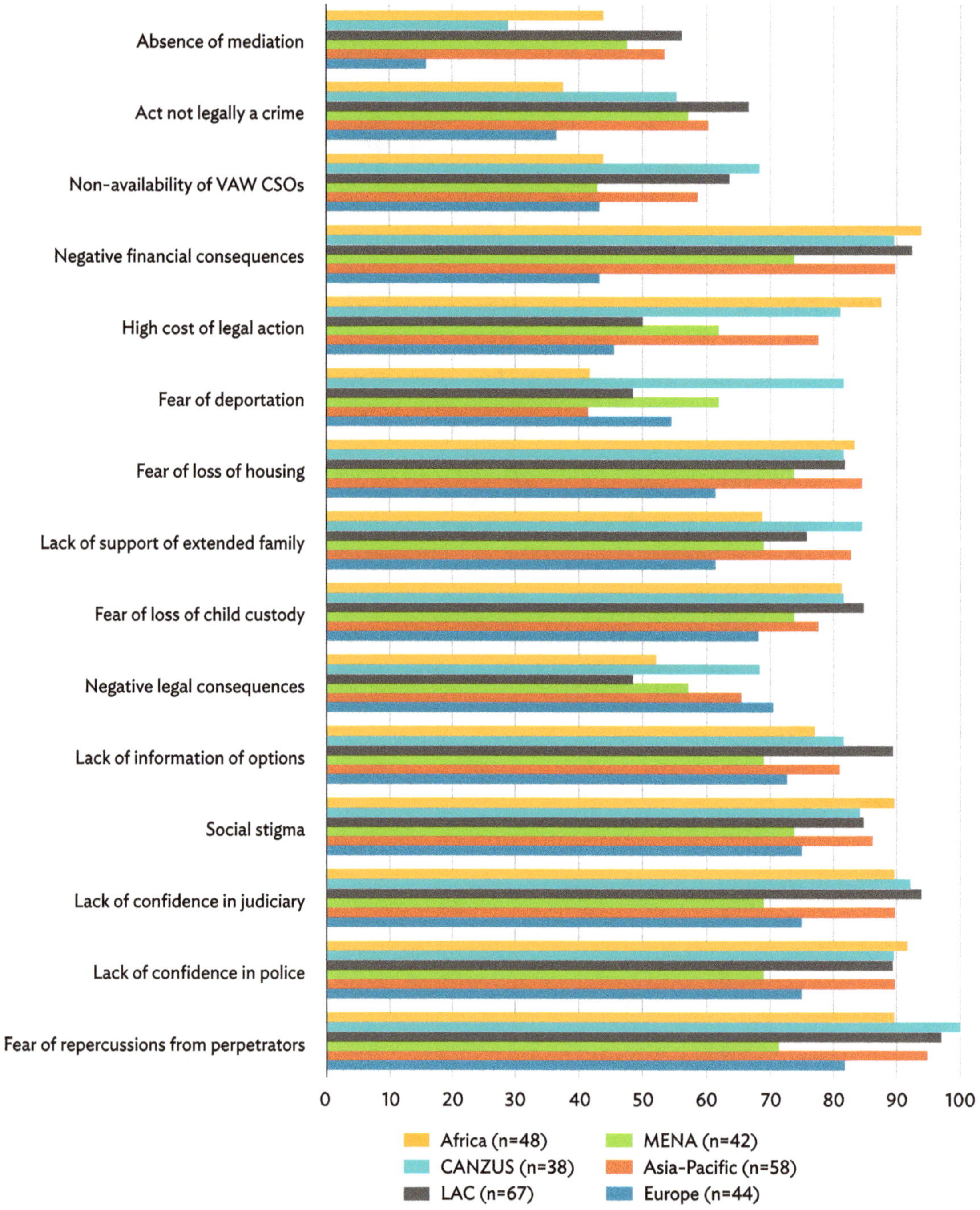
Absence of mediation
Act not legally a crime
Non-availability of VAW CSOs
Negative financial consequences
High cost of legal action
Fear of deportation
Fear of loss of housing
Lack of support of extended family
Fear of loss of child custody
Negative legal consequences
Lack of information of options
Social stigma
Lack of confidence in judiciary
Lack of confidence in police
Fear of repercussions from perpetrators
0
10
20
30
40
50
60
70
80
90
100
Africa (n=48)
CANZUS (n=38)
LAC (n=67)
MENA (n=42)
Asia-Pacific (n=58)
Europe (n=44)

CANZUS = Canada, Australia, New Zealand, and the United States; CSO = civil society organization; LAC = Latin America and the Caribbean; MENA = Middle East and North Africa; n = number; VAW = violence against women.

Source: Z. Abdul Aziz and J. Moussa. 2013, reprint 2016. *Due Diligence Framework: State Accountability Framework for Eliminating Violence against Women*. Penang.

1. General Protection Orders

Courts have some inherent powers that can be exercised for the following purposes: (i) ensure convenience and fairness in legal proceedings, (ii) prevent inefficacious proceedings, (iii) prevent abuse of process, and (iv) aid courts and tribunals.[22] These inherent powers include developing rules of court and practice directions and can be exercised by superior courts. The District and Sessions Courts have used their powers to summon witnesses or issue warrants under Sections 68, 75, or 90 of the CrPC and to order the police to provide protection to a witness to come to court and return. This comes under the purview of ensuring efficacious proceedings and preventing abuse of processes.

In practice, a written application or verbal request can be made by an accused, complainant, or witness. The court then hears the application. The order is set out in the proceedings and thereafter the police station house officer is directed to provide protection to the witness.

A common example is an application by a woman to a Magistrate for an order that she be admitted in a government shelter because she fears her life is in danger. Similarly, in habeas petitions, often the Sessions Court or the High Court, as the case may be, may send women to *dar ul aman* (shelters). In summary, any court that is adjudicating a case of a woman can grant permission or order a *dar ul aman* to provide safe accommodation if the woman applies to the court. Further, in case of female minors, the court may, if it considers that the situation warrants it, send female minors to a shelter.

Gender-Based Violence Court General Protection Orders

A GBV Court is a specialized District and Sessions Court in a particular province or territory. A GBV Court is empowered once the court has received the *Challan* (charge sheet), to take certain actions as set out in the General Protections Orders.

The *Practice Note for the Model Gender-Based Violence Court*, endorsed by the Lahore High Court, requires a judge to consider protection orders when a summons is being issued to a victim or witnesses (see Appendix 2). The judge may include a direction asking whether they require police protection. Directions are given to the process server who is required to contact the relevant superintendent of police cell without delay to make arrangements and report back to the court on what was arranged. A judge may, at any time, make orders to provide protection for victims and witnesses.

In order for these protection orders to be effective in practice, the superintendent of police cell must ensure the protection orders are implemented.

---

[22] W. Lacey. 2003. Inherent Jurisdiction, Judicial Power and Implied Guarantees under Chapter III of the Constitution. *Federal Law Review*. 31 (1). Citing (i) I. H. Jacob. 1970. The Inherent Jurisdiction of the Court. *Current Legal Problems*. 23; and (ii) K. Mason. 1983. The Inherent Jurisdiction of the Court. *Australian Law Journal*. 57.

2. Laws Providing Specific Protection Orders

There are two types of laws that provide for protection orders: (i) protecting persons in cases of domestic violence under domestic violence legislation, and (ii) protecting a witness under witness protection legislation.

Protection Orders: Domestic Violence

Four provinces have laws providing for protection orders in relation to domestic violence. The Islamabad Capital Territory does not have a specific law. The laws that have been enacted from 2013 to 2021 are the Sindh Domestic Violence (Prevention and Protection) Act, 2013; the Balochistan Domestic Violence (Prevention and Protection) Act, 2014; the Punjab Protection of Women Against Violence Act, 2016; and the Khyber Pakhtunkhwa Domestic Violence (Prevention and Protection) Act, 2021. They each have similar protections for victims but also have significant differences:

Common Elements of All Laws

- Protection orders can be made in favor of a victim and prohibit an accused from having any communication with or causing violence against an accused or relatives;

- Interim protection orders;

- Residence orders to ensure the accused or their family do not evict the victim from her home; and

- Monetary orders requiring the accused to pay certain expenses.

Additional Similarities and Differences between the Laws

- Orders can be made by a first-class Magistrate in Sindh and Balochistan,[23] the Family Court in Punjab, and the Court of District and Session Judge and/or Session Judge in Khyber Pakhtunkhwa.

- In Sindh and Balochistan, protection orders also protect anyone who has been subjected to violence by a defendant in the household.

- In each province, protection orders can be granted after a *prima facie* domestic violence is established (Section 11 of the Sindh Domestic Violence (Prevention and Protection) Act, 2013; Section 8(1) of the Balochistan Domestic Violence (Prevention and Protection) Act, 2014; and Section 14 of Khyber Pakhtunkhwa Domestic Violence (Prevention and Protection) Act, 2021). In the case of the Punjab Protection of Women Against Violence Act, 2016, Section 7 states that protection orders can be granted if the court is satisfied that any violence "has been committed or is likely committed."

---

[23]   The Balochistan Domestic Violence (Prevention and Protection) Act, 2014 mentioned the Sub Divisional Magistrate who had been an executive magistrate, but after the termination of the executive magistracy, the functions were automatically transferred to the judicial magistrates.

- The definitions of domestic violence are detailed and differ slightly, with the most expansive being Section 2(p) of Khyber Pakhtunkhwa Domestic Violence (Prevention and Protection) Act, 2021.

- In all provinces, there is a provision for a protection committee and a female protection officer (or in Khyber Pakhtunkhwa, the Secretary of the District Protection Committee, who is not required to be a woman), to assist the victim in various ways set out in the Acts. This role is very important in assisting a victim to get access to shelter and services. In Sindh and Balochistan, a protection committee may also file an application for a protection order on behalf of the aggrieved person.

- In Punjab, Section 13 of the Punjab Domestic Violence (Prevention and Protection) Act, 2016 establishes protection centers (one-stop center) and shelter homes. In addition, a Women's Protection Officer can make certain orders such as directing the defendant to immediately move out of the house for a period not exceeding 40 hours (Section 14 of the Punjab Domestic Violence (Prevention and Protection) Act, 2016).

- A significant point of difference is that the Sindh Domestic Violence (Prevention and Protection) Act, 2013 (Section 6) and the Balochistan Domestic Violence (Prevention and Protection) Act, 2014 criminalize the act of domestic violence; whereas the Punjab Domestic Violence (Prevention and Protection) Act, 2016 and the Khyber Pakhtunkhwa Domestic Violence (Prevention and Protection) Act, 2021 criminalize breaches of a court order and not the domestic abuse itself. Violators in Punjab and Khyber Pakhtunkhwa can only be imprisoned for 'breach of a court order' (Section 20 of Punjab Domestic Violence (Prevention and Protection) Act, 2016 and Section 17 of the Khyber Pakhtunkhwa Domestic Violence (Prevention and Protection) Act, 2021) and not for the domestic abuse itself.

In practice, it appears that these laws are not implemented effectively. This is due to a general lack of awareness that must be addressed. District and Sessions Courts and GBV Courts, although they do not have specific jurisdiction to make protection orders under the Acts (save for the jurisdiction given to District and Sessions Courts under the Khyber Pakhtunkhwa Domestic Violence [Prevention and Protection] Act, 2021), can assist in inspiring protection orders that utilize the practices set out above.

Protection Orders: Witness Protection Legislation

Three provinces of Pakistan have specific laws on witness protection, in addition to the Federal Witness Protection, Security and Benefit Act, 2017. The provisions of Sindh Witness Protection Act, 2013 and the Balochistan Witness Protection Act, 2016 are the same, while the Punjab Witness Protection Act, 2018 gives broader and improved measures of protection for witnesses. The Federal Witness Protection, Security and Benefit Act, 2017 is less detailed and less developed.

Common Procedure

All four laws have common procedure involving witness protection boards and units that enable non-court measures of protection to be provided. The provisions in each law include protection of witnesses that enable them to give evidence in criminal proceedings, which includes rape and indecent assault on a child less than 16 years of age involving grievous bodily harm. The Punjab Witness Protection Act, 2018 extends more broadly to a "sexual offence," referring to Sections 366A, 367A, 376, and 377 of the PPC.

Person Protected

The Sindh and Balochistan laws provide protection for a "threatened witness" who is defined as one in respect of whom "there is likelihood of danger to the safety of his or her life or life of his or her close relatives; or serious danger to his or her property or property of his or her close relatives" (Section 2(o)). This is a high threshold for protection. The Punjab law refers to a witness being "fearful or under stress owing to the nature of the offence or proceeding relating thereto or is intimidated or labours under intimidation that harm may come to his person or family or property" (Section 7(1)(a)), as well as persons who suffer from physical or mental disorder (Section 7(1)(c)).

Protection Type and Process

In Sindh and Balochistan, a court order can be made through a formal process if the court is "satisfied that the life or safety of that person may be endangered by virtue of the person being a witness" (Section16(2)). The Punjab Act enables the court to make orders under Section 8, which refers to "special measures" that enable a witness to give evidence. They also include screening to prevent the witness being seen (Section 9), use of video link (Section 10), rules of cross-examination limiting the circumstances in which the witness may be cross-examined by an accused (Section 12), and reporting of criminal proceedings (Section 13).

The protections offered to witnesses could potentially apply in proceedings before District and Sessions Courts and GBV Courts, if it is part of the overall witness protection program. In Punjab, the law requires the Witness Protection Unit to be established and operational in the State (Section 7).

In summary, witness protection laws may not be readily available to provide protection for GBV witnesses. However, they may be used if the administrative arrangements are put in place.

Protection for Victims and Witnesses in Trafficking of Persons

Section 11 of the Federal Prevention of Trafficking in Persons Act, 2018 prescribes the protection measures that may be taken by the government for victims and witnesses of trafficking to safeguard "the[ir] physical safety." Section 12 gives examples of the protections that may be available. No mention is made on making court orders, but reference is made on rules that enable certain measures to be taken including proceedings in camera and permitting evidence behind a screen or similar or using a video link. Section 13 specifically mentions compensation to victims.

B.   Domestic Violence Laws: Case Examples

The cases below describe some of the court cases that have applied Pakistan's domestic violence laws. These cases demonstrate how courts can make a difference by assisting women victims of violence when earlier processes have failed them.

Case 1: *Mst Rukkiya Iqbal v. Faisal Hayat,* Cr Petition No. 457 of 2017, Court of the Judicial Magistrate–XV, West Karachi, 23 February 2019

On 23 February 2019, a Karachi court sentenced a man—under the Sindh Domestic Violence (Prevention and Protection) Act, 2013—to 6 months imprisonment and to pay Pakistan rupees (PRs) 45,000 in compensation to the victim. The man was also sentenced under Sections 337A and 337L of the PPC and ordered to pay PRs5,000 as *Daman* (compensation determined by the Court to be paid by the offender to the victim) and sentenced to 6 months imprisonment. This took place after his wife filed a complaint 2 years earlier. She was so badly beaten that she fled from home, which led her to filing the complaint. The accused was found guilty of "physical abuse" as well as "emotional, psychological, and verbal" abuse under the Sindh Act, as well as for inflicting "hurt" under the PPC.

The court declared that domestic violence was a human rights violation, stating "[The law] was enacted to provide protection to the weakest classes [of] society, i.e., women and children, as normally we [carry] a presumption of living [in] a 'male-dominant society' where [the] aggrieved even does not dare to tell about 'domestic violence' because of threats of being abandoned or dispossessed/removed from [the] household."

Other significant features of the case are as follows:

    (i)   The victim's mother-in-law and father-in-law entered the room, but they made no attempt to stop their son.

    (ii)   Soon after the attack, the survivor managed to escape. Her mother took her to the police station.

    (iii)   The police twice refused to register a First Information Report (FIR) against the perpetrator, even after the accused went to the hospital and obtained a medical report.

    (iv)   The complainant filed a petition before a magistrate to seek protection orders against the accused for her and her family. The magistrate then framed charges against the accused.

Part of the assault history includes forced aggressive sex that resulted in bruising and vaginal infection. This case epitomizes the barriers that women have to overcome because of attitudinal responses from society, the police, and medical professionals.

Case 2: *Mst Hina v. Province of Sindh,* PLD 2019 Sind 363

A Sindh High Court took notice of delays in the implementation of the Sindh Domestic Violence (Prevention and Protection) Act, 2013. A number of petitions came before the High Court judge. The judge found that the Sindh Act was not being implemented due to negligence of the Sindh government. The Chief Secretary of the Sindh government was directed to submit a report and ensure that (i) the Commission and Committees established under the Act are notified within a month, and (ii) the Act is widely publicized.

Case 3

The Express Tribune News on 27 August 2020 reported a case registered under the Sindh Domestic Violence (Prevention and Protection) Act, 2013.[24] A Malir civil court in Karachi issued a restraining order and barred the husband, who was accused of physically assaulting his wife, from entering her workplace and her household. The court directed the relevant SHO of the Malir Cantt Police Station to provide security to the petitioner and take a security bond of PRs100,000 from the accused to prevent the commission of domestic violence in accordance with Section 11 (4) of the law.

IV. Legal Aid

The Constitution of Pakistan provides for inexpensive and expeditious justice (Article 37(d)), a right to a fair trial as a fundamental right (Article 10 (a)), and equality before the law (Article 25).

Section 340 of the CrPC provides for an accused to be represented by a counsel at the expense of the State. Section 161A of the CrPC also entitles victims of sexual abuse to free legal aid. The police must inform victims of this right after registering the case and provide her with the list of lawyers maintained by the Provincial Bar Councils for this purpose.

The Sindh Domestic Violence (Prevention and Protection) Act, 2013; the Balochistan Domestic Violence (Prevention and Protection) Act, 2014; the Punjab Protection of Women Against Violence Act, 2016; and the Khyber Pakhtunkhwa Domestic Violence (Prevention and Protection) Act, 2021 make it a duty of a protection officer and Secretary of the District Protection Committee (as the case may be) to ensure that an aggrieved person or complainant is provided with legal aid.

The Public Service Defenders and Free Legal Aid Ordinance, 2009 was applicable until it was repealed in 2012. The formal sources of legal aid now include the following:

- The Legal Practitioners and Bar Council Act, 1973 makes provision for legal aid. The Pakistan Bar Council Free Legal Aid Committee Rules, 1999 sets up Free Legal Aid Committees to deliver legal services through federal, provincial, and district legal aid committees. Those eligible include the poor, destitute, orphan, indigent, and deserving persons entitled to *Zakat* (a Muslim annual payment calculated based on income and specified property) who cannot afford legal services. Eligible cases include persons involved in succession certificates, ejectment, illegal detention, and family law.

- The District Legal Empowerment Committees (Constitution and Functions) Rules, 2011 establishes District Legal Empowerment Committees, headed by District and Session Judges, to administer and manage free legal aid. The funds available can be used for lawyers' fees. This fund appears to be underutilized due to a number of factors including lack of awareness.

- The Punjab Legal Aid Act, 2018 establishes a government-administered agency to provide legal aid. However, it has only recently approved the agency and does not appear to be in operation to date.

---

[24] *The Express Tribune.* 2020. Court Issues Restraining Order. 27 August.

- The Khyber Pakhtunkhwa Legal Aid Act, 2019 limits legal aid to an indigent person who is defined as a person involved in the commission of an offense or a female involved in a domestic dispute and does not have the financial capacity to engage an advocate on his/her own (Section 2(g)). The domestic dispute is defined as disputes relating to divorce, maintenance, dowry, dower or custody of children (Section 2(e)).

- The Federal Legal Aid and Justice Authority Act, 2020 is supposed to apply to the whole of Pakistan and is to come into force, in whole or in part, on a date appointed by the Federal Government as notified in the official gazette. It has not happened so far.

There is often a lack of awareness about the availability of legal aid, not only among the public but also among lawyers. Well-informed courts can be a source of information for litigants and lawyers alike and individual judges may also be able to alert litigants to potential services within their province or district.

V. Conclusory Remarks

If there is to be a real change for victims of GBV, first responders and the courts need to have a sound understanding of the complex issues that confront victims in pursuing their cases before the court, and how that can be improved. Judges, prosecutors, the police, medical officers, and lawyers must work together to achieve this. Protection orders are fundamental for women to feel safe to come forward to pursue their case.

Model Gender-Based Violence (GBV) Court. Former Lahore High Court Chief Justice (now Justice of the Supreme Court) Syed Mansoor Ali Shah inaugurates the model GBV Court in Lahore, Pakistan on 23 October 2017. The GBV Court has since been replicated in all judicial districts of Pakistan (photo c/o Justice Syed Mansoor Ali Shah).

Chapter 8

THE COURT ENVIRONMENT

I.   Introduction

In this chapter, victims of gender-based violence (GBV) have now reached the court. A new set of challenges await them. Research reveals that women generally describe experiencing indifferent, insensitive, or harsh treatment by the police, prosecutors, and judges, who often minimize or trivialize, and dismiss the violence or blame the victims. Victims equate this to a "second assault"[1] or "second rape," which can be more traumatic than the first."[2] Women feel they are on trial by both the prosecutor and defense counsel.[3] "[They] are rarely allowed to tell their story; the prosecution does not protect their reputation; and the discrediting information put forward by the defense often remains unchallenged."[4] Similar views are expressed by women in Pakistan who were unwilling to pursue trial due to weak judicial procedures, fear of being re-traumatized, and not being given protection.[5]

II. Gender-Based Violence Specialized Courts

One of the most promising measures taken by countries internationally is establishing specialized GBV Courts with designated judges and special measures to assist victims and give evidence in combination with guidelines, protocols, and bench books. Such measures have been evaluated and found to be effective. They can improve gender sensitivity of judges and efficiency of case management and create a hospitable court environment.[6] Some victims reported that such courts gave them a sense of control and safety and even if there was an acquittal, they were supported, informed, and consulted throughout the process. They did not

---

[1]   L. Kelly. 2005. *Promising Practices Addressing Sexual Violence.* Expert paper prepared for the Violence against Women: Good Practices in Combating and Eliminating Violence against Women Expert Group Meeting. Vienna. 17–20 May 2005.

[2]   Women's Centre for Change. 2007. *Seeking More Effective Prosecution of Sexual Crimes: Background Paper for Dialogue with Prosecutors.* Penang. Cited in United Nations Office on Drugs and Crime. 2019. *Handbook for the Judiciary on Effective Criminal Justice Responses to Gender-Based Violence against Women and Girls.* Vienna. p. 16.

[3]   O. Smith and T. Skinner. 2012. Observing Court Responses to Victims of Rape and Sexual Assault. *Feminist Criminology.* 7(4).

[4]   United Nations Office on Drugs and Crime. 2019. *Handbook for the Judiciary on Effective Criminal Justice Responses to Gender-Based Violence against Women and Girls.* Vienna. p. 16.

[5]   Punjab Commission on the Status of Women (PCSW). 2018. *Punjab Gender Parity Report 2018.*

[6]   UN Women. 2012. *Handbook for National Action Plans on Violence against Women.* New York.

regret pursuing the case even if the outcome was disappointing.[7] Also, the satisfaction of victims was directly proportional to the sensitivity and dignified treatment they received from court personnel.[8] The overall features of such specialized courts are discussed in the United Nations Office on Drugs and Crime's 2019 *Handbook for the Judiciary on Effective Criminal Justice for Women and Girls* and research by A.R. Klein on domestic violence in 2008.[9]

A. Overview of Specialized Gender-Based Violence Courts in Pakistan

The first specialized Model GBV Court was set up in Lahore in October 2017. This historically followed the directions given by the Supreme Court in *Salman Akram Raja v. The Government of Punjab through Chief Secretary, Civil Secretariat, Lahore and Others*[10] (*Salman Akram Raja Case*) and also Section 13 of the Criminal Law (Amendment) (Offenses Related to Rape) Act, 2016.[11] The initial GBV Court in Lahore was set up in accordance with the *Guidelines to be Followed in Cases of Gender-Based Violence* (*Guidelines*, Appendix 1) issued by the Lahore High Court that closely followed the directions in the *Salman Akram Raja Case*.

At the same time, discussions took place with stakeholders (including judges from the High Court of Lahore, District and Sessions Court, police, prosecutors, and the Bar Association). The *Practice Note* was issued by the Lahore High Court initially in 2017, but later revised in February 2018 (*2018 Practice Note*, Appendix 2). The *2018 Practice Note* was later discussed and refined by the District and Sessions Court

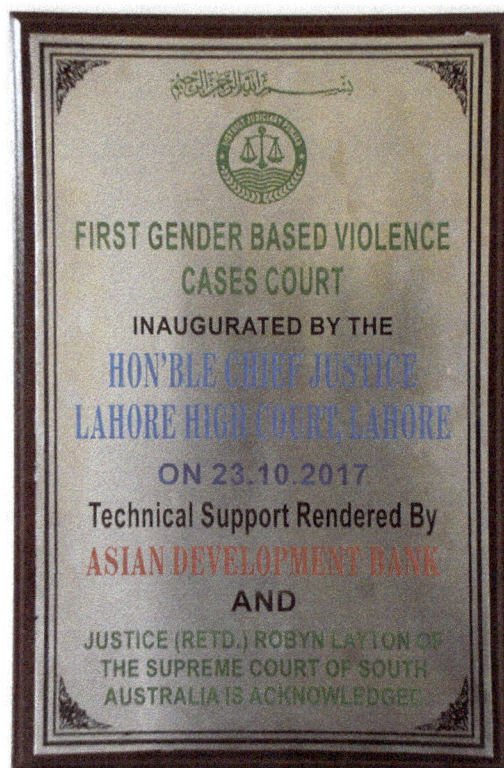

Lahore Gender-Based Violence (GBV) Court. The plaque outside the model GBV Court indicates the Lahore High Court's appreciation for ADB's support in setting up the court (photo courtesy of Justice Syed Mansoor Ali Shah).

---

[7] A.R. Klein. 2008. *Practical Implications of Current Domestic Violence Research, Part II: Prosecution*. Report submitted to the National Institute of Justice, United States.

[8] K.D. Muller. 2017. A Study to Determine the Satisfaction Level of Victims Accessing Services at Identified Sexual Offences Courts in South Africa. *The Child Witness Institute*.

[9] United Nations Office on Drugs and Crime. 2019. *Handbook for the Judiciary on Effective Criminal Justice Responses to Gender-Based Violence against Women and Girls*. Vienna; and A.R. Klein. 2008. *Practical Implications of Current Domestic Violence Research, Part II: Prosecution*. Report submitted to the National Institute of Justice, United States.

[10] 2013 SCMR 203.

[11] Section 13 provides for the amendment of Section 352 of the Criminal Procedure Code (CrPC), including the trial of offenses under Sections 354A, 376,376A, 377, and 377B of the PPC to be conducted in camera, adopting appropriate measures, including holding of trial through video link or usage of screens, for the protection of the victim and the witnesses.

Gender-Based Violence Court inauguration. Then Chief Justice of the Lahore High Court (now Justice of the Supreme Court of Pakistan) Syed Mansoor Ali Shah presents a plaque of appreciation to ADB principal capacity development specialist (consultant) Robyn Layton, who represented ADB during the Gender-Based Violence Court inauguration ceremony on 23 October 2017 (photo courtesy of Justice Syed Mansoor Ali Shah).

judges in Lahore to include additional offenses and special procedures for child witnesses, and used for subsequent trainings (*Updated Practice Note*, Appendix 2A).[12] The *2018 Practice Note* and the *Updated Practice Note* are collectively referred to as "*Practice Notes*" in this publication. They provide practical details on how the *Guidelines* would be implemented in practice.

The Model GBV Court in Lahore has significantly increased conviction rates for GBV cases from 4.37% to 16.5% in a little over 12 months of operation. In 2019, directions were given by the Chief Justice of the Supreme Court and the National Judicial Committee that similar *Guidelines* and *Practice Notes* would be issued by the High Courts in each of the other provinces and territories for the setting up of GBV Courts in 114 districts of Pakistan.

The *Guidelines* and *Practice Notes* for hearing GBV cases do not require legislation to support them, as they are procedural matters which are within the province of the courts and not the legislature (see discussion on inherent powers of a court in Chapter 7). This was made clear when the Chief Justice of the Supreme Court and Judges in the National Judicial Committee directed the process.

Even if the High Court in a province or territory has not issued the *Guidelines* and *Practice Notes*, a court dealing with a GBV case can follow the directions in the *Salman Akram Raja Case*. For example, the Sindh High Court had reinforced and strengthened the directions given in the *Salman Akram Raja Case* to be implemented in Sindh across relevant courts, including all magistrate courts.[13]

---

[12] The refinements to the *2018 Practice Note* are underlined in Appendix 2A. The *2018 Practice Note* and the *Updated Practice Note* will collectively be referred to as "*Practice Notes*."

[13] *Kainat Somro and Ors v. Province of Sindh and Ors*, PLD 2020 Karachi 611.

It is noted that the *Guidelines* and *Practice Notes* essentially reiterate the *Salman Akram Raja Case* directions and enable their implementation. Many similar topics and procedures are also contained in other laws that are relevant to a GBV Court and District and Sessions Courts:

- The Khyber Pakhtunkhwa Domestic Violence Against Women (Prevention and Protection) Act, 2021, Section 12(2) (decide a case within 60 days and no adjournments for more than 2 days);

- Sindh Witness Protection Act, 2013, Section 16 (protection orders);

- Balochistan Witness Protection Act, 2016, Section 16 (protection orders);

- Punjab Witness Protection Act, 2018, Section 7 (protection order), Section 8 (use of screen), Section 10 (evidence by video link), and Section 12 (limit cross-examination of the victim by the accused);

- Prevention of Trafficking in Persons Act, 2018, Section 12 (rules for in-camera hearing, use of screen, and video link);

- Criminal Procedure Code 1898 (CrPC), Section 352 (trial of offenses under Sections 354A, 376, 376A, 377, and 377B of the **Pakistan Penal Code 1860** (PPC) to be conducted in camera, adopting appropriate measures, including trial through video link or usage of screens), and Section 344A (3-month time limit for conclusion of the trial of the above offenses); and

- Qanun-E-Shahadat Order, 1984 (QSO) Articles 146 and 148 (prohibiting indecent, scandalous, insulting, annoying or offensive questions).

B. Gender-Based Violence Court Guidelines and Practice Notes

The overriding purpose for a GBV Court is to try and minimize distress to victims and enable them to give their best evidence, but at the same time to ensure that fairness is given to the accused. Sometimes the accused may themselves be vulnerable, having mental and other disabilities, which may mean that they too need to be given sensitivity in court and when giving their evidence. The ultimate aim is to provide equal justice for all within the GBV Court.

Some of the key features of the *Guidelines* and *Practice Notes* are discussed below with additional reference to laws on similar topics. It is recognized that, for various reasons, it may not be possible to comply with all elements of the *Guidelines* and *Practice Notes*.

C. Who Is Covered and for What Offenses?

The *Guidelines* and *Practice Notes* recognize that the victims are mainly women and girls. Additionally, victims of GBV may regard themselves as transgender male or female or nonconforming genders. The gender sensitivity approach also extends to the treatment of other vulnerable witnesses in a GBV case in the court, including witnesses with mental and other disabilities. The list of offenses covered are set out in footnote 1 of the *Updated Practice Note* (see Appendix 2A).

D. Fast Tracking Trial Dates and Finalization with Strict Hearing Schedules

Research undertaken in Lahore District and Sessions Courts prior to setting up the GBV Court reveals that multiple adjournments of cases are a common feature, some up to 40 times, with cases often being partly heard before different judges. Consequently, the deciding judge is required to make decisions on the credibility and acceptance of evidence of witnesses that the judge may not have even heard. Delays in the trial process can lead to cases being consigned to record, or a resiling of the victim or witnesses or dismissal of the case.

The processes for dealing with GBV cases commence from the time when the *Challan* (charge sheet) is forwarded to the court. GBV cases allocated to the GBV Court are fast tracked, given priority hearing and strict hearing schedules. Cases are listed for a day or week or month. The trial continues without a break, unless a short adjournment is required for a valid reason.[14] Fast tracking of older cases is done at the same time as the listing of new cases. Certainty is helpful not only for the victim, but also for the accused, the counsel, other witnesses, and for court management. The defense bar has so far supported this certainty of hearings.

Other laws with time limits for hearings are Section 344A of CrPC, 3 months from cognizance to conclusion of the trial in cases of stripping a woman naked in public (Section 354A, PPC), rape (Section 376, PPC), disclosure of identity of a victim of sexual offense (Section 376A, PPC), unnatural sexual act, sodomy (Section 377, PPC), and sexual abuse (Section 377B, PPC). Also, Section 12(2) of the Khyber Pakhtunkhwa Domestic Violence Against Women (Prevention and Protection) Act, 2021 requires deciding a case in 60 days with no adjournments for more than 2 days.

E. Attending to Victims When They Arrive at the Court Precinct

The court environment is a busy and intimidating environment for a victim to arrive at before they even give their evidence. They are concerned that they may meet up with either the accused or alternatively the family and friends of the accused. It is also well-known that aggression can occur between an accused family and their supporters and a victim within the court environs.

The GBV Court practice provides for a "Female Support Officer" who is a designated trained employee of the court (*Updated Practice Note*, paras. 5–9) to meet and escort the victim to a waiting room and then later to the court room. If a female support officer is not available, then a court staff or security officer may escort the victim to a protected place .

F. Courtroom Set Up and Design

Judges and lawyers regard the courtroom as a familiar workplace, but not so for victims. The rooms are formal, bureaucratic, and somber. The judge and lawyers are dressed formally and

---

[14] *Guidelines*, para. 5; *Updated Practice Note*, paras. 25, 26, and 31.

Protected place for victims. The GBV Court in Lahore has a waiting room for vulnerable witnesses (photo by Samar Minallah Khan).

speak in unfamiliar technical, legal language. There is proximity of lawyers, police officers, accused persons, and witnesses.

The GBV Court set up is designed to address these daunting features. Most courts in the District and Sessions Courts presently have a configuration where a table for lawyers is immediately in front of the judge's bench and is flanked at either end with the dock and the witness box. All save the judge are required to stand.

The *Updated Practice Note* describes the basic set up as well as the procedures to be followed.[15]

A central feature of the GBV Court is that there are two ways in which evidence can be given by a victim.

- The first is in the trial courtroom with the modification of a screen near the witness box to enable the victim to be protected from having to face the accused when giving evidence.

- A second is through a TV link where the victim does not go into the courtroom but instead gives evidence outside the trial court and be seen and heard on a screen in the trial court.

Figure 8.1 depicts the suggested layout of a GBV Court with a bar table for lawyers distanced from the judge's bench and the witness box. A screen, either solid or a curtain, is situated next to the seated witness box. The witnesses, lawyers, and the accused are seated. All have water and tissues. The TV screen allows witnesses to give evidence remotely.

Other accommodations may be made by the judge, for example, for persons with disabilities.

If the victim gives evidence in the court room, they should enter the court room in the absence of the accused and be seated behind a screen before the accused returns to the court room. The accused should not be visible to the victim.

---

15   *Updated Practice Note*, paras. 10–24.

Figure 8.1: Layout of a Gender-Based Violence Court

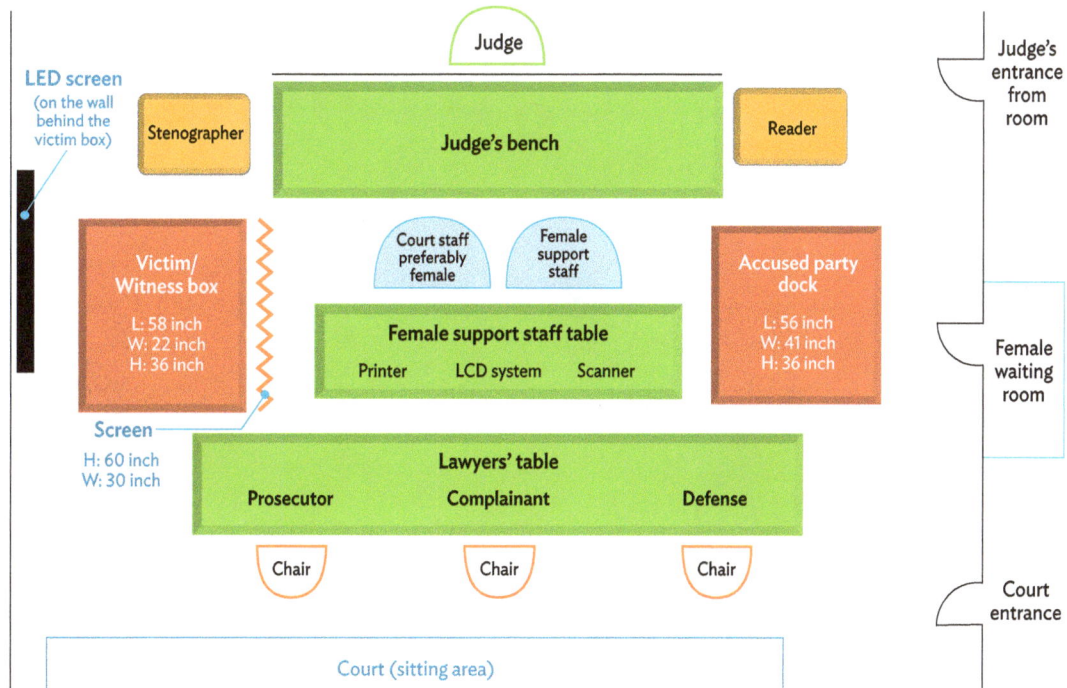

Judge

Judge's bench

Stenographer

Reader

LED screen
(on the wall behind the victim box)

Judge's entrance from room

Victim/ Witness box

L: 58 inch
W: 22 inch
H: 36 inch

Court staff preferably female

Female support staff

Accused party dock

L: 56 inch
W: 41 inch
H: 36 inch

Female support staff table

Printer   LCD system   Scanner

Screen

H: 60 inch
W: 30 inch

Female waiting room

Lawyers' table

Prosecutor   **Complainant**   **Defense**

Chair   Chair   Chair

Court entrance

Court (sitting area)

H = height, L = length, LCD = liquid crystal display, W = width.
Source: Authors.

Set up of Gender-Based Violence Court. A photo of the GBV Court in Lahore showing the judge, stenographer, and reader; the female support officer/staff; clerk and court officer; bar table for counsel, witness box and screen to shield view of the dock; and TV screen (photo by Samar Minallah Khan).

View of the Gender-Based Violence Court from the judge's bench. The door on the left leads to the waiting room for vulnerable witnesses (photo by Samar Minallah Khan).

G.   Hearing in Camera

Paragraphs 9 to 11 of the *Guidelines* provide that the hearing of GBV cases should be in camera and that irrelevant persons be excluded from the court. Section 352 CrPC provides that a court be open to the public, but it is not mandatory, and a judge can order that the court be closed to the general public or a particular person. Section 352(2) CrPC requires that the trial of offenses under Sections 354A, 376, 376A, 377, and 377B be conducted in camera but permits a judge to allow presence of any particular person to be in court. Section 352(4) CrPC prohibits printing or publishing of any trial held in camera except with court permission.

H.   Set Up and Use of the e-Courtroom

The best arrangement for most witnesses is the use of video facilities that permit evidence to be given by the victim from outside the trial court and be seen and heard on a screen in the trial court (Figure 8.2). This can be a small but comfortable space. A female support officer should be seated near the victim.

For child witnesses, suitable comfort items such as toys can be placed on the table (Figure 8.3). If the accused

Figure 8.2: Video Facilities in e-Courtrooms

Source: Authors.

needs to be removed from the court, the facility can also be used for the accused to see and hear proceedings from the e-court space. Other laws also provide for the use of video link or usage of screens. Section 352(3) CrPC provides that the government may adopt such measures for protection of victim and witnesses in cases of stripping a woman naked in public (Section 354A PPC), rape (Section 376 PPC), disclosure of identity of a victim of sexual offense (Section 376A PPC), unnatural sexual act, sodomy (Section 377 PPC),

Figure 8.3: e-Courtrooms for Child Witnesses

Source: Authors.

and sexual abuse (Section 377B). The Prevention of Trafficking in Persons Act, 2018, Section 12, also adopts such rules.

III. Role of Judges in Gender-Based Violence Courts

A. Judicial Role: Before Evidence Commences

It is the responsibility of the judge to create a calm and organized court environment. Making a witness comfortable before they give evidence has a twofold benefit of assisting the witness to give her/his best evidence and showing that the judge is there to listen to what they have to say and is interested in their welfare.

B. Settling the Victim and Witnesses

A good practice for settling witnesses is set out in the *Updated Practice Note* (paras. 27–30). Different judges have their own ways, but it is suggested they introduce themselves and the others in the courtroom to the victim and ask what name she prefers to use. They should also be asked whether they have security concerns so that orders can be made. It is well known that that is a time of high risk for victims.

C. Settling a Child Victim or Witnesses

Different considerations apply when settling a child, depending on their age, educational level, cultural background, as well as their physical or mental disabilities.[16] The settling questions should be few, and not in any way connected to the offending circumstances. For example, it is inappropriate to ask a child details about their family, when a family member may be the perpetrator. Similarly, if a teacher is involved, questions about the child's grade or favorite subjects are also inappropriate. Instead, simple questions can be what she/he did before coming to court, or her/his favorite breakfast and hobbies.

The manner of questioning should be empathetic but not overly friendly and allow a child to respond in her/his own way. Questions should be open and short, and simple (one topic at a time in age-appropriate language and expressions). The answers given may assist the judge in understanding the communication capacity of the child and also their competency. Appendix 3 provides helpful best practices for questioning of children. This has been drawn up with input of child psychologists and can be adapted to suit a particular child.

D. Settling Persons with Disability

Victims or witnesses with a disability require special attention. Hopefully, the prosecution or the counsel assisting the victim have already considered and agreed what is needed for them to give evidence. Their requirements may include an interpreter communication assistant and/or communication aids, such as paper, markers, cards, or objects to enable their evidence to be understood.[17]

E. Interpreter or Communication Assistant for Victims or Witnesses

Victims or witnesses who have language issues, a disability, incapacity, and/or is a child may require an interpreter or communication assistant. A good practice is to have them freely available for those who require it.

The role of an interpreter is to faithfully interpret into the appropriate language of the witness, given that the witness answers the question in the language that will be understood by the court. An interpreter should not be asked to interpret long questions or answers.

A communication assistant helps witnesses who have physical or mental impairments to give their evidence. The role is to communicate the question being asked of a witness such that they will be able to understand given their particular impairment; then to communicate the answer that the witness has given in a manner that may be understood by the counsel, the prosecutor, and the court.

---

[16] *Updated Practice Note*, para. 46–49.
[17] See footnote 6 of the *Updated Practice Note*.

An interpreter under Section 543 CrCP is required to be bound over to interpret truthfully. A similar requirement should also apply to a communicator.

Sometimes courts tend to use a family member for these roles. This is far from ideal as family members are not independent and may have already heard the witness before and may be relaying previously told information rather than what the witness says in the court. They may also "improve" the witnesses' evidence.

The role of the judge should be to inform the assistant as to how the evidence will be taken and request they indicate any problem with the form of the question so that it can be rephrased. Or, if there is some ambiguity about an answer, that should be indicated so it can be clarified by further questions.

Additionally, Sections 360, 361, and 364 of the CrCP essentially require that if a witness does not understand the language being used, it shall be interpreted to them in a language they understand. Also, as evidence is normally recorded in narrative (Section 359 CrCP), it is to be read over to the witness, and if they deny the correctness of any part, the judge is to make a note of it (Section 360(2) CrPC).

F.   Conduct in the Courtroom

The judge at all times controls conduct in the courtroom and, at the commencement of a trial, should ask whether the counsels are familiar with the *Guidelines* and the *Practice Notes*, particularly the trial processes in the *Updated Practice Note* (paras. 31–35).

A major role of the judge in a GBV Court is ensuring that all questions are asked with gender sensitivity and appropriate language, and having regard to the victim's age, educational level, cultural background, physical or mental disabilities. This also applies to other witnesses in a trial.

G.   General Observations about Language and Questioning of Victims

There are two aspects to be considered with regard to questioning of a witness. The first is the content of the questions and the second is the manner of questioning.

1. Content of the Question

Article 146 QSO gives the court discretion to forbid any questions or inquiries which it regards as "indecent or scandalous." Article 148 QSO allows the court to forbid any questions which appear to be "intended to insult or annoy" or otherwise appear to be "needlessly offensive."

Many common law jurisdictions have similar evidentiary rules that sometimes prohibit "improper" questions. "Improper" covers inappropriate language or language that is misleading, annoying, harassing, intimidating, offensive, oppressive, or repetitive (e.g., Section 26, Australian Evidence Act, 1995).

Article 148 QSO could potentially include misleading, confusing, or harassing questions, including questions with more than one question contained within it and questions that can be differently understood by the witness. Examples of harassing questions is where a counsel asks the same question in slightly different ways over and over to trick or wear down the witness and get the answer they are looking for.

Other questions that are forbidden are "insulting" or "needlessly offensive" questions that demonstrate ignorance by the questioner about victims of sexual offenses, including questions such as "Are you seriously suggesting that my client raped you when you had no injuries?"

Further, Section 12(3) Punjab Witness Protection Act, 2018 expressly forbids questions being asked of the victim of a sexual offense, about any sexual behavior of the victim on any previous occasion with the accused or other person, unless it is a relevant fact in the case.

2. Manner of Questioning

The court should prohibit questioning that is bullying, aggressive, angry or said in a loud voice. A judge should prohibit body language or aggressive eye contact which can be threatening, including "rapid fire" questions.

The court needs to be aware of the impact of this conduct on an individual witness and in the overall circumstances of the questioning. It just takes one offensive or inappropriate question to unsettle a witness for the remainder of their evidence.

H. Cross-Examination of Victims by Defense Counsel

To prevent intimidatory questioning behavior by the defense counsel of victims, the *Guidelines* (para. 14) and the *Updated Practice Note* (para. 34) require cross-examination questions to be in writing or as the court thinks fit. The judge then asks the questions of a witness in a manner and language that can be understood. The judge may give directions on how this can be implemented in practice. A suggested procedure is set out in Appendix 4.

There are also laws that limit cross-examination of a victim by an accused with a similar purpose in mind. For example, Section 12 of Punjab Witness Protection Act, 2018 prohibits an accused charged with a sexual offense from in-person cross examination of a witness without the express permission of the court. Permission shall not be granted when in the court's opinion, such cross examination "is likely to affect the voluntariness or quality of evidence" [Section 12(2)].

In addition, the judge should watch witnesses carefully to see whether they appear to understand a question. If there is uncertainty, the judge can (i) ask the witness whether they would like the question repeated, or (ii) ask the witness to repeat the question they thought had been asked. The latter is a particularly effective way of addressing the issue with a child or a person with disability.

The procedures in the *Guidelines* and the *Practice Notes* do not prevent defense counsels from adequately putting their case and questioning the victims, but they control the way in which their questions are put so that they do not re-traumatize the victims by their manner or language. This requires counsels to be organized before their appearance in court. Modifications can be made to this procedure where appropriate, in the interests of the overall justice to both the accused and the victim, according to circumstances as they arise in a case.

I.   A Good Practice to Obtain Truthful Evidence

A good practice in eliciting truthful evidence from a victim witness is by asking open questions and allowing them to tell their story. Open questions usually begin with the words, what, when, who, or which. This is especially important for children or persons with a mental disability as referred to in Appendix 3. There is a well-known tendency for witnesses who are stressed or vulnerable to answer "yes" to closed or leading questions, making cross-examination style, closed questions, the least effective way of gaining truthful evidence.

Closed questions or leading questions usually contain a positive assertion followed by words such as an assertive "that's right, isn't it?" Common leading questions include, "You didn't cry out because nothing happened—isn't that right?" or "You just made all of that up, didn't you." Many times such questions should be the subject of objection because they are too broad and lack specificity as to what the question is referring to. Further, they are often not questioning at all but are counsel's assertions.

In order to reduce the intimidating effect of cross-examination and assertions being put to the victim, a preferable way is for the defense counsel to put their case and questions in writing and use words such as "I suggest to you that X did not hit you, do you agree with me?" or "I suggest that you didn't cry out, do you agree with me?" This allows the victim to answer "yes," "no" or give an alternative answer, so they can fairly provide their evidence.

J.   Conclusory Remarks on the Role of Judges

The overall duty of the judge is to ensure that there is a fair trial for both the victim and the accused in the court. The duty requires ensuring that all witnesses in a GBV case are able to give their best evidence, otherwise the very point of a fair trial is rendered useless.

The court should also not turn a "blind eye" as to whether the police and prosecution have undertaken their obligations. If the obligations to properly investigate have not been taken, then the court can make appropriate orders and/or draw attention of deficiencies to the appropriate authority. This may result in punishable offenses under Sections 166(2) and 186(2) PPC.

In addition, the court can exercise its powers under Section 540 CrPC and Article 161 QSO to summon witnesses, recall and reexamine witnesses, ask questions, and order productions of documents as referred to in the *Updated Practice Note* (paras. 53–56). This does not in any way suggest that the GBV Court is an investigative court, instead it enables the court to have all reasonably available evidence before it to make a just decision. This process assists the accused and the victim and does not alter the burden of proof.

IV. Role of Prosecutors in Gender-Based Violence Courts

Prosecutors have a vital role in fulfilling the requirements of the State to provide access to justice for persons who are victims of GBV and to ensure that offenders are properly charged and fairly brought to justice for their crime. A prosecutor, in realizing that requirement, needs to be fiercely independent, fair, and courageous.

Deciding whether to prosecute a case is one of the most important steps in the prosecution process. The United Nations Guidelines on the Role of Prosecutors (UN Guidelines) emphasize that prosecutors need to keep in mind the public interest as well as the interests and concerns of victims when carrying out their duties.[18] Article 13(d) of the UN Guidelines reaffirms the *Declaration of the Basic Principles of Justice for Victims of Crime and Abuse of Power,* and mandates that prosecutors "allow the views and concerns of victims to be presented and considered at appropriate stages of the proceedings where their personal interests are affected, without prejudice to the accused and consistent with the relevant national criminal justice system."

Additionally, good practice requires that only specialized or trained prosecutors should take such cases. Such training should give prosecutors an improved understanding of the needs of victims and avoid stereotyping and bias in the decisions as to whether a prosecution should be commenced and continued (see Chapter 2).

The role of the prosecutor is relevant at a number of crucial points. It starts from responding to a bail application, recalling a bail application, reviewing police reports, and formulating an opinion as to whether there are defects in the investigation or further lines of inquiry that should be pursued by the police prior to the *Challan* (charge sheet) being forwarded to the court.

Police and prosecution should collaborate to ensure that all evidence that is reasonably available is obtained, appreciating the different roles that each play in that process. Further, the prosecution critically assists the court in the framing of appropriate charges that will then provide the basis for the prosecution.

The role of the prosecutor is also provided for in various sections of the CrPC, such as Sections 158, 173, 227–231, and particularly 265. Other provinces also have provisions in Chapter III in laws such as the Punjab Criminal Prosecution Service (Constitution, Functions and Powers) Act, 2006; Sindh Criminal Prosecution Service (Constitution, Functions and Powers) Act, 2016; and Khyber Pakhtunkhwa Prosecution Service (Constitution, Functions and Powers) Act, 2005.

Even before a trial commences, the prosecution is required to consider the interests of the victim and of the public. Sometimes there will be tension. A victim may be keen to pursue a prosecution, but the prosecution does not consider that there is a realistic prospect of conviction

---

[18]   United Nations Human Rights Office of the High Commissioner. *Guidelines on the Role of Prosecutors.* The guidelines were adopted by the 8th United Nations Congress on the Prevention of Crime and the Treatment of Offenders in Havana Cuba (28 August to 7 September 1990).

on the available evidence. Alternatively, the victim may be reluctant to continue with the case because of fear of recrimination, the court processes, family pressure, or threats to resile. The latter is more likely in a GBV case (see Chapter 12).

A. Preparing for Trial

Before a GBV case commences in court, good practice requires the prosecutor to personally speak with the victim to explain the court processes including the different ways in which their evidence may be given. This meeting enables the prosecutor to understand how they can best adduce the victim's evidence and inform the victim about the approach that the defense may have. Further, there should be a discussion with any counsel acting on behalf of the victim about special witness requirements such as interpreters, communication assistants, and communication aids, to ensure a smooth process during trial.

Additionally, prosecutors should consider whether the witness requires counselling, protection orders, or other assistance to enable her to feel secure. Unless the witness is assured of her safety, they may resile. In this situation, the prosecution must be well-trained in how to undertake an effective hostile witness cross-examination.

B. The Trial Process

Throughout the trial processes, prosecutors should ensure that the *Guidelines* and *Practice Notes* are followed in the court room and defense counsel. They should object to any questions that are inappropriate for the witness.

Finally, in the event of a successful prosecution, the prosecutor has a further role with regard to sentencing and ensuring that a strong but fair submission is made to the court on the sentence which should be imposed in all of the circumstances (see Chapter 11).

C. Conclusory Observations on the Role of Prosecutors

In conclusion, it may often occur that the prosecutor has more experience on the appropriate way to deal with GBV cases than does the judge. This makes it even more important that they are able to assist the GBV Court on the *Guidelines* and *Practice Notes*.

V. Role of Defense Counsel in Gender-Based Violence Courts

Defense counsels are officers of the court who are obliged to conduct themselves in a way which contributes to fairness and justice in the court processes. Unlike prosecutors, they are not required to be independent, but instead represent their clients to the best of their ability within the requirements of the law and procedures. Their role as officers of the court requires that they familiarize themselves with the directions in the *Salman Akram Raja Case* and any *Guidelines* or *Practice Notes* of the court.

No longer is a defense counsel entitled to make spurious, personalized observations or humiliating strategies against a victim in order to achieve an acquittal of an accused. The court should stop defense counsels from adopting such strategies. This is demonstrated by the criticism made by the Delhi High Court of an experienced counsel who used techniques of maligning a deceased victim in the Nirbhaya gang rape trial in India to obtain an acquittal.[19]

Best practice indicates that trials proceed more smoothly when there is communication between the prosecutor and defense counsel about procedural issues including any use of interpreters, communication assistance or communication aids; the listing of the case; the time required for the trial; and any needs for adjournment.

Another matter that is relevant to the role of defense counsel concerns the court's approach to procedures when the victim or other witnesses resile from previous statements (see Chapter 8). The *Practice Notes* set out a procedure that the judge may adopt or a combination of procedures to address this issue. The defense counsel should make themselves familiar with this process.

VI. *Amicus Curiae*

An *amicus curiae* (friend of the court) has a long history. It applies to a person/lawyer not having interest in the case, who uses their own knowledge to make suggestions on a point of law or fact for the information of the court or to prevent uninformed court error. It now more commonly refers to a lawyer who is appointed by the court or civil society organizations in cases of public interest, human rights, political issues, or cases that have broad impact or ramifications (interest group amicus).

An amicus may represent an accused person who lacks representation or support one of the parties. This is referred to as an endorsing amicus. An amicus may also provide independent advice to the court on complex legal issues, or gather information and inquiries, and report to the court. This is the more traditional disinterested amicus.

The Supreme Court of Pakistan has increasingly allowed amicus counsels to appear and make submissions. The broader use of *amicus curiae* are matters a court can consider so that justice can be provided in the case at hand and serve as a precedent for future cases.

---

[19]   *News18.* 2020. AP Singh, the Lawyer Whose Defence of Nirbhaya Rapists Began with "Would Have Burnt My Daughter If…" 10 February.

VII. Conclusory Remarks

A combination of the *Guidelines* and the *Practice Notes* provides the best practice for courts in improving access to justice for the victims of GBV. Even if a particular province or territory has not formally endorsed them, it does not mean that the processes set out in those two documents cannot be followed. As indicated, they reflect practices and procedures that are already applied under other related laws, and in particular the directions in the *Salman Akram Raja* case.

The *Guidelines* and *Practice Notes* do not imply that the court take an inquisitorial approach; it is of course not for the court to run the case. Instead, the court is urged to exercise its proper power to ensure that the processes that take place in the GBV Court are fair for all parties.

Ending rape culture. A rally is held in Islamabad, Pakistan for women's rights. The placard reads, "There's no excuse for rape! No matter who she is or what she wears or where she is" (photo by Tanveer Shahzad).

Chapter 9

EVIDENCE AND CREDIBILITY

I.   Introduction

This chapter connects interlocking elements affecting gender-based violence (GBV) claims and outcomes. These elements include the myths and stereotypes about women who have been subjected to GBV, negative societal attitudes about GBV claims, deficient evidence gathering, misconceptions about corroboration and virginity testing, and court processes and delays (Figure 9.1). These interlocking elements lead to high case attrition and offender impunity (see Chapter 12).

Figure 9.1: Interlocking Elements Affecting Gender-Based Violence Claims and Outcomes

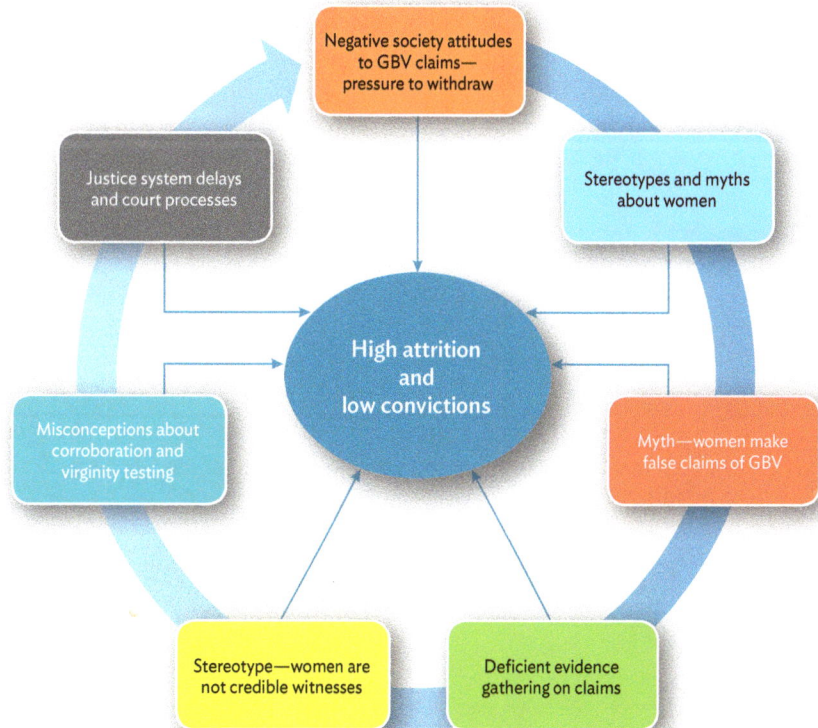

Negative society attitudes to GBV claims— pressure to withdraw

Justice system delays and court processes

Stereotypes and myths about women

High attrition and low convictions

Misconceptions about corroboration and virginity testing

Myth—women make false claims of GBV

Stereotype—women are not credible witnesses

Deficient evidence gathering on claims

GBV = gender-based violence.
Source: Authors.

It is extremely important that evidence is gathered in a prompt and efficient manner because thorough and rigorous gathering of evidence is necessary to support the victim's allegations. Evidence which falls short of this standard significantly contributes to low conviction rates. GBV crimes against women are usually perpetrated in private without witnesses. Although circumstantial evidence is obtainable and could be collected, oftentimes it is not. This lack of independent evidence may lead a judge to mistrust and doubt a victim's credibility and consequently, the case cannot be proven beyond a reasonable doubt.

Impediments to justice as a result of poor evidence collection are compounded by court delays and fear of court processes allow for the accused to place pressure on the victim and her family. Even if the victim and her family are brave enough to make a complaint and pursue proceedings, they may later resile, resulting in acquittal of the accused.

To redress this injustice, a combination of approaches is required—starting with the police adopting a sensitive and empathetic approach to evidence collection and policing, and ensuring that a rigorous and timely investigation that obtains evidence and statements is conducted.

II. Police Evidence

The police, as first-line investigators, must provide an effective, prompt, impartial, and thorough investigation.

Devastating consequences occur when the police conduct deficient investigations. The following cases highlight the importance of a proper investigation. Courts have an important role in ensuring that deficiencies in police investigation are addressed and remedied.

A. Cases from Pakistan

- *Human Rights Case No. 42389–P of 2013*[1]
  Supreme Court of Pakistan

Facts: Gang rape of a hearing-impaired mother of three on 9 October 2013; the police would not register her case. She went before a magistrate who ordered that she be medically examined on 12 October 2013. The report revealed she had sustained vaginal injuries. On 14 October 2013, a first information report (FIR) was registered by the victim's brother; the victim's statement was still not recorded. The Chief Justice of Pakistan took notice through a newspaper report on 4 November 2013. The Court called for a report from the inspector general of police (IGP) on 6 November 2013. Instead of taking prompt action, the IGP handed the matter to a subordinate. No report was provided, so the Court ordered that a date of hearing be fixed.

The district police office (DPO) report stated that the victim accused three persons of raping her on the roof of a house. The victim's brother stated that there were six accused inside the house. The DPO found these to be contradictions and exonerated the accused.

---

[1]   2014 SCMR 515.

The Supreme Court appointed a District and Sessions Court judge to conduct an inquiry, who told the Court the "police showed slackness and negligence."

Held: The Supreme Court concluded that on account of criminal negligence, the poor lady who is hearing- and speech-impaired was subjected to a "criminal act and the police knowing well about their negligence were trying to cover up their defects." The Court directed the IGP to initiate criminal proceedings against all delinquent police officers, including the supervising DPO, as early as possible. The Court further directed an independent investigation in order to initiate disciplinary proceedings against the supervising DPO and others, and referred the matter to the concerned authority in accordance with law.

- ***Mst Rukkiya Iqbal v. Faisal Hayat***[2]
  Court of the Judicial Magistrate–XV, West Karachi

The case of *Mst Rukkiya Iqbal v. Faisal Hayat*, previously referred to in Chapter 7, is an example of a domestic violence case where the police were reluctant to register an FIR, and did not investigate the evidence.

B.   Cases before Regional Courts or Commissions

Treaties often provide that litigants may appeal their cases to international or regional courts or commissions, where they allege that their domestic court system had failed and they exhausted the domestic court processes. International tribunals' decisions often apply international norms and good practices. Pakistan courts have on numerous occasions applied international norms. The Court in *Najib Zarab Ltd.* held, "[T]he community of nations requires that rules of international law may be accommodated in the municipal law even without express legislative sanction provided they do not run into conflict with the Acts of the Parliament."[3] (See Chapter 1.)

- ***M.C. v. Bulgaria***[4]
  European Court of Human Rights

Facts: A victim alleged she was raped twice on two consecutive days by two perpetrators who were friends of each other and acquaintances of hers. She was 14 years old and 10 months over the age of consent in Bulgaria where the rapes took place. Medical examination indicated her hymen was freshly torn and she had abrasions on her body. Initially, the victim reported the first rape, but not the second due to shame. Later she reported the second rape. The investigator found no evidence that the accused had used threats or violence and proposed that the proceedings be terminated.

Held: The Court noted the presence of two irreconcilable versions of the facts and called for a contextual assessment of the credibility of the statements and for verification of all the surrounding circumstances. The Court found that the authorities had failed to investigate the surrounding circumstances as they put undue emphasis on "direct" proof of rape such as

---

[2]   Cr Petition No. 457 of 2017.

[3]   *M/s Najib Zarab Ltd v. The Government of Pakistan*, PLD 1993 Karachi 93.

[4]   Application No. 39272/98, 4 December 2003.

stranger rape, serious injuries, eyewitnesses, and proof of physical resistance. The prosecutors also forwent the possibility of proving the perpetrators' *mens rea* by assessing all the surrounding circumstances, such as evidence that they had deliberately misled the applicant in order to take her to a deserted area, thus creating an environment of coercion. Thus, the authorities' approach erroneously equated lack of physical resistance by the victim to a defining element of the offense.

Finally, the Court found that "the approach taken by the investigator and the prosecutors in the case fell short of the requirements inherent in the States' positive obligations—viewed in the light of the relevant modern standards in comparative and international law—to establish and apply effectively a criminal-law system punishing all forms of rape and sexual abuse."[5]

- ● *Jessica Lenahan (Gonzales) v. United States*[6]
  Inter-American Commission on Human Rights

Jessica Gonzales was subjected to recurring controlling abusive behavior and physical and sexual assaults by her husband. She obtained protection orders, however, the police repeatedly neglected to respond to her calls or enforce her restraining orders against her husband, which, tragically led to her children's deaths. The Supreme Court of the United States found that Ms. Gonzales had no right to expect the police to enforce the protective order. Consequently, she brought her case before the Inter-American Commission on Human Rights (IACHR).[7] The IACHR held that the Government of the United States was responsible for human rights violations against Ms. Gonzales and her three children, as it had a positive duty to protect Ms. Gonzales whom it knows is a person at risk (due to the restraining orders against her husband).

C. Police Good Practice

It is good practice for the police to have a Code of Practice and develop a checklist of evidence to apply in notoriously underinvestigated domestic violence cases. In 2010, the United Nations Office on Drugs and Crime produced the *Handbook on Effective Police Responses to Violence against Women*, which includes examples of police practices from many countries.[8] The handbook states that effective and thorough investigations should

- ● determine whether an offense was committed;
- ● identify victims and witnesses;
- ● gather and preserve any and all relevant evidence;
- ● discover cause, manner, and location of offense;
- ● prove the identity of the suspect or person(s) responsible;
- ● where appropriate, formulate grounds to bring charge;
- ● document the investigation and evidence, and prepare to present evidence at trial; and

---

5   Footnote 4, para. 185.
6   Report No. 80/11 (2011).
7   See American Civil Liberties Union (ACLU). Jessica Gonzales' Statement before the IACHR.
8   United Nations Office on Drugs and Crime. 2010. *Handbook on Effective Police Responses to Violence against Women*. New York.

- prevent further victimization (includes both the victim and others who may be affected, such as children).[9]

Drawing from this list, and with regard to the Pakistani context, the police should develop a checklist of investigation elements for GBV cases. (See Chapter 12 on victimless prosecution and pro-prosecution policy.)

A basic investigation also includes the collection of circumstantial evidence and the recording and obtaining of evidence about circumstances that draw inferences about an accused's guilt from the accused's own conduct.

III. Corroboration: Concept and Application

A thorough investigation by the police may fortify the allegations made by the victim, nonetheless, evidence must be collected. Failure to do so can result in missing evidence that could have corroborated allegations.

What is meant by corroboration? Simply put, corroborating evidence is evidence that supports some other evidence of an offense. Two simple examples are as follows:

(i)   If A gives evidence she was hit by B, then C gives evidence that he saw B hit A—that would be regarded as direct evidence and would corroborate A's evidence if accepted.

(ii)   If A gives evidence she was hit by B, and C gives evidence he heard A scream and saw B coming out of a house with a stick, followed by A who had blood on her face, then C's evidence is circumstantial evidence from which it can be inferred that B hit A. If it were accepted, it would corroborate A's evidence.

There are many ways in which corroborating evidence can be given in court. Sometimes laws require corroborating evidence for the case to be proven beyond a reasonable doubt.[10] On the whole, whether corroboration is required in a particular case is left for judges to decide under their judicial prudence. The Qanun e-Shahadat Order 1984 (QSO) addresses relevancy of evidence but not credibility, reliability, or corroboration.

A general application of judicial prudence, as expressed in Pakistan's case law, is that if direct/ original evidence is trustworthy and sufficient to establish the charge, then corroboration from another source is not required. Corroboration is a 'rule of abundant caution,' not a default rule. Its application is desirable only when the judicial conscience is not satisfied as to the truthfulness of evidence.[11]

As a Peshawar High Court said, if there are minor discrepancies in the complainant's statements, they are inconsequential and not fatal to the case. If the original evidence does not suffer from

---

9   Footnote 8, pp. 46–47.
10   S. A. Cheema. 2015. *Corroborating Evidence in Pakistan: A Mechanism to Fill Reliability Void.*
11   *Abdul Rashid v. State*, 2003 SCMR 799.

'any major or significant contradiction,'[12] or, if the Court is satisfied as to the 'truthfulness of direct/original evidence,' then corroboration of the same would not be of consequence.[13] The Court continued that such direct evidence could not be cast aside only on the basis of the relationship between prosecution witnesses and the deceased.

S.A. Cheema (2015) sets out a useful collection of examples of the application of corroboration in Pakistan's superior courts:

a. Nature and extent of corroboratory evidence may vary from case to case and depends on judicial discretion of the court (*Shera Masih v. State, 2002 PLD 643*).

b. The corroborative evidence should prove guilt of an accused (*Haq Nawaz v. Sultan Khan, 1977 SCMR 99*). Or at least it must connect or tend to connect the accused with the crime (*Shahzad v. State, 2002 SCMR 1009*).

c. The corroborative evidence is not required to confirm the whole story narrated by a witness whose evidence is being corroborated, it is sufficient if it supports the ocular/original evidence in material particulars (*Shera Masih v. State, 2002*).

d. The corroborating evidence is not required to come from an independent witness: it may come from anything (*Shah Nawaz v. State, 2002 PCr LJ 388*). Corroboration may be sought from direct or even from circumstantial evidence (*Shera Masih v. State, 2002*). However, corroboration cannot be sought from the evidence of the witness whose evidence is required to be corroborated (*Zahida Saleem v. Muhammad Naseem, 2006 PLD SC 427*).

e. A corroborative piece of evidence cannot corroborate another corroborative piece of evidence (*Dr. M. Sarwar Ch. v. State, 2001 YLR 2478*). A piece of evidence which is tainted cannot be used for corroboration of similar evidence (*Manzoor v. State, 1973 PLD Lahore 714*).[14]

IV. Corroboration: Credibility of Women's Evidence in Gender-Based Violence Cases

The approach taken with respect to corroboration of women's evidence in GBV cases has not been used in cases relating to other offenses. Misconceptions regarding women's credibility (for example, that they are untrustworthy) in sexual assault and rape cases previously dictated that the law require corroboration. Although the law has now changed, the underlying and insidious stereotype that women are untrustworthy and that their testimony requires outside attestation remains. The stereotype is that women are untruthful due to shame and stigma, so they will not admit to having consensual sex outside of marriage; they lie and say the premarital or extramarital sex was nonconsensual. Another myth is that women make rape allegations to cause harm or seek

---

12 *Rahim Shah v. State*, 2004 PCrLJ 1129.

13 *Muhammad Panah v. State*, 2011 YLR 1811.

14 Footnote 10, p. 5.

revenge. These discriminatory and stereotypical attitudes remain an impediment to successful convictions. These presumptions that women 'lie' are also erroneously made when women are compelled by their family to resile subsequent to their families 'compromising' or entering into settlements with the accused (see Chapter 12).

Early common law regarded rape as "an accusation easily made and hard to be proved, and harder to be defended by the accused, though never so innocent."[15] The legal requirement mandating corroboration in sexual assault cases exemplifies historical skepticism of women alleging sexual assault.

Now it is increasingly accepted and understood that alleging sexual assault is not easy. As the South Africa Court of Appeal stated in *S v. J*, "[F]ew things may be more difficult and humiliating for a woman than to cry rape: she is often, within certain communities, considered to have lost her credibility; she may be seen as unchaste and unworthy of respect; her community may turn its back on her; she has to undergo the most harrowing cross-examination in court, where the intimate details of the crime are traversed ad nauseam; she (but not the accused) may be required to reveal her previous sexual history..."[16] The notion that women "cry rape" is highly inaccurate. In fact, data shows that the percentage of women who fabricate sexual assault complaints is very low.[17]

A.   International Case Examples of Corroboration of Women's Evidence

- **Kenya**
  Mukungu v. Republic[18]

The facts of this case concern a victim who alleged she was raped by two men. The accused was not medically examined and could not be connected with the offense.

The appellant appealed his conviction to the Court of Appeal of Kenya. The Court discussed the history of corroboration in previous court decisions and the stereotype about girls and women telling false stories, then stated:

> [12.] It is noteworthy that the same caution is not required of the evidence of women and girls in other offences. Besides there is neither scientific proof nor research finding that we know of to show that women and girls will, as a general rule, give false testimony or fabricate cases against men in sexual offences. And yet courts have hitherto consistently held that in sexual offences testimony of women and girls should be treated differently. Perhaps there was nothing objectionable about that discriminative treatment before Kenya became a republic in 1964. The Republic

---

15   M. Hale, ed. 1847. *The History of the Pleas of the Crown*. Philadelphia: Robert H. Small. pp. 633–636 (particularly 634).

16   1998 (2) SA 984.

17   See for example, Victoria Law Reform Commission. 2001. *Sexual Offences Discussion Paper*. p. 156.

18   [2003] 2 EA 482.

Constitution has various provisions against discriminatory treatment on the basis of, inter alia, race and sex. Section 82 of the Constitution [...]

[13.] [...] The Constitution has no provision authorising any discriminatory treatment of witnesses particularly with regard to matters of credibility. It is noteworthy that even the Evidence Act (Chapter 80) Laws of Kenya, has no provision on the issue of corroboration of the testimony of adult women and girls.

[14.] For the foregoing reasons we think **that the requirement for corroboration in sexual offences affecting adult women and girls is unconstitutional to the extent that the requirement is against them qua women or girls.** (emphasis added)

- **Committee on the Elimination of Violence against Women**
  R.P.B. v. The Philippines[19]

This case concerns a rape which occurred in 2006 of a hearing and speech impaired 17-year-old girl, R.P.B. In 2011, the Regional Trial Court of Pasig City acquitted the victim's neighbor of the rape. R.P.B. later submitted a communication to the Committee on the Elimination of Violence against Women (CEDAW Committee), claiming the trial court discriminated against her. In particular, she noted that the stereotypes and myths imposed peculiar evidentiary burdens on, and undermined the credibility of, women rape victims. "Those who satisfy the stereotypes," she said, "are considered credible, while the others are met with suspicion and disbelief, leading to the acquittal of the accused."

The CEDAW Committee concluded that the Philippines violated CEDAW by engaging in stereotyping which resulted in 'material and moral damage and prejudice.'[20] After explaining how the trial court's reliance on stereotypes led to the acquittal, the Committee outlined the obligations of States Parties concerning judicial stereotyping. The Committee indicated that "stereotyping affects women's right to a fair and just trial and [...] **the judiciary must take caution not to create inflexible standards of what women or girls should be or what they should have done when confronted with a situation of rape based merely on preconceived notions of what defines a rape victim.**" (emphasis added)

- **Bangladesh**
  Al Amin & Ors v. Bangladesh[21]

The Bangladesh High Court held that "the testimony of a victim of sexual assault is vital, and unless there are compelling reasons which necessitate corroboration of her statement, the court should find no difficulty in convicting an accused on her testimony alone if it inspires confidence and is found to be reliable."[22] To do so, the Court noted, "would be to treat victims of sexual violence equally with other victims and witnesses of violent crimes, for whom decisions

---

[19] CEDAW/C/57/D/34/2011, Communication No. 34/2011.

[20] Footnote 19, para. 8.8.

[21] 51 DLR (1999) 154. The case was cited in a compilation of judgments by South Asian Regional Initiative Authority/Equity Support Program.

[22] South Asia Regional Initiative/Equity Support Program. *Landmark Judgments on Violence against Women and Children from South Asia.* p. 107.

of credibility are made on a case-by-case basis and not subject to general rules. **The per se imposition of a requirement that a victim's testimony be corroborated in sexual assault cases is discriminatory and contradicts the duty of the authorities, outlined by the Committee on the Elimination of Discrimination against Women to ensure that "legal procedures in cases involving crimes of rape and other sexual offenses [...] be impartial and fair, and not affected by prejudices or stereotypical gender notions"** (emphasis added, footnote 21).

- **India**

Three Supreme Court cases from India eloquently articulate that corroboration is not required by law and insignificant discrepancies in testimony should not be the basis for rejecting evidence.

In the case of *State of Punjab v. Gurmit Singh*,[23] the Supreme Court stated:

> Corroboration as a condition for judicial reliance on the testimony of the prosecutrix is not a requirement of law but a guidance of prudence under given circumstances. It must not be overlooked that a woman or a girl subjected to sexual assault is not an accomplice to the crime but is a victim of another person's lust and it is improper and undesirable to test her evidence with a certain amount of suspicion, treating her as if she were an accomplice. Inferences have to be drawn from a given set of facts and circumstances with realistic diversity and not dead uniformity lest that type of rigidity in the shape of rule of law is introduced through a new form of testimonial tyranny making justice a casualty. Courts cannot cling to a fossil formula and insist upon corroboration even if, taken as a whole, the case spoken of by the victim of sex crime strikes the judicial mind as probable.

In *The State of MP v. Dayal Sahu*,[24] the Supreme Court of India held that the victim's testimony in a sexual assault case should be given great weight and that corroborative evidence is neither imperative nor was it a critical component of judicial credence in every case. The Court held that the complainant and her husband could not be expected to know that they should have rushed to a doctor following the assault and the fact that the complainant deposed that she had taken a bath and washed her clothes after the incident was not evidence of dishonesty. Furthermore, the Court held that, under the circumstances, the inability of the victim to produce a medical report was not consequential since the other evidence on record was believable:

> Corroboration of testimony of the prosecutrix as a condition for judicial reliance is not a requirement of law but a guidance of prudence under the given facts and circumstances. It is also noticed that minor contradictions or insignificant discrepancies should not be a ground for throwing out an otherwise reliable prosecution case. Non-examination of doctor and non-production of doctor's report would not cause fatal to the prosecution case, if the statements of the prosecutrix and other prosecution witnesses inspire confidence. It is also noticed that the Court while acquitting the accused on benefit of doubt should be cautious to see that the

---

23   (1996) 2 SCC 384.
24   AIR (2005) SC 3570.

doubt should be a reasonable doubt and it should not reverse the findings of the guilt on the basis of irrelevant circumstances or mere technicalities.

In another of India's Supreme Court decisions, *Bharwada Bhoginbhai Hirjibhai v. State of Gujarat,*[25] the Court reversed the decision to not act on the testimony of a victim of sexual assault in the absence of corroboration. This was, according to the Court, adding insult to injury. The Court compared the requirement of corroborating evidence to be like reading with the aid of spectacles fitted with lenses tinted with doubt, disbelief, or suspicion.

B.   Pakistani Case Examples of Corroboration of Women's Evidence in Sex Cases

Case law in Pakistan affirms that corroborating evidence is not required in the prosecution of crimes such as rape, and that a conviction can be based on the sole testimony of the victim if her evidence is credible. Such was the court's ruling in *Shakeel and Others v. The State*, which found that the victim's witness statement was sufficient and corroborating evidence not necessary.[26] The case illustrates the challenges women face when pursuing their cases.

- *Shakeel and Others v. The State*
  Supreme Court of Pakistan

The facts involve a dreadful ordeal in which the victim was held by four accused and given sedatives. This rendered her semiconscious and she was subjected to *zina-bil-jabr* (rape) by the accused. One of the accused, Shakeel, compromised with the victim's father and brother. The victim reported 3 days later through an FIR. On appeal to the Supreme Court, appellants argued (i) the victim was a "lady of easy virtue," (ii) her statement should be discarded, (iii) delay in reporting indicated concoction, (iv) the FIR was lodged by her and "not supported by any member of her family," and (v) semen did not prove rape and it did not identify the appellants. Furthermore, they contended there was no corroboration of her evidence.

The Supreme Court held that there is no reason to disbelieve the victim and conviction could be awarded on her solitary statement. In addition, even if she was "a girl of an easy virtue" by reason of the two-finger test, "no blanket authority can be given to rape her by anyone who wishes to do so" (footnote 26). The Court further said:

> It is well settled by now that the extent and nature of corroboration required may, no doubt, vary from witness to witness and from case to case, but as a rule it is not necessary that there [should] be corroboration in every particular, all that is necessary is that the corroboration must be such as to effect the accused by connecting or tending to connect him with the crime. [...] To say that certain witnesses require corroboration and then to lay down that the corroborative evidence must

---

[25]   AIR (1983) SC 753.
[26]   2011 PLJ SC1.

show that the accused did not do the precise act attributed to him by the witnesses is tantamount to doing away with the evidence of those witnesses. [...]

By now it has been well settled that if the statement of the prosecutrix is considered trustworthy, no corroboration would be needed. [This is necessary only in] circumstances indicating the possibility of her [consenting] to sexual intercourse, [...] a rare [phenomenon] in cases of *zina-bil-jabr*. [In such cases, corroboration of evidence does not need to be] direct evidence but it may be independent evidence of such a character which would connect the accused directly or indirectly with the alleged offence (footnote 26).

- ### *The State v. Abdul Khaliq and Others*[27]
  Supreme Court of Pakistan

A case with a complex fact history is *The State v. Abdul Khaliq and Others*, which was a *suo moto* proceeding following public outcry.

The *suo moto* application concluded with two majority judges holding that the appeals should be dismissed, and a minority judge who disagreed. The description of the facts by the majority, compared with that of the dissenting judge, read like two separate cases.

In its reasoning, the Court focused specifically on certain factors, such as the chronology of events; delay in lodging an FIR (8 days); alleged inconsistencies of evidence (including specifics as to the extent of the state of undress of the victim after the events); whether there were marks of injuries on the victim's body; evidence not called; and whether there was corroboration.

The minority judge dealt with each issue and highlighted facts that the majority had hardly focused on. For example, the judge examined the details regarding the negotiations of the *Panchayat* (village council) between the Mastoi Tribe and the Gujjars, and how a compromise was reached on the prosecution case that was not honored by the Mastoi tribe and which resulted in the rape of the prosecutrix. Contrary to the majority's opinion, delay of FIR was regarded by the minority judge as justifiable. Although the majority and minority judges applied the same legal tests, clearly the outcomes were vastly different.

The outcome of a particular case is oftentimes contingent on judicial discretion. The extent to which a judge may appreciate the very real circumstances that a victim has faced, or adopts or denounces stereotypes and discriminatory assumptions of victims of GBV, will immensely impact a judge's discretion. Therefore, it is important for judges to recognize their own personal preconceptions and biases toward victims' credibility and witness behavior to ensure that they are not using stereotypes when considering the evidence and circumstances of a particular case before them.

It is vital that the justice system recognize and appreciate the plight of GBV victims who have been subjected to horrific cases of violence and who faced immense societal and cultural pressure to stay silent, so that justice is achievable for those individual courageous women who bring their cases forward. It is possible to do this without compromising the presumed innocence of the accused.

---

[27]   PLD 2011 Supreme Court 554.

V. Court Processes Impacting on the Credibility of Women Victims

Two further examples of court processes and judicial attitudes that impact the credibility of women victims of sexual assault are discussed. The first is with regard to character attacks and the second is virginity testing.

A. Character Attacks

Traditionally, perpetrators were allowed to present their victims as immoral and unchaste through allegations of a victim's past sexual history. Character attacks were mounted mainly on the argument that the victim was "impure," and therefore, not credible. Victims were humiliated at the police station and in courts (i.e., they were re-victimized at the hands of the law and law enforcers).

Gradually, the law evolved to emphasize that the character, morality, and sexual history of victims are irrelevant; that like any other crime, what is significant is whether the offense complained of had occurred. For example, in a trial where a businessman had been robbed and his credit cards used by the accused, the following are irrelevant:

    (i)   The bank should not have approved these credit cards (through testimonies of bank managers and credit card officers to suggest they had special and inappropriate relationships with the victim);

    (ii)   The victim earned his wealth dishonorably (through testimonies of the victim's business partners that they thought the victim was a disreputable businessman or that the victim had them); and

    (iii)   The victim abused his employees (through evidence of former employees that the victim had not paid his employees fairly and was a 'bad' or immoral employer).

Nor does the court have the discretion to decide, solely based on these business dealings that

    (i)   The victim could not possibly have been robbed; or

    (ii)   The victim must have voluntarily handed the credit cards to the accused, and therefore, the accused is to be found not guilty.

At law, such a scenario is preposterous. Yet in rape trials, and only in rape trials, Section 151 of the Evidence Act gave the defense counsel special permission to attack the victim's character by suggesting that she was immoral (usually, if she was unmarried, that she was habituated to sex, and if she was married, that she was otherwise immoral). This rule was applicable only to rape trials, and not to any other offenses:

QSO
Article 151: Impeaching credit of witness

The credit of a witness may be impeached in the following ways:

[...]

(4) when a man is prosecuted for rape or an attempt to ravish, it may be shown that the prosecutrix was of generally immoral character (Repealed Am 2016).

This provision was repealed in 2016. Some provinces expounded upon the 2016 provision repeal and further clarified that past sexual conduct of the victim is immaterial and irrelevant. For example:

Punjab Witness Protection Act, 2018
Section 12(3) Rules of cross-examination

The court shall forbid a question to the victim of a sexual offence relating to any sexual behaviour of the victim on any previous occasion with the accused or any other person, unless such a question, in the opinion of the court, is a relevant fact in the case.

Even though Article 151 of the QSO was repealed, judges have continued to allow character attacks on the victim. This is legally incorrect and should not be tolerated.

The Supreme Court of Pakistan in *Atif Zareef v. The State* sternly warned against the 'twin myths,' i.e., the false presumption that **past sexual history** has any bearing on whether a victim **consented** or is worthy to be believed.[28] The Court reiterated, "[T]he real fact-in-issue is whether or not the accused committed rape on her. If the victim had lost her virginity earlier, it does not give to anyone the right to rape her. In a criminal trial relating to rape, it is the accused who is on trial and not the victim. The courts should also discontinue the use of painfully intrusive and inappropriate expressions, like 'habituated to sex', 'woman of easy virtue', 'woman of loose moral character', and 'non-virgin', for the alleged rape victims even if they find that the charge of rape is not proved against the accused. Such expressions are unconstitutional and illegal."[29]

In addition, as discussed in detail in Chapter 8, it is the role of the Court to ensure that witnesses (including victims) are not asked indecent, scandalous or offensive questions (QSO Article 146), and to forbid questions that insult or annoy (QSO Article 148).

B. Virginity Testing

Penetration, no matter how slight, is sufficient to prove the offense of rape. Yet, there are still some who believe the primary evidence of rape must be obtained through virginity testing. But what does virginity testing actually prove?

Is tearing of the hymen necessary to prove rape? The short answer is 'no.' Evidence of a torn hymen is not necessary to prove rape.

---

[28] Criminal Appeal No. 251/2020 and Criminal Petition No. 667/2020 (January 2021).
[29] Footnote 28, para. 12.

Does an intact hymen prove no penetration has occurred? The short answer is 'no.'

In the case of *Ranjit Hazarika v. State of Assam*, the Supreme Court of India held that the "mere fact that no injury was found on the private parts of the prosecutrix or her hymen does not belie the statement of the prosecutrix as she nowhere stated that she bled per vagina as a result of the penetration. [...] To constitute the offence of rape, penetration, however slight, is sufficient."[30]

In any case alleging rape, it is critical to understand what a hymen is. Judicial officers and prosecutors, when asked during training programs, were largely unfamiliar with what a hymen looks like. The hymen is not a flat piece of tissue covering the vagina that is punctured during intercourse (if this were the case, there would be no outlet for menstrual blood). Usually, the hymen looks like a fringe of tissue around the vaginal opening. Some girls are born without a hymen, others have only a scanty fringe of tissue. Hymens can be torn during sex or physical activity, but it does not "break." Torn areas can bleed, but not always.

Similarly, the Verma Committee concluded that virginity testing is not only without probative value, it is also forbidden because it is humiliating and harmful. Doctors should not conclude whether rape has occurred based on a medical examination. That conclusion can only be made by the court.[31]

Does a torn hymen prove that previous sexual intercourse had taken place? The short answer is 'no.'

The Verma Committee further underlined that the size of the vaginal introitus has no bearing on a sexual assault case, and, therefore, testing to ascertain the laxity of the vaginal muscles, commonly referred to as the two-finger test, must not be conducted.[32]

> On the basis of this [two-finger] test observations/ conclusions such as 'habituated to sexual intercourse' should not be made and this is forbidden by law.
>
> Routinely, there is a lot of attention given to the status of hymen. The "finger test" is also conducted to note the distensibility of the hymen. However it is largely irrelevant because the hymen can be torn due to several reasons. An intact hymen does not rule out sexual assault, and a torn hymen does not prove previous sexual intercourse. Hymen should therefore be treated like any other part of the genitals while documenting examination findings in cases of sexual assault. Only those that are relevant to the episode of assault (findings such as fresh tears, bleeding, oedema etc.) are to be documented (footnote 32).

It is clear that virginity testing and the two-finger test are used to attack a victim's character. Moreover, the test is used to insinuate that the victim is immoral and not credible; it perpetuates the stereotype that a victim who is unmarried should be a virgin and, if she is not, then her rape complaint is false and that she is an immoral woman (i.e., it was legally improbable that she would have not agreed to have sex with the rapist). Two case examples are as follows:

---

[30] (1998) 8 SCC 635.

[31] J.S. Verma, L. Seth, and G. Subramanium. 2013. *Report of the Committee on Amendments to Criminal Law*. pp. 274–275.

[32] Footnote 31, p. 275.

- The Lahore High Court in *Fahad Aziz v. State* disregarded the victim's rape complaint as "she appeared to be a woman of easy virtue [and] indulged in sexual activities."[33]

- The Lahore High Court accepted the testimony of the victim in *Amanullah v. State* as the "vagina admitted two-finger tight fully and painfully which showed [...] she was not a woman of easy virtue and was not used to committing sexual intercourse."[34]

The two-finger test has no probative value and should be discontinued. It is no longer permissible to attack the character of a victim by reference to her alleged 'easy virtue,' or to impute that if she has had sex with a man, she would have also consented to have sex with the accused.

The World Health Organization (WHO), the United Nations Office of the High Commissioner for Human Rights, and UN Women have called an end to virginity testing, categorically declaring that there is no examination that can prove whether a girl or a woman has had sex and that the two-finger test MUST NEVER be carried out.[35] Figure 9.2 shows, for example, WHO's social media campaign to end this practice.

The Criminal Procedure Code (CrPC) was amended in 2016 and provides specific requirements for the medical examination of victims. Section 164A of the CrPC (Am Act 2016) provides that the victim shall be examined by a registered medical practitioner (for rape, a female registered medical practitioner) who shall prepare a report containing a set of particulars.

The two-finger test and forensic medical examination for rape were also exhaustively considered in *Sadaf Aziz v. Pakistan*.[36] After referring to domestic cases and cases from apex courts which "all held that there is no scientific or medical basis to carry out virginity testing in the form of two-finger test or to rely on the status of the hymen whether it is torn or intact as it has no relevance to the investigation into the incident of rape or sexual abuse," as well as to Pakistan's international treaty obligations, the Lahore High Court declared the two-finger test and the hymen test carried out for purposes of ascertaining the virginity of a female victim of rape or sexual abuse as unscientific with no medical or forensic value. Further, added the Court, virginity tests are discriminatory and unconstitutional as it offends the dignity of the victim and therefore violates the right to life and right to dignity.

The use of the two-finger test was strongly criticized by the Supreme Court of Pakistan in *Atif Zareef v. The State* (footnote 28). The Court affirmed that "the two-finger test must not be conducted for establishing rape-sexual violence, and the size of the vaginal introitus has no bearing on a case of sexual violence."[37] The Supreme Court further held, "Dragging [the] sexual history of the rape survivor into the case by making observations about her body including observations like 'the vagina admits two fingers easily' or 'old ruptured hymen' is an affront to the reputation and honour of the rape survivor and violates Article 4(2)(a) of the Constitution..."[38]

---

[33] 2008 YLR 2846.

[34] PLD 2009 542.

[35] World Health Organization, United Nations Office of the High Commissioner for Human Rights, and UN Women. 2018. *Eliminating Virginity Testing: An Interagency Statement*. Geneva: World Health Organization.

[36] WP No.13537 of 2020.

[37] Footnote 28, para. 9.

[38] Footnote 28, para. 11.

Figure 9.2: Tweets by the World Health Organization on Virginity Testing

World Health Organization (WHO) ✔
@WHO

Replying to @WHO @WHO_Europe and 5 others

#VirginityTesting is an act of violence against women.

"Virginity testing" aka "two-finger testing" has no scientific or clinical basis. It is an inspection of female genitalia designed to determine whether a 👧 or 👩 has had vaginal intercourse.

We must #EndViolence #16Days ♀

End Virginity Testing 🚫

Virginity testing, also called "two-finger testing", is unscientific, harmful, and a violation of women's and girls' human rights.

World Health Organization

👤 WHO EMRO and 5 others

10:58 PM · Nov 30, 2019 · Twitter Web App

320 Retweets   **12** Quote Tweets   **374** Likes

World Health Organization (WHO) ✔
@WHO

Replying to @WHO

There is NO examination that can prove a girl or woman has had sex.

So-called #Virginitytesting is often performed by inspecting the hymen for tears or its size of opening, and/or inserting fingers into the vagina (the "two-finger" test).

It must NEVER be carried out!

End Virginity Testing 🚫

It is not possible to tell a "virgin" hymen from a "non-virgin" hymen.

World Health Organization

👤 WHO/Europe and 5 others

12:09 AM · Dec 1, 2019 · Twitter for iPhone

1,776 Retweets   **63** Quote Tweets   **1,062** Likes

Source: World Health Organization (Official Twitter Account). Tweets on (left to right) 30 November 2019, 10:58 PM and 1 December 2019, 12:09 AM.

An ordinance issued by the Pakistan Minister of Law and Justice made virginity testing unlawful, quoting that it is in violation of the Constitution.[39]

In conclusion, forensic medical examination should include a rape kit that is provided for collecting forensic medical evidence. This kit would include immediate care, head-to-toe examination, follow-up care, and preventive treatment for sexually transmitted infections.[40] At no point does the medical forensic examination involve a two-finger test. The two-finger test is traumatic for victims and has no evidential value and, therefore, no place in the judicial system.

---

[39]   To date, the ordinance has yet to be promulgated into legislation.

[40]   Rape, Abuse & Incest National Network (RAINN). What Is a Sexual Assault Forensic Exam?

VI. Conclusory Remarks

This chapter highlights the importance of thorough and efficient gathering of evidence in GBV cases, including circumstantial evidence to ensure that appropriate corroborating evidence is available to support the victim's case. It also clarifies that corroborating evidence for rape and GBV is not necessary for proving an accused's guilt if the victim's testimony is sound under evidentiary rules.

This chapter also emphasizes how judges applying the same legal test can arrive at very different outcomes. This is because outcomes are very much contingent on the exercise of judicial discretion which, in turn, is highly dependent on the extent to which a judge may stereotype victims of GBV and witnesses. It is vital for judges to recognize their individual preconceptions and biases to ensure that they are not using stereotypes when applying legal principles.

Further, judges need to ensure that GBV victims are not exposed to character attacks concerning their irrelevant past sexual conduct, such as character attacks that insinuate or alleged 'easy virtue' or the myth that if she has had sex with a man, that she would have also consented to have sex with the accused. Also, virginity testing using a two-finger test is banned because not only is it a traumatic invasion and "an affront to the reputation and honour of the rape survivor and violates Article 4(2)(a) of the Constitution" but also because it cannot prove whether a girl or woman has had sex. Addressing these issues can have a significant effect on improving the extremely low conviction rates in GBV cases and reducing resiling and attrition (see Chapter 12).

A view of the Lahore High Court hearing room.
The Lahore High Court held in *Sadaf Aziz v. Pakistan*
that virginity testing is unscientific with no medical or
forensic value (photo by Maria Cecilia T. Sicangco).

Chapter 10

JUDGMENT WRITING

I. Introduction

This chapter moves from the courtroom to decision-making and sentencing which are two of the hardest jobs for a judge or court to undertake. This is because the decision and sentence must be just and contain reasoning that articulates the court's thought process and explain how the decision was reached. It is a two-part process. Firstly, the court must decide whether the accused is guilty, and secondly, the court must choose what the punishment should be while considering imprisonment and matters of compensation in their decision-making (see Chapter 11).

After handing down a guilty decision, the court must decide on a sentence which requires a reasoning process that takes into account specific compulsory elements such as the facts of the case, legal principles, and sentencing guidelines. Similar to the court's judgment, the sentence that is handed down must be clear and concise and contain all of the court's reasoning used in reaching its conclusion.

II. Content

This chapter is not concerned with judgment writing as a craft, but rather, the content of a particular judgment.[1] Specifically, this chapter focuses on the reasoning used in decisions and considers how the language used in gender-based crimes must take into account the vulnerabilities and sensitivities of the victims.

The primary purpose of a judgment is to explain the court's decision to the parties, and to articulate its reasoning to the public. Sometimes though, judges focus too much on making a judgment "appeal proof;" at times this tends to garner more attention than it should.

Judgments serve as judicial precedents. As such, an issue that may arise when looking at judicial precedent is that judgments from higher courts are inconsistent; this can result in conflicting authorities. Discrepancies in precedent may create a predicament for a judge since judges are expected to follow the finding of the more senior judge and/or larger bench. When faced with conflicting judicial precedent,

---

[1] For judges interested in the craft of judgment writing, see J.C. Raymond. 2015. *Pacific Judicial Development Program: Judicial Decision-Making Toolkit.* The Pacific Judicial Development Program is funded by the Government of New Zealand and managed by the Federal Court of Australia.

the best approach is for a judge to consider his or her conscience with the knowledge that he or she has decided the case impartially and with intellectual honesty.

The following elements, not necessarily in this order, are commonly present in well-constructed judgments:

- introduction
- overview of facts
- clear statement of the factual issues that arise for consideration or determination
- evidence proving each factual issue
- reasoning and findings on the facts
- applicable law
- application of the law to the facts of the case
- conclusion

A frequent approach in dealing with disputed facts is to have separate headings stating the issue and the conclusion reached. Findings of fact also require an assessment of a witness' credibility. Credibility of a witness should not be based solely on the physical or visual appearance of a witness, but rather on the plausibility of their evidence either inherently or with regard to other evidence in the case. It requires looking at all of the evidence tendered in the case.

III. Gender-Sensitive Language

A judgment should be easy to read and use everyday language. Legal jargon should be avoided unless necessary. Short sentences are preferable over complex sentences. Every judge has their own way of writing and judgments should be expressed in a style that suits the judge, however, when choosing words, the judge should be conscious of the effect of the judgment on those concerned. Care should be taken to avoid intemperate language, injection of personal views, flamboyant flourishes, and hyperbole. Further, as the former Chief Justice Muhammad Munir of the Supreme Court said in *Muhammad Sharif v. The State*, a judge should not "assume the role of an advisor or a theologian."[2]

Gender-insensitive language can be one of the most pernicious ways to reinforce gender stereotypes. Hence, in the context of gender-based violence (GBV) crimes, gender-sensitive language is vital. Sexist language is not only inappropriate, but it reinforces the gender inequality that causes GBV in the first place.

A. The Importance of Gender-Sensitive Language

A case example that underscores the importance of language is the Supreme Court of India's decision in *The State of Punjab v. Gurmit Singh and Ors.*[3]

---

[2]   PLD 157 SC 201.
[3]   1996 AIR 1393.

The facts involve the abduction and rape of a girl under 16 years old. The accused were acquitted, which was appealed. The appeal was successful; the court found that the accused was guilty beyond a reasonable doubt. In doing so, the court castigated the trial court for using language that cast stigma on the character of the rape victim:

> The trial court not only erroneously disbelieved the prosecutrix, but quite uncharitably and unjustifiably even characterized her as a girl 'of loose morals' or 'such type of a girl.' What has shocked our judicial conscience all the more is the inference drawn by the court, based on no evidence and not even on a denied suggestion, to the effect:
>
>> 'The more probability is that (prosecutrix) was a girl of loose character. She wanted to dupe her parents that she resided for one night at the house of her maternal uncle, but for the reasons best known to her she does not do so and she preferred to give company to some persons.'
>
> We must express our strong disapproval of the approach of the trial court and its casting a stigma on the character of the prosecutrix (footnote 3).

The court highlighted why the language used in judgments in GBV cases differs from criminal cases:

> Such like stigmas have the potential of not only discouraging an even otherwise reluctant victim of sexual assault to bring forth [a] complaint for trial of criminals, thereby making the society suffer by letting the criminal escape even a trial. The courts are expected to use self-restraint while recording such findings which have larger repercussions so far as the future of the victim of the sex crime is concerned and even wider implications on the society as a whole—where the victim of crime is discouraged—the criminal encouraged and in turn crime gets rewarded! Even in cases, unlike the present case, where there is some acceptable material on the record to show that the victim was habituated to sexual intercourse, no such inference like the victim being a girl of "loose moral character" is permissible to be drawn from that circumstance alone (footnote 3).

The Court also explained why the previous sexual conduct is irrelevant:

> Even if the prosecutrix, in a given case, has been promiscuous in her sexual behaviour earlier, she has a right to refuse to submit herself to sexual intercourse to anyone and everyone because she is not a vulnerable object or prey for being sexually assaulted by anyone [and] everyone (footnote 3).

Finally, the court powerfully stated:

> No stigma, like the one as cast in the present case should be cast against such a witness by the Courts, **for after all it is the accused and not the victim of sex crime who is on trial in the Court**.[4]

---

4   Footnote 3, emphasis added.

B. Gender-Sensitive and Gender-Insensitive Language

In the context of GBV, **gender-sensitive language** is exemplified when the words used in a judgment convey the discrimination and roadblocks that victims of GBV encounter in pursuing justice (such as being faced with barriers to lodging complaints).

Sometimes, **gender-insensitive language** is used in judgments even when the court is sympathetic to the plight of the victim. On other occasions, the lack of sensitivity is because of accepted normalization of GBV against women in society and minimization of the effect of GBV on victims.

Examples of Gender-Insensitive Language

- *People v. Matrimonio*[5]
  Supreme Court of the Philippines

The complainant alleged two counts of rape by her father when she was 14 years old. She became pregnant after the first rape, but it was after she was raped the second time that she made the complaint. She gave evidence that the father threatened her life and the lives of her family. The father admitted sexual intercourse but denied coercing her.

The court upheld the conviction of the father. In relation to delay, the Supreme Court was sympathetic:

> The complainant [...] was also aware that by testifying, she made public a painful and humiliating secret which others would have simply kept to themselves forever, **jeopardized her chances of marriage or foreclosed the possibility of a blissful married life as her husband may not fully understand the excruciatingly painful experience** which would haunt her. She further realized too well that **her denunciations against her own father would only bring down on her and her family shame and humiliation.**[6]

The emphasized wording highlights acceptance of negative community attitudes toward rape victims by their family. The language does not encourage victims to come forward and instead suggests that, if she brings a complaint, she will never have a happy marriage and her family will denounce her. This reinforces negative community attitudes toward victims.

- *Abdul Sattar v. The State*[7]
  Lahore High Court

The accused was charged with throwing acid on a woman which resulted in "superficial to deep burns" to her body and permanent blindness in her right eye. The accused was found guilty and appealed. The Lahore High Court had no hesitation in dismissing the appeal and stated:

---

[5]   G.R. Nos. 82223-24, 13 November 1992.

[6]   Footnote 5, emphasis added.

[7]   2016 PCr LJ 122.

[A]nd to disfigure or disfeature the most beautiful part of a woman, i.e., face, permits punishability to a maleficent but may be regarded as sin the schadenfreude had visioned incessant plight and **pity of the hapless victim till death. Oh! What a yelling and moaning, anyhow, Allah Almighty has absolute powers to dispense the real and ultimate justice.**[8]

The prominence placed by the judge on the face of the victim "being the most beautiful part of a woman," indicates a limited appreciation of women. "[P]ity of the hapless victim till death" does not give a hopeful message to the victim for the future and is florid and inappropriate language for a judgment.

- *Ali Muhammad v. The State*[9]
  Lahore High Court

The case came before the Lahore High Court as an appeal against a refusal of bail. The Court decided that the petitioner should be given bail subject to deposit of the requisite amounts. When setting out the facts of the case, the following language was used:

> According to the F.I.R . itself the situation had degenerated into violence at the spur of the moment upon arrival of the petitioner's son (the complainant's stepson) at the matrimonial home of the petitioner and the complainant where they were present together quite peacefully immediately prior to the occurrence. **The petitioner had allegedly picked up a sota from the spot and he and his son had then collectively given only three injuries to the complainant. The case was, thus, a run of the mill case of domestic violence based upon estranged matrimonial relations.**[10]

In describing the violence committed against the woman by her husband and stepson, the highlighted language that she was given "**only** three injuries" is a shameful minimization of her experience and it takes no account of the psychological trauma that such an attack would have on her. To add that it was "a run of the mill case of domestic violence based upon estranged matrimonial relations" demonstrates acceptance of GBV as normalized behavior.

Examples of Gender-Sensitive Language

Gender-sensitive language in the context of GBV is when the judgment conveys the experience that women have as victims of GBV and recognizes the barriers victims face in pursuing justice.

---

[8]   Footnote 7, emphasis added.
[9]   2009 PLD Lahore 312.
[10] Footnote 9, emphasis added

- *The State v. Abdul Khaliq and Others*[11]
  Supreme Court of Pakistan

The following are observations made in the context of a *suo moto* case brought to appeal against an acquittal.[12]

> 9. It follows that it is quite normal that crimes of rape are not reported promptly. The devastating effects of rape on the victim and her family itself furnish explanation for delay in its reporting. Delay per se would not cast any reflection on the truthfulness of the allegations made in the report. There is another compelling reason that discourages a rape victim to prosecute the accused. She is deterred by the embarrassment and humiliation she would have to suffer in narrating the incident to strangers, more so, to the police recording the F.I.R., followed by probes during investigation into matters personal to her. She would further have to bear the agony of narrating the story in the open court in the presence of men and face searching and harassing questions from the cross-examiner. It is said that a rape victim relives the trauma every time she narrates the incident.

> 10. [...] **To bring the rapist to justice, they invariably require permission and approval of their men-folk.** This is amply demonstrated by the facts of this case. P.W. Maulvi Abdul Razzaq claims that when he learnt about the incident, he approached the father of the complainant, Ghulam Fareed. It was only after he managed to persuade the father that the complainant was taken to lodge the report.[13]

Paragraph 10 above reflects the reality that in most cases, it is the male family members who decide whether a police complaint should be lodged, whom to name as the accused in the complaint, and whether a court case should continue or the matter withdrawn and when. The victim is usually compelled to comply with the wishes of their male family members.[14]

- *Mst Rukkiya Iqbal v. Faisal Hayat*[15]
  Court of the Judicial Magistrate–XV, West Karachi

The case addressed a protection order:

> Therefore, in order to get rid of the mischief of domestic violence, the legislatures, in its wisdom, enacted the Sindh Domestic Violence (Prevention and Protection) Act, 2013, which came into force on 19th March, 2013. Undoubtedly the Act is meant to protect the women from domestic violence committed against them by the husband and his family members. The Act has recognized the fact that domestic violence is limited not only to physical and mental cruelty, but can also extend to verbal and emotional abuse, and even to economic abuse. The Act has recognized the fact that

---

[11]   PLD 2011 Supreme Court 554.

[12]   *Suo moto* cases are cases where the court, relying on its inherent powers, initiates the hearing.

[13]   Footnote 11, emphasis supplied.

[14]   Asian Development Bank (Office of the General Counsel). 2017. Consultation Mission to Punjab, Pakistan: Legal Literacy for Women Technical Assistance. Needs Assessment Report (internal).

[15]   Cr Petition No. 457 of 2017.

mental cruelty can take the form of verbal and emotional abuse. [...] Prima facie, it was enacted to provide protection to the weakest classes [of] society, i.e., women and children, as normally we [carry] a presumption of living [in] a 'male-dominant society' where [the] aggrieved even does not dare to tell about 'domestic violence' because of threats of being abandoned or dispossessed/removed from [the] household. The perusal of the Act shows that [the] term 'domestic violence' has no limited definition but has been extended thereby making it[s] applicability to cover all sort[s] of situation[s] including 'stalking' (footnote 15).

This paragraph uses language thoughtfully and sensitively to articulate the reality that many victims do not report domestic violence out of fear.

IV. Victim Blaming

Another common issue is "victim blaming," where women are regarded as responsible for violence committed against them. Recently, there was a public example of victim blaming by a senior police officer. In September 2020, the Lahore Capital Police Officer was giving evidence before a Senate human rights panel about a woman who was gang raped in front of her children. He stated she was raped because she travelled late at night without her husband's permission.[16] Public outcry against his statement ensued.

By contrast, more than 60 years ago in *Muhammad Sharif v. The State*,[17] the Supreme Court rejected victim blaming and illustrated the absurdity of it:

> The measure in which [a] girl should be allowed freedom is essentially the responsibility of those who manage an educational institution. It may be that the college authorities considered that girls are as much entitled to fresh air as boys and that by permitting them to go unescorted and without *perdah* they are foresting (fostering) in them a feeling of independence, confidence and self-reliance. The fact that a girl old enough to look after herself decides to walk in a public place without someone to look after her and without her *perdah* can never be a ground for a miscreant to tease or annoy her for that reason. If the ld. Judge thought that the appearance of educated girls in public places furnishes excusable provocation to the young men who come or happen to be at that place, then he was propounding an extremely pernicious doctrine that because a mother adorns her infant daughter with costly ornaments and permits her to go to a neighbour's house, an evil-minded person would have a justifiable excuse to rob her ornaments.

Judges need to be aware of how they express themselves in judgments, so they do not retraumatize the victim or perpetuate discriminatory and false stereotypes.

---

16   N. Siddiqui. 2020. Motorway Rape Occurred Because Victim Travelled 'Late Night without Husband's Permission', CCPO Tells Senate Panel. *Dawn*. 28 September.

17   PLD 1957 Supreme Court Pakistan 201.

V.   Disparaging Language

Judges should also refrain from using disparaging language, such as referring to a person as disabled, physically handicapped, mentally retarded, or crippled. Two recent important judgments—one from the Lahore High Court and the other from the Supreme Court of Pakistan—addressed this issue.

The first is *Asfandyar Khan v. Government of Punjab*.[18] In this case, there was a challenge to the wording used in the Disabled Persons (Employment and Rehabilitation) Ordinance, 1981, namely, references to persons as "disabled," "physically handicapped," and "mentally retarded." The then Chief Justice of the Lahore High Court (now Justice of the Supreme Court) Syed Mansoor Ali Shah stated:

> The use of the terms or words like **"disabled", "physically handicapped" and "mentally retarded"** characterize and label a person on the basis of an impairment, which negates reasonable accommodation as they deny persons with disabilities the enjoyment or exercise on an equal basis with others of all human rights and fundamental freedoms. **These words also amount to discrimination on the basis of disabilities** as they have the effect of impairing or nullifying the recognition, enjoyment or exercise of persons with disabilities, on an equal basis with others, of all human rights and fundamental freedoms. **These words, labels and characterization seriously offend the right to be a person thereby infringing constitutional guarantees like right to life, right to human dignity and right to non-discrimination of persons with disabilities, thereby violating Articles 9, 14 and 25 of the Constitution**.
>
> [...]
>
> In addition to the above[,] the Federal Government, as well as the Government of the Punjab[,] is directed to discontinue the use of these words in official correspondence, directives, notifications and circulars and shift to persons with disabilities or persons with different abilities.[19]

In *Mst Beena v. Raja Muhammad and Others*, the Supreme Court took up the issue of disparaging references made by a High Court Judge to a petitioner as a 'crippled/disabled lady having no source of income.'[20] The Court concluded that neither the mother's physical condition nor her income is determinative in a custody case. The petitioner had a disability, but should not be called "crippled" or "disabled." She also earned an honest living contrary to the notion that she had "no source of income." The Court stated, "To denigrate such a lady was wholly inappropriate. Instead[,] she should be admired for demonstrating remarkable determination and perseverance" (footnote 20).

The Supreme Court then cited and endorsed the above passages from *Asfandyar Khan Tareen v. Government of Punjab*, adding:

---

18   Case No. WP No. 29131.

19   Footnote 18, paras. 16 and 20, emphasis supplied.

20   PLD 2020 Supreme Court 508.

[P]ejorative words, like 'crippled' or 'disabled,' seriously offend the right to be a person thereby infringing constitutional guarantees like right to life, right to human dignity and right to non-discrimination of persons with disabilities, thereby violating Articles 9, 14 and 25 of the Constitution. We may add that the Constitution permits 'the State from making any special provision for the protection of women and children' but does not permit discrimination (footnote 20).

In conclusion, the words used by the then Chief Justice in *Asfandyar Khan Tareen v. Government of Punjab* are apt and have broader application.

The use of outdated language and words to describe people with disabilities helps to continue old stereotypes. **Being aware of the words we choose when we communicate is the first step toward correcting injustice.** These portrayals led to unwanted sympathy, or worse, pity toward individuals with disabilities. Respect and acceptance is what people with disabilities would rather have. **By carefully choosing our words, we can make a tremendous difference in the lives of other youth with disabilities. Using respectful language can dramatically change our communities for the better.**[21]

VI. Language Favoring Males

The use of "blue-eyed boy" of the law is another example of outdated, inappropriate, and discriminatory language that is used in judgments.

In ordinary usage, the expression "blue-eyed boy" refers to a male who is treated with special favor and held in high regard by a person in authority. The "blue-eyed boy" is treated better than others, both male and female. For example, the boss of an organization may have a male that they recognize and treat more favorably than other workers, either male or female, in that organization. He is regarded as the boss's "blue-eyed boy." It is both sexist and discriminatory.

The use of the expression "blue-eyed boy" to refer to a male accused in a criminal law context is concerning. While the accused may be innocent until proven guilty, and the law builds in protections to make sure an innocent person is not wrongly punished, the accused is neither favored by the law nor given special treatment.

Illustrations of usage in case law follow below.

- *Dost Muhammad v. The State*[22]
  Sindh High Court

  It is [a] well- settled principle of law [that] every accused would be presumed to be blue eyed boy of [the] law until and unless he may be found guilty of alleged charge and [the] law cannot be stretched upon in favour of the prosecution, particularly, at bail stage.

---

21   Footnote 18, para. 17, emphasis supplied.
22   2017 YLR 1320. The same language was used verbatim in *Ayaz Hussain v. The State*, 2020 P Cr. L J 737.

- *Muhammad Gulzar v. Adalat Hussain and Others*[23]
  Lahore High Court

> It is a legal parlance that every accused is blue eyed child of [the] law and is presumed to be innocent unless and until he is held guilty by due course of [the] law.

The expression is very offensive for female victims especially because the "blue-eyed boy" is the very one who is on trial for the crime. The expression suggests that, in the eyes of the law, the accused is favored over the victim and held in higher regard. It suggests that the victim is accusing the court's favorite person and that the victim has an even greater onus before a "blue eyed boy" can be found guilty.

This expression is outdated and discriminatory and should not be used in court language or judgments, particularly in GBV cases. In a criminal trial, it is the accused who is on trial and not the victim. As declared by the Pakistan Supreme Court, "The rule of giving benefit of doubt to accused person is essentially a rule of caution and prudence."[24] Giving the accused "the benefit of doubt" should not transfigure the accused into a "blue-eyed boy."

VII. Burden of Proof in Gender-Based Violence Offenses

A review of some judgments in the District and Sessions Courts' decisions on GBV offenses reveals another concerning feature, namely, the way the burden of proof in criminal cases is expressed. Frequently, the expression used by judges is that the burden is "beyond a shadow of a doubt." This is in fact not the correct wording of the burden of proof in a criminal case, which in many apex court decisions has been indicated as being proof "beyond a reasonable doubt."

Unfortunately, the phrase "beyond a shadow of doubt" has crept in and is commonly being used in criminal cases. This expression wrongly suggests that guilt is not proved if merely "a shadow of a doubt" exists. A "shadow of a doubt" may not amount to a "reasonable doubt," but instead implies something less. A "shadow of doubt" is more akin to a slight suggestion or hint of a doubt. This is important because a wrongly expressed burden of proof can lead to an ill-considered result.

The correct expression and meaning of "beyond a reasonable doubt" have been discussed in the following cases.

In *The State v. Manzoor Ahmed*, the Court defined "reasonable doubt" as "a doubt such as would assail a reasonable mind and not any and every kind of doubt and much less a doubt conjured up by preconceived notions."[25]

---

[23]   2012 M L D 1321.

[24]   *Atif Zareef v. The State*, Criminal Appeal No.251/2020 & Criminal Petition No.667/2020, 4 January 2021.

[25]   PLD 1966 SC 662.

In *The State v. Mushtaq Ahmed*, the Court discussed how the law allows persons accused of criminal offenses the benefit of a "reasonable" and not an imaginary doubt.[26] A reasonable doubt is not a question of law. Rather, it is a question for human judgment by a prudent person to be determined in each case in the light of day-to-day experience in life after "taking in account fully all the facts and circumstances appearing on the entire record." It is the antithesis of a haphazard assumption or reaching a decision in a case in a fitful manner.

In *Shamoon Alias Shamma v. State*, the Court held that the prosecution must prove its case against the accused beyond reasonable doubts irrespective of any plea raised by the accused in his defense.[27]

To a similar effect, the Court in *Shamshad v. The State* discussed how the prosecution is to prove its case beyond a reasonable doubt.[28] Such burden cannot be discharged by a weakness in the defense's case.

In *Ali Ahmad v. State and Ors.*, the Court explained that the accused cannot be convicted on the ground that his defense appears unconvincing.[29] The prosecution is duty-bound to prove its case and is not absolved of this duty even if the accused takes a defense plea. This case also discussed the shifting onus and summarized the principles to be applied when the accused takes a specific plea or has produced evidence in his defense, and the role of the court and burden of proof having regard to Article 121 of the Qanun e-Shahadat Order 1984 (QSO) and Section 342 of the Criminal Procedure Code (CrPC).[30]

In summary, the expression "beyond a reasonable doubt" remains the correct burden of proof. Other alternative expressions should not be used as it can lead to error in the application of the burden. This is particularly important in GBV cases that are difficult enough and should not be saddled with an erroneous extra barrier.

VIII. Conclusory Remarks

In summary, the language in a judgment provides a powerful way to denounce GBV and empower victims to feel confident and protected in coming forward to make complaints. Judgments should be gender-sensitive and nondiscriminatory. Judgments are highly influential and can change the mindsets and attitudes of those who read them.

---

[26]   PLD 1973 SC 418, 430.
[27]   1995 SCMR 1377.
[28]   1998 SCMR 854.
[29]   PLD 2020 SC 201.
[30]   Footnote 29, para. 23.

The facade of the Supreme Court of Pakistan. In *Atif Zareef v. The State*, the Supreme Court held that dragging the sexual history of a rape victim into the case by making observations about her body is an affront to her reputation and honor, and violates Article 4(2)(a) of the Constitution (photo by Tanveer Shahzad).

Chapter 11

SENTENCING, COMPENSATION, AND FORGIVENESS

I. Introduction

Holding perpetrators accountable for gender-based violence (GBV) against women is fundamental to the principle of punishment. Accountability creates predictability and certainty, and mandates that perpetrators will have to answer for violence against women (VAW).[1] Failure to hold perpetrators accountable sends a detrimental message to society that VAW is tolerated.

The role of the court is to provide effective judicial remedies to any person whose rights or freedoms are violated. Effective judicial remedies should include both criminal and civil remedies. Resorting to remedies by appealing to the constitutional jurisdiction of the court is always available when there is no efficacious remedy available.

At the outset, it is material to add here an observation of the Singh High Court: "'domestic violence,' targeting the weakest of society i.e., women and infirm old (parents), has been increasing abnormally. The aggrieved, normally, resorts to constitutional jurisdiction when there is no efficacious remedy available at [the] doorstep."[2]

Punishing the perpetrator and doing little else is insufficient in ensuring that the victim can rebuild her life (see section on Reparation below). The State must ensure that the perpetrator is unable to commit further crimes against the victim or society and, in addition, with regard to the victim, the State must ensure that she is safe and protected from further violence and is able to rebuild her life thereafter.

The State's obligation to provide effective judicial remedies serves as a means for citizens to hold States and organs of States accountable. Keeping in mind that the State has this obligation is important especially since the potential infringement comes not only in its misfeasance, but also through a duty-bearer's failure to act (omission).

---

[1] Z. Abdul Aziz and J. Moussa. 2013, reprint 2016. *Due Diligence Framework: State Accountability Framework for Eliminating Violence against Women.* Penang. p. 65.

[2] *Mst. Hina v. Province of Sindh through Secretary Home Department Sindh at Karachi and 4 Others,* PLD 2019 Sindh 363.

II. Punishment

Punishment must meet international standards and be commensurate to the severity of the offense. Some punishments are enhanced due to aggravating factors such as severity of the violence, relationship between perpetrators and victims (*loco parentis*, spouse), capacity of victims (minor), and recidivism of perpetrators.

Still, the severity of crime must be examined in a nuanced manner since the level of injury suffered may not always correctly reflect the gravity of the crime. For example, when assessing the injury sustained from crimes such as domestic violence and sexual harassment, it is vital to consider the repetitive nature of such violence since such acts, when examined individually, may not appear to have caused grievous hurt. The challenge in sentencing of such repetitive crimes is that oftentimes, there is a tendency to "down-criminalize" the offense.

The effectiveness of criminal law and a robust justice system depends on the law's capacity to prevent recidivism, rehabilitate perpetrators and prepare them for reintegration, and deter others from committing similar offenses.[3] States must ensure that punishment protects public interest and ultimately eliminates VAW. This accords with the Punjab Sentencing Act, 2019 which lays out the sentencing policy, including provisions for aggravating and mitigating factors:

> A court dealing with an offender in respect of his offence shall have regard to the purposes of sentencing being the:
>
> (a) punishment of offenders;
> (b) reduction of crime including its reduction by deterrence;
> (c) reform and rehabilitation of offenders;
> (d) protection of the public; and
> (e) making of reparation by offenders to persons affected by their offences.[4]

Politicians respond to public outcry denouncing GBV and VAW by increasing the sentence for a crime or enacting mandatory minimum sentences, for example, for rape and other sexual offenses. A case in point is the response to the motorway gang rape. Politicians called for rapists to be hanged or chemically or surgically castrated.[5] Knee-jerk reactions that increase the punishment for crimes are unlikely to actually prevent all future crimes, but on the contrary, are more likely to lengthen the court process, increase pressure on victims to withdraw cases, and cause prosecutors and judges to down-criminalize offenses.

While incarceration appears to be the most common form of punishment, sometimes, incarceration may not be sought or preferred by victims, especially in cases of domestic violence. The punishment of incarceration may even discourage women from reporting the violence since

---

3   See also United Nations (UN), General Assembly, *In-Depth Study on All Forms of Violence against Women: Report of the Secretary General*, A/61/122/Add.1 (6 July 2006). para. 76.

4   Punjab Sentencing Act, 2019. Sec. 4.

5   Following from the public outcry in relation to the motorway rape, politicians called for increased penalties, including death and castration. See *Dawn*. 2020. Rapists Should Be Publicly Hanged or Chemically Castrated: PM Imran. 14 September.

it would render their partners, possibly the sole breadwinners of the family, unemployed. Their partners could also retaliate harshly.[6] Where the law allows, perpetrators can continue working to pay compensation and/or maintenance to victims; however, this option should be exercised only if the safety of victims can be guaranteed. Irrespective of whether there are broad punishments provided under the law, due diligence in punishment focuses on perpetrator accountability. States should ensure punishment is premised on VAW not being justifiable or excusable.

III. *Jinayat* and Forgiveness

In *fiqh* (Islamic jurisprudence), modern jurists have identified three categories of offenses: *hudood* (offenses for which punishment is described in the Qur'an), *jinayat* (offenses of homicide and bodily harm), and *ta'zir* (offenses for which the punishment is within the discretion of the State or the judge). The punishment or consequences for committing *jinayat* can be divided into three categories: (i) *qisas* (law of retaliation [*lex talionis*]) and *diyat* (compensation), (ii) *badal-i-sulh* (compounding), and (iii) *awf* (waiver and forgiveness) (Figure 11.1).

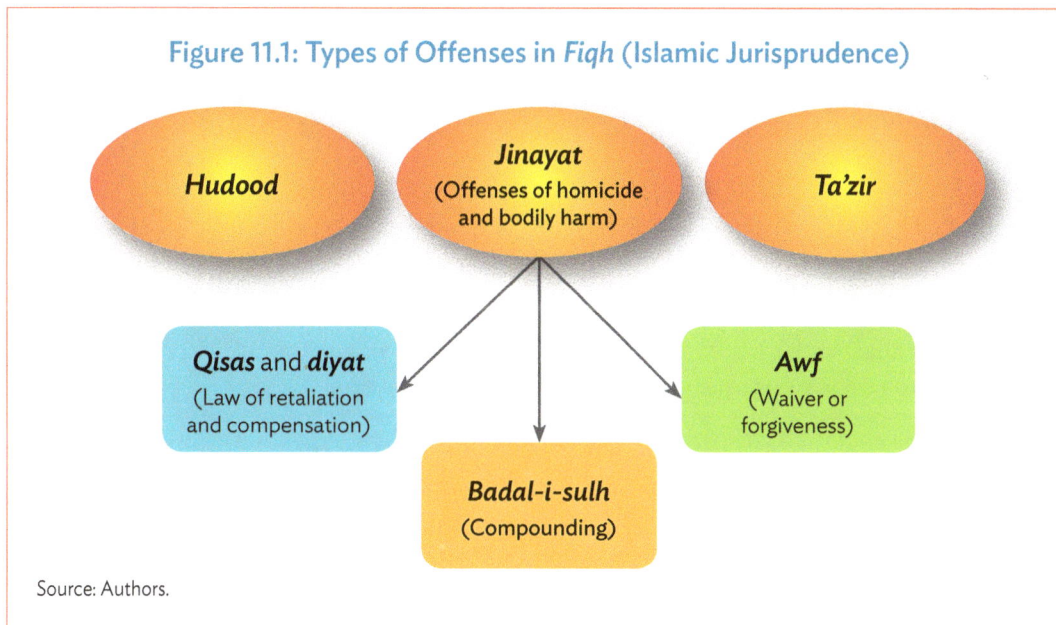

Figure 11.1: Types of Offenses in *Fiqh* (Islamic Jurisprudence)

Hudood

Jinayat
(Offenses of homicide and bodily harm)

Ta'zir

Qisas and **diyat**
(Law of retaliation and compensation)

Badal-i-sulh
(Compounding)

Awf
(Waiver or forgiveness)

Source: Authors.

Scholars suggest that the law of *qisas* was meant to avert the ancient custom of blood feuds among Arab tribes. *Qisas* should be understood as a means to end the practice of unrestrained revenge rather than just infliction of equal punishment on the offender. *Diyat* was the alternative to revenge.[7]

---

6   Footnote 1. The findings of the Due Diligence Project survey suggest that States must address fear of repercussions since it is the most-quoted complaint of victims and is deemed a significant obstacle to women reporting VAW by civil society organization respondents globally (see Figure 7.1 on p. 102).

7   S. El-Awa. 1982. *Punishment in Islamic Law: A Comparative Study*. Indianapolis: American Trust Publications. p. 70. Cited in M. Perven. 2016. Law of Murder under Islamic Criminal Law: An Analysis. *Journal of Law, Policy and Globalization*. 53. p.143.

In the law of equality, there is (saving of) Life to you,
O ye men of understanding; that ye may restrain yourselves.
Al-Qur'an Surah Al-Baqarah 2:179, translation Yusuf Ali

The Pakistan Penal Code (PPC) provisions that are relevant to offenses of murder and bodily harm include the following:

Section 305. *Wali*: In case of *qatl*, the *wali* shall be—

(a) the heirs of the victim, according to his personal law [but shall not include the accused or the convict in case of *qatl-i-amd* if committed in the name or on the pretext of honor]; and

(b) the Government, if there is no heir.

Section 309. Waiver (*Awf*): Adult *wali* may at any time, without compensation, waive his right to *qisas* in murder cases except in cases of *fasad-fil-arz*.

Section 310. Compounding of *qisas* (*Sulh*): An adult sane *wali* may compound his right to *qisas* which may be paid on demand or on a deferred date except in cases of *fasad-fil-arz* where Section 311 shall apply. A female person cannot be given by way of *sulh*.

Section 311. *Ta'zir* after waiver or compounding of right of *qisas* in *qatl-i-amd*: Notwithstanding anything contained in Section 309 or Section 310, where all the *wali* do not waive or compound the right of *qisas*, or [if] the principle of *fasad-fil-arz* the Court may, having regard to the facts and circumstances of the case, punish an offender against whom the right of *qisas* has been waived or compounded with [death or imprisonment for life or] imprisonment of either description for a term of which may extend to fourteen years as *ta'zir*.

Provided that if the offence has been committed in the name or on the pretext of honour, the imprisonment shall not be less than ten years.

> **Explanation:** For the purpose of this Section, the expression *Fasad-fil-Arz* includes the past conduct of the offender, or whether he has any previous convictions, or the brutal or shocking manner in which the offence has been committed by him which is outrageous to the public conscience, or if the offender is considered a potential danger to the community or if the offence has been committed in the name or on the pretext of honour.

Section 338E. Waiver or compounding of offences: (1) Subject to the provisions of this chapter and section 345 of the Code of Criminal Procedure, 1898 all offences under this chapter may be waived or compounded and the provisions of sections 309, 310 and 311 shall, *mutatis mutandis* apply, to the waiver or compounding of such offences.

Provided that where an offense has been waived or compounded, the court may, in its discretion having regard to the facts and circumstances of the case, acquit or award *ta'zir* to the offender according to the nature of the offense.

Provided further that where an offence under this chapter has been committed and the principle of *fasad-fil-arz* is attracted the court having regard to the facts and the circumstance of the case shall punish the offender with imprisonment or fine as provided for that offence.

The provision in Article 345 of Pakistan Criminal Procedure Code (CrPC) relevant to compounding of offenses and waiver, as mentioned in Section 338E, lists the offenses under the Penal Code which can be compounded.

> **Article 345. Compounding offences:** Offences mentioned in the list under subsection 1 can be compounded without permission of the court, but offences under subsection 2 require prior permission of the court for compounding.

There is a further restriction for compounding and that is subject to subsection 7 of Article 345 CrPC.[8] Subsection 7 states that "no offence shall be waived or compounded save as provided by this section and section 311 of PPC."

Non-Compounding of *Fasad-fil-arz* Offenses

Section 302 (murder) is included in the list of offenses under subsection 2 of Article 345 of the CrPC, but its compounding is subject to Section 311 PPC.[9]

Consequently, murder, where the principle *fasad-fil-arz* is applicable, shall be punishable irrespective of whether all the *wali* (a person entitled to claim *qisas*) have agreed to waive or compound the right of *qisas*. These include crimes of honor and crimes that are particularly brutal.

Article 345(5) further provides that when the accused has been convicted and an appeal pending, composition shall only be with leave of the court before which the appeal is to be heard.

Article 345(6) provides that the composition shall have the effect of an acquittal of the accused.

Note that Section 338E PPC determines waiver or compounding of all the offenses mentioned in Chapter XVI of the PPC. While an application for compounding is moved under Article 345 CrPC, it is Section 338E PPC which gives discretion to the court to either accept compounding or reject it. It also makes offenses falling in the category of *fasad-fil-arz* non-compoundable.[10]

Zahid Rehman v. The State is also instructive regarding the application of Section 311 of the PPC.[11] The judgment clarified that Section 311 applies only to murders liable to *qisas* punishment. It also clarified that three categories of offenders mentioned in Section 306 of the PPC can be punished if the murder is liable to *qisas*, otherwise they are liable under Section 302(b) of the PPC. In addition to these two key issues, there are many other points of legal clarification.

---

[8] Added through 2016 PPC amendments.
[9] Amended through 2016 PPC amendments. Murder, where the principle *fasad-fil-arz* is applicable, shall be punishable irrespective of whether all the *wali* have agreed to waive or compound the right of *qisas*.
[10] See *Sanobar Khan v. The State*, 2018 PCrLJ Note 181.
[11] PLD 2016 SC 77.

IV. *Jinayat*: State's Interest and Victim's Interest

Today, most States adopt dual processes:

- the criminal justice process—the State assumes the obligation to prosecute and punish the perpetrator; and

- the civil process—the victim assumes the responsibility to prosecute.

Some offenses may constitute both crime and civil offense. *Qisas* and *diyat* focus on the rights of the victim, and in the event of her death, the rights of her/his next of kin. It has a strong retributive focus in extracting retaliation or remitting punishment. While the emphasis of the limitation of these rights to the victim or her next of kin implies that these offenses are often regarded as private prosecutions, the severity of retaliation makes it similar to criminal punishments.

That leaves the question of State obligation. Under the concept of the modern State, the State assumes the duty to exercise due diligence to keep every member of society safe. The State is the guardian of the rule of law and has the obligation to provide certainty of the law and punishment. Punishment must have consequences for both the accused and society.

Under the theory of punishment (penology), the State has the obligation to ensure that punishment has a strong deterrence effect. Therefore, punishment must prevent recidivism, rehabilitate the perpetrators (ensure that the perpetrator is fit to rejoin society), and deter others (prevent other would be perpetrators from committing similar crimes).

An effective criminal justice process must satisfy both the State interest and the victim's interest. There are instances where the compounding of an offense may satisfy the *wali* (a person entitled to claim *qisas*) or victim; however, allowing the *wali* or victim to compound may endanger society. For example, a wealthy offender who beats up and murders multiple people may compound with the victims or their *wali*. But the State may regard the offender as a danger to society and therefore the compounding of the offenses may not satisfy the State's interest in protecting society. Under the principle of *fasad-fil-arz*, the State can still punish the perpetrator under Section 311 PPC regardless of whether the victims or *wali* have waived or compounded with the offender.

Similarly, the State has an interest to eliminate crimes committed under the pretext of honor. Under these circumstances, the State can still punish the offender irrespective of whether the *wali* or victim had waived, forgiven or compounded with the offender.

Rape is not a compoundable crime

In relation to rape, the State has established that rape is not a compoundable crime. Other countries have also defined rape as a heinous crime where the sentence cannot be reduced. The Brazilian Federal Supreme Court, for example, denied the application of a rapist to have his sentenced reduced.[12] The Court held that as rape is a heinous crime, the sentence should remain without reduction.

Firstly, it is imperative to note that waiver (*awf*) or compounding of *qisas* is applicable only to murder and hurt. Rape and offenses categorized as *fasad-fil-arz* are not compoundable and they both must be prosecuted even if the victim or her family has 'compromised' with the accused. Despite this, it is common for the accused in rape cases to be acquitted due to a 'compromise' with the victim's family.

A case in point reportedly occurred in September 2020. A woman who had been repeatedly raped became pregnant, and the accused allegedly disposed of the body of the infant. In court, the accused stated that the victim had forgiven him and that they had decided to get married. Their marriage was solemnized in the courtroom and the accused was released.[13] The court's role in sanctioning the alleged illegal/unlawful acts is of grave concern. There were two crimes committed—the

Let's take the money and marry her to the rapist. That will save the family honor.

Rape cannot be compounded.

first is that of rape, and the second is that of concealment of birth by secret disposal of a dead body, which is a crime under Section 329 of the Penal Code. Furthermore, the 'out-of-court compromise' to exculpate the accused, is specifically prohibited under the law.

In the case of *Rustam v. State*, a victim committed suicide after a rape.[14] An out-of-court compromise between the victim's family and the accused parties resulted in the acquittal of the accused at the appellate stage. The Trial Court considered evidence on record and held that it sufficiently proves that the incident had occurred but that the parties compromised. Due to the compromise, all of the prosecution witnesses turned hostile and resiled from their evidence. Unfortunately, although the Court had the power, there was no order by the court against these hostile witnesses (see Chapter 12 on Resiling and Attrition).

In the case of *Manzoor Chachar v. State*, the Sindh High Court reduced the sentence of a rape convict from life imprisonment to 10 years based on an out-of-court settlement.[15]

The Supreme Court decision in *Salman Akram Raja v. The Government of Punjab through Chief Secretary, Civil Secretariat, Lahore and Others* was prompted by a compromise in a rape case.[16] The victim in this case, aggrieved by the attitude of investigative agencies, had attempted suicide. The case was highlighted in the media, and the Supreme Court took *suo moto* notice of

---

12 Cornell Law School, Legal Information Institute. Rape Defined as Heinous Crime for Sentencing Purposes: Habeas Corpus No. 81.288-1 (in Portuguese).
13 *Naya Daur*. 2020. Rapist Granted Bail for Marrying Woman He Had Raped for Months. 24 September.
14 2013 YLR 2600 [Sindh].
15 2015 P Cr. LJ 690 [Sindh].
16 2013 SCMR 203.

the matter.[17] It is unfortunate that even in this case, which was prompted by a compromise, the Supreme Court did not make an outright declaration on the compromise itself, as requested by the petitioner.

It is noteworthy that in several Middle East countries, it is no longer legal for perpetrators to escape rape punishment by marrying the victim.[18] Discussions with judges and police officers indicate that this practice, although disallowed under the law, is accepted and practiced because families erroneously rationalize that since murder is compoundable, rape—like murder—should similarly be compoundable. Furthermore, *diyat* and *Badal-i-Sulh* are also incorrectly associated with compensation for the injury to the family's 'honor.' Under these circumstances, the sum received is utilized by the victim's family members instead of using it to compensate the victim for the crime perpetrated against her or to enable her to rebuild her life.

In *Sanobar Khan v. The State*, the Peshawar High Court rejected a compromise in the case of a double murder of a man and a woman which occurred under the pretext of honor (footnote 10). The Court held that the offense was non-compoundable under the 2016 PPC amendments, which declared that honor killing is non-compoundable as it is categorized as *fasad-fil-arz*. The accused's death sentence was upheld by the Supreme Court.

V.   Impact of Forgiveness

What is the impact of a 'compromise'? The law provides that the composition "shall have the effect of an acquittal of the accused." As mentioned above, it is critical to recognize that there are two interests at stake: the first is the interest of the State in prohibiting crimes and deterring crimes, and the second is the interest of the victim or his/her *wali*. Consequently, there can be two outcomes: the first is when the State interest or obligation converges with the victim's interest, and the second is when these respective interests do not converge. This poses two important questions: (i) does the State forfeit its interests if the victim or his/her *wali* decide to forgive the perpetrator or compound the offense, or (ii) does the State retain its interest separately from the interest of the victim or his/her *wali*?

In *Ghulam Yasin v. The State*, the Lahore High Court rejected bail and stated that the fact that the heirs of the deceased had pardoned the petitioner was not sufficient to entitle the petitioner to a pre-arrest bail since the offense alleged against the petitioner was perpetrated against the State as well.[19]

The latter interpretation, namely, that the State retains its interest separately from the interest of the victim, was exemplified in the principle of *fasad-fil-arz*. The State clearly relied on its obligation to protect society when it insisted on the ability to sentence the accused even if the accused is forgiven by its *wali*.

These issues relating to the impact of forgiveness were further dealt with by the Supreme Court in three cases with differing outcomes.

---

[17]   HRC No. 13728-P of 2012.

[18]   *BBC*. 2017. Lebanon Rape Law: Parliament Abolishes Marriage Loophole. 16 August.

[19]   PLD 2017 Lah 103.

- *Chairman Agriculture Development Bank of Pakistan v. Mumtaz Khan*[20]

Here, the respondent was implicated in a murder and sentenced to life imprisonment and fines. The respondent was removed from service with the applicant bank. Two years later, he paid the *wali* of the victim for the purpose of compounding the offense (*Badal-i-Sulh*) and was released. He then filed an appeal for reinstatement and back pay. The bank appealed.

The respondent argued that, by reason of the compound, he was entitled to reinstatement and back pay. He relied on Section 345(6) of the CrPC which states, "The composition of an offence under this section shall have the effect of an acquittal of the accused with whom the offence has been compounded."

The Supreme Court held that, "*Awf* (waiver) of *Sulh* (compounding) in respect of an offence has the effect of purging the offender of the crime." Therefore, the Court ordered that the respondent be reinstated because there was "no material available [...] to conclude or hold that the respondent's departmental appeal was barred by time and [...] on what basis the said appeal had been dismissed."

With all due respect, the decision means that third parties are not able to rely on the certainty of the law and therefore cannot take appropriate measures based on the court's decision at the relevant date. What if the employer was not a bank but a modest company and the vacated position had since been filled by a competent and well-liked employee for the past several years? Must the employer dismiss the employee and reinstate the convict with several years worth of back pay?

- *Suo Moto Case No. 3 of 2017*

In this case, the appellant, after being convicted of murder and sentenced to death, filed to reappraise the evidence in the interest of administration of justice. During the pendency of this appeal, the convict filed an application seeking acquittal on the basis of a compromise. The majority was of the opinion that the convict should be acquitted. Qazi Faez Isa J said,

> The judgment has two components, conviction, which means he is guilty, and the sentence, which is the punishment awarded to him. If the legal heirs of the deceased compound the offence, it does not mean that the appellant/convict was not guilty of the murder for which he was convicted. [...] Subsection (6) of section 345 also avoids creating such a fiction as it provides that the 'composition of an offence [...] shall have the effect of an acquittal', which means that the punishment (sentence) part of the judgment is brought to an end. [...] The law permits the legal heirs of a murdered person to compound the offence with the convict, with or without receiving *badal-i-sulh/diyat* (sections 310 and 323 PPC). When the legal heirs compounded the offence, they elected not to seek retribution or the enforcement of the sentence. [...] The aforesaid interpretation of subsection (6) of section 345 is in conformity with a number of verses of the Holy Qur'an: surah Al-Baqarah (2) verses 178-9, surah Al-Maidah (5) verse 45, surah Al-Isra (17) verse 33 and surah Ash-Shura (42) verse 40. In these verses our Merciful Creator suggests that forgiveness and

---

[20] PLD 2010 SC 695.

reconciliation is preferable to revenge or retaliation. A person can only be forgiven if he is guilty. The cited verses neither state nor imply that the finding of guilt is effaced.

The matter was then brought before a three-member bench of the Supreme Court. The Supreme Court comprising Asif Saeed Khan Khosa CJ, Ijaz ul Ahsan J, and Syed Mansoor Ali Shah J, decided,

> We find that the controversy over 'acquittal' and 'effect of an acquittal' in the context of section 345(6), Cr.P.C. and drawing a distinction in this regard between guilt and punishment may be quite unnecessary. [...]

> The issues highlighted by our learned brother Qazi Faez Isa, J. and mentioned above may be relevant to the concerned court at the time of granting or refusing permission or leave in respect of the proposed composition but after such permission or leave has been granted by the court and the proposed composition is successfully completed the accused person or convict is to be acquitted and such acquittal is to entail all the fruits and effects of a lawful acquittal.

- *Shafqat @ Shafaat v. The State*[21]

In 2016, the petitioner was convicted for murder as *ta'zir* (offenses for which the punishment is within the discretion of the State or the judge) to imprisonment for life and to pay PRs100,000 to the heirs of the deceased. In 2018, an application was made stating that a "compromise has been affected [effected] and the legal heirs of the deceased have forgiven the convict/accused in the name of Allah," which was verified and accepted by the Court. The question before the Court was whether the petitioner's conviction should be set aside or whether he should just be saved from punishment.

The Court affirmed that forgiveness earns the mercy and reward of Almighty Allah, but noted that there was not "a single verse of the Holy Qur'an which states that if a person is forgiven/ pardoned, his/her crime is erased, effaced, obliterated or washed away." The Court explained, "It is our understanding that forgiveness or pardon does not erase or obliterate the crime, it simply withholds the punishment. The Qur'an negates the concept of obliteration of the crime, even if it has been forgiven, and its repetition attracts punishment—'Allah forgives what is in the past, for repetition Allah will punish.'[22] The record therefore remains intact."

Furthermore, the Court held that, "If however the conviction of a murder is set aside and he is acquitted, it means that he/she did not commit the crime, which creates a factual fiction. And, such factual fiction has repercussions. Applying for employment, a pardoned convict need not disclose his conviction, including when seeking employment in respect of role model positions, of a teacher or in respect of sensitive jobs or where moral integrity is an employment prerequisite." The Court also added that such a "factual fiction" may also negate the provisions of the PPC and the CrPC which take into account the previous convictions and conduct of the offender.

---

21   PLJ 2019 SC (Cr.C.) 323.
22   Surah Al-Maidah (5) verse 95.

The convict was therefore released. A larger bench of the Supreme Court would be constituted to decide whether the convict, as a consequence of accepting the compromise, was also to be acquitted.

Another question that may arise is when can the compromise be concluded? In the case of *qisas*, any adult sane *wali* can compound at any time except in case of *fasad-fil-arz*. In *ta'zir* cases, all heirs of the deceased must be party to *qisas*. For the compromise to take effect, all the deceased victim's *wali* must agree. However, if one person disagrees, technically, the convict can wait for that particular *wali* to die and then enter into a compromise with the remaining *wali*.

In *Abdul Rashid alias Teddy v. The State*, a convict was sentenced to death by way of *ta'zir* for killing a woman who refused to marry him.[23] One of the deceased's heirs was adamant during his lifetime not to compound the offense with the convict. After his death, all the heirs agreed to compound the offense. A five-member bench of the Supreme Court declared the compound to be valid.

On the other hand, in *Azmat v. The State*, a brother and sister killed their father, stepmother, and two minor stepsisters.[24] Three siblings of the two accused forgave them and both the accused submitted an application for acquittal. The Trial Court rejected the application and ordered the prosecution to proceed with evidence. The Supreme Court upheld the order rejecting the application.

The Court laid out the following considerations when deciding on whether to approve the compound:

- Verify whether all the heirs joined in the compromise.

- If any *wali* was a minor, determine whether the minor reached the compromise in accordance with Section 313(2) of the PPC.

- In cases of compromise by all the heirs, discern whether the case was one of *fasad-fil-arz* and thus not a case of acquittal despite such a compromise, but rather a case of punishment under Section 311 of the PPC.

- Determine whether any facts exist which could persuade the court to prohibit the compromise in accordance with Section 345(2) of the CrPC.

Despite these directions, the Court added, "It is neither possible nor desirable to categorise cases where such approval should be granted or withheld. Such a decision shall have to be taken by the concerned court after applying its judicial mind and of course whether the act in question amounted to *fasad-fil-arz*."

In *Naseem Akhtar and Another v. The State*, a man with his accomplice killed his paternal uncle, his wife, and two daughters.[25] The Supreme Court held that the requirement of leave of the court cannot be an automatic act of affixing a "judicial stamp" upon a compromise, particularly if the compromiser and the offender are both beneficiaries of the crime (e.g., the offense is committed for an obvious objective of grabbing the property of the deceased by the compromiser).

---

[23] 2013 SCMR 1281.
[24] PLD 2009 SC 768.
[25] PLD 2010 SC 938.

In *Gulam Farid alias Farida v. The State*, the Supreme Court further held that only compromises that are above any blemish, either mild or strong, would qualify for acceptance by the Court.[26]

VI. Reparation

Redress and reparation are remedies made available to victims of GBV for the harm they have suffered. The purpose of reparation is to mitigate the effects of the violence committed against the victims.

While punishment looks at action taken against the perpetrator, redress and reparation focuses on the victim and requires consideration of the victim's needs so that she may rebuild her life after the violence. Without reparations or redress, victims would be reluctant to seek the court's intervention.

Reparations must fit the victim's needs, which requires the court to focus on the rights, dignity, and reputation of the victim.[27] Reparations must also be proportional to the harm suffered.

The Committee on the Elimination of Discrimination against Women interprets Article 2(b) of the Convention on the Elimination of Discrimination against Women[28] as requiring State parties to provide reparation to those whose rights have been violated.[29] Without reparation, the obligation to provide an appropriate remedy is not discharged. This requires that the court understands the gravity of the harm of GBV and adopts a victim-oriented perspective.

The most common form of reparation is monetary compensation for any economically assessable damage as appropriate and proportional to the gravity of the violation, including physical or mental harm, lost opportunities for employment, education and social benefits, and material and moral damages. The compensation may approximate the amount of damages that may be awarded to the victim. Domestic violence legislations in several jurisdictions, including Balochistan, Punjab, and Sindh, empower the court to "order monetary relief to meet the expenses incurred and losses suffered."

---

[26]   PLD 2006 SC 53.

[27]   *Diyat* and *arsh* (compensation specified in Chapter XVI to be paid to the victim or her/his heirs) are not included in this section as the amounts are already specified under the Penal Code and therefore the court does not have the discretion to decide on the amount based on its assessment of, among others, the loss, damages and harm suffered, and costs and expenses incurred.

[28]   *Convention on the Elimination of All Forms of Discrimination against Women*, New York, 18 December 1979, *United Nations Treaty Series*, Vol. 1249, No. 20378, p. 13. Art. 2(b) requires States Parties "[to] adopt appropriate legislative and other measures, including sanctions where appropriate, prohibiting all discrimination against women."

[29]   UN Committee on the Elimination of Discrimination against Women, *General Recommendation No. 28 on the Core Obligations of States Parties under Article 2 of the Convention on the Elimination of All Forms of Discrimination against Women*, CEDAW/C/GC/28 (16 December 2010); UN Committee on the Elimination of Discrimination against Women, *General Recommendation No. 30 on Women in Conflict Prevention, Conflict and Post-conflict Situations*, CEDAW/C/GC/30 (1 November 2013); and UN Committee on the Elimination of Discrimination against Women, *General Recommendation No. 33 on Women's Access to Justice*, CEDAW/C/GC/33 (3 August 2015).

There are two kinds of orders that grant the court the discretion to order reparation to the victim. These are daman (compensation determined by the Court to be paid by the offender to the victim for causing hurt not liable to arsh [compensation specified in Chapter XVI to be paid to the victim or her/his heirs]) under the Penal Code and compensation under the Criminal Procedure Code. Daman technically is a mandatory punishment,[30] while Article 544A of the CrPC is compensatory. Both daman and compensation may be awarded simultaneously.[31]

The Penal Code provides that the court may order the convict to pay *daman*. The value of *daman* may be determined by the court by assessing

(i)   the expenses incurred due to the treatment of the victim,

(ii)   loss or disability caused in the functioning or power of any organ, and

(iii)   the compensation for the anguish suffered by the victim.

Further, the CrPC mandates the court to order compensation to be paid to the victim or her/his heirs; otherwise reasons must be provided as to why compensation is not awarded:

> **Article 544A. Compensation to the heirs of the person killed, etc.** (1) Whenever a person is convicted of an offence in the commission whereof the death of or hurt, injury, or mental anguish or psychological damage to any person is caused, or damage to or loss or destruction of any property is caused, the court shall when convicting such person, unless for reasons to be recorded in writing it otherwise directs, order the person convicted to pay to the heirs of the person whose death has been caused, or to the person hurt or injured, or to the person to whom mental anguish or psychological damage has been caused, or to the owner of the property damaged, lost or destroyed, as the case may be, such compensation as the court may determine having regard to the circumstances of the case. [...]

For example, the court in *Nadeem Masood v. The State*, a child was born to a victim as a consequence of rape.[32] The Lahore High Court on appeal affirmed the conviction for rape and awarded PRs 1 million as compensation.

The Sindh Domestic Violence (Prevention and Protection) Act, 2013 provides for two kinds of monetary relief. The first is the conversion of a fine into compensation. Under Section 6(2), the court may sentence the accused to imprisonment or fine "to be paid as compensation to the aggrieved person" for certain offenses. The court may also, under Section 12, order monetary relief "to meet the expenses incurred and losses suffered by the aggrieved person and such relief may include, but is not limited to compensation for suffering as a consequence of economic abuse, loss of earning, medical expense, the loss caused due to the destruction, damage or removal of any property and maintenance for the aggrieved person as well her children." Monetary relief is

---

30   *Daman* is mentioned as one of the punishments in Section 53 of the PPC, which lists the types of punishments offenders are liable under the provisions of the PPC.

31   See *Rukkiya Iqbal v. Faisal Ahmad*, Cr. Petition No. 457/2017 (Court of Judicial Magistrate–West Karachi).

32   2015 P Cr. LJ 1633.

also provided under Section 15 of the Khyber Pakhtunkhwa Domestic Violence Against Women (Prevention and Protection) Act, 2021.[33]

The ability to convert a fine into compensation is also provided under Article 545 of the CrPC. It allows courts to order payment of the entire fine or part of it to the victim. The fine recovered may be applied in

(i)   defraying expenses properly incurred in the prosecution, and

(ii)   the payment to any person of compensation for any loss, injury or mental anguish or psychological damage caused by the offense, when substantial compensation is, in the opinion of the court, recoverable by such person in a Civil Court.

The punishment for rape mentions a fine although it is not specified. However, in sexual abuse cases, the minimum fine is PRs500,000.

The rigor with which the court ensures adequate reparation may subsequently result in a decrease of compromises since the victim will be able to recuperate her loss and receive compensation.

Another issue that the court may need to consider is the ability of victims to recuperate compensation from perpetrators independently of processes described above. Victims who pursue compensation from perpetrators may however be exposed to additional risk and trauma from continued contact with the offenders. As such, the court may need to consider alternative ways for victims to recuperate compensation from perpetrators, such as attachment of property.

Reparation can also take the form of rehabilitation, including medical and psychological care, legal and social services, as well as restitution to restore victims to their original situations. The court should also be aware that victims may require continued medical/psychological care long after the crime. While the pain experienced during and immediately after the crime is well documented, subsequent long-term pain is often disregarded. For example, fire and chemical burn victims often experience long-term pain. A study states that, "Few burn survivors (those referred to us for persistent pain long after their last burn-related hospitalization) are aware that

---

[33]   Section 15 provides:
15. Monetary Relief.---(1) The Court may, at any stage of the trail, on an application by the complainant, direct the complainee to deposit expenses incurred and losses suffered by the complainant and such relief may include-
(a) compensation to the complainant for suffering as a consequence of economic abuse to be determined by the Court;
(b) loss of earning;
(c) medical expense;
(d) the loss caused due to the destruction, damage or removal of any property from the control of the complainant; and
(e) the maintenance for the complainant and his children, if any, under family laws for the time being enforce.
(2) The complainee shall provide monetary relief to the complainant within the period specified in the order issued under sub-section (1) and in accordance with terms, thereof:
Provided that upon failure of the complainee to make payment, the Court may pass any order as deemed appropriate.

neuropathic pain resulting from burns may be chronic, relatively resistant to opioids, and the physiological basis for persistent pain years after the trauma."[34]

Victims may also seek out and need acknowledgment of the crimes perpetrated against them and for the accused to exhibit/demonstrate accountability which may include a public apology and/or a guarantee of non-repetition. Judgments can address underlying causal factors of GBV against women. As the courts are called upon to interpret relevant laws and practices, they can use the procedures discussed in this chapter to deliver justice for the violations of constitutional and human rights of victims, as well as bring about transformative changes.[35] They can also aim to guarantee non-repetition.

Ordering reparation during the court's sentencing of the perpetrator is a good practice as it reduces court time, costs, and the trauma experienced by the victim if she is forced to commence a new civil suit for damages. It can also result in less compromises and less resiling as victims need not rely on compromises in order to obtain reparation for their loss, pain, and suffering.

---

[34] A. Dauber et al. 2002. Chronic Persistent Pain After Severe Burns: A Survey of 358 Burn Survivors. *Pain Medicine.* 3 (1). pp. 6–17.

[35] Footnote 1, p. 76; and UN Human Rights Council, *Report of the Special Rapporteur on Violence against Women, Its Causes and Consequences, Rashida Manjoo,* A/HRC/14/22 (23 April 2010). para. 12.

Judicial training. ADB expert and trainer Saima A. Khawaja speaks with participant judges Rahila Omer and Hassan Ahmad during the Judicial Training on Gender Sensitization and Gender-Based Violence held at the Punjab Judicial Academy in September 2017 (photo by Maria Cecilia T. Sicangco).

Chapter 12

RESILING AND ATTRITION

I.   Introduction

This chapter discusses resiling and attrition, their relationship to evidence and credibility, why they occur, and the best ways to reduce them.

Regrettably in Pakistan, the most likely outcome of gender-based violence (GBV) cases that manage to reach the District and Sessions Court is acquittal, mostly due to resiling of witnesses. Figure 12.1 shows the number of convictions as against acquittals and cases consigned to record in Punjab before the GBV Court was set up in Lahore. In 2017, there were 7,219 GBV cases decided by courts across Punjab, of which 315 cases resulted in convictions (4.37%) and 6,904 (95.63%) in acquittals.[1] In addition to these cases, there were 5,949 cases consigned to record. Cases consigned to record are cases deemed concluded for reasons other than conviction or acquittal, e.g. cases where the complainant, victim or witnesses had resiled or where the accused could not be found or had absconded. When added to the acquittal numbers, this results in convictions being only 2.39% of the total cases. The highest numbers of those consigned were for rape (1,806) and assault to outrage the modesty of a woman (1,165).[2]

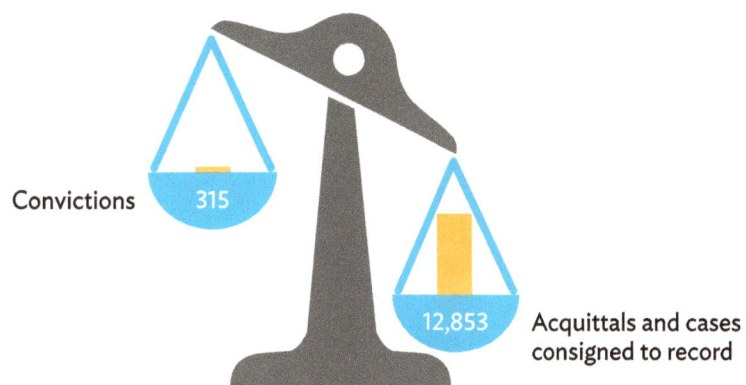

Figure 12.1: Convictions vs. Acquittals and Cases Consigned to Record in Violence against Women Cases in Punjab, 2017

Convictions 315

12,853 Acquittals and cases consigned to record

Source: Punjab Commission on the Status of Women. 2018. *Punjab Gender Parity Report 2018*. p. 185. Data from the Public Prosecution Department.

---

1   Punjab Commission on the Status of Women (PCSW). 2018. *Punjab Gender Parity Report 2018*. pp. 184–185.

2   Footnote 1, p. 185.

Figure 12.2 shows the breakdown of the disposal of rape cases. There were 104 (3.4%) convictions and 2,957 (96.6%) acquittals in 2017 in Punjab (footnote 2). Of those that resulted in acquittals, there were 2,483 (81.1%) cases where witnesses resiled; 367 (12%) acquittals on merit after a case had been heard; and 107 (3.5%) acquittals due to deficient evidence gathering. In addition, there were 1,806 cases consigned to record.

Figure 12.2: Disposal of Rape Cases in Punjab, 2017

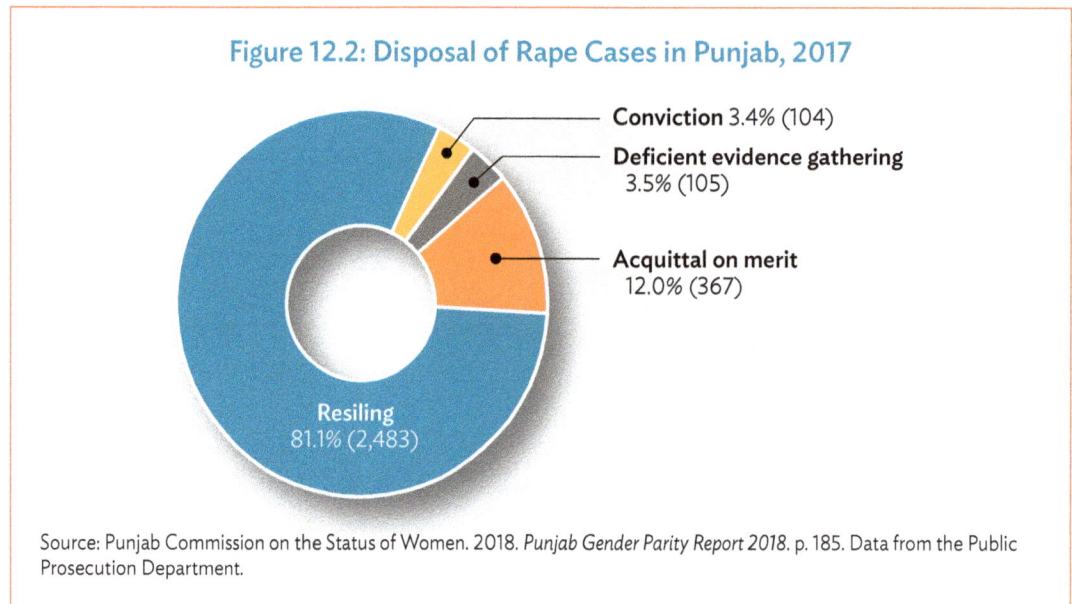

Conviction 3.4% (104)

Deficient evidence gathering
3.5% (105)

Acquittal on merit
12.0% (367)

Resiling
81.1% (2,483)

Source: Punjab Commission on the Status of Women. 2018. *Punjab Gender Parity Report 2018*. p. 185. Data from the Public Prosecution Department.

These figures are only the tip of the iceberg. These are the women that have had the courage to go to the courts. What does this say about the level of impunity for perpetrators of GBV? They are not being convicted and punished for their crimes. The cycle of violence just continues through the generations.

This sorry state of affairs was underscored by interviews conducted with District and Sessions Court judges from Lahore, Sheikhupura, Gujranwala, Kasur, Rawalpindi, Multan, and Bahawalpur.[3] Commonly expressed views are as follows:

- Most rape cases were compromised, with witnesses and complainants resiling from their statements;

- "Genuine" rape cases (e.g., *Wanni*, exchange and early marriages) were not brought to the courts and the cases brought to court were generally not "genuine";

- Male family members decided whether any case was to be filed, especially a rape/sexual assault case (both false and genuine cases);

- Male family members decided whether a case should be settled or withdrawn (either because of monetary compensation or fear of retribution);

---

[3] Asian Development Bank (Office of the General Counsel). 2017. Consultation Mission to Punjab, Pakistan: Legal Literacy for Women Technical Assistance. Needs Assessment Report (internal).

- Judges generally allow the cases to be withdrawn when witnesses or complainants resiled (even if other evidence exist, such as photos, medical evidence, or similar evidence to support a rape);

- There was general dissatisfaction over the insufficiency of police evidence to support convictions; and

- Judges were confident that they were able to assess whether a rape complaint was genuine or not.

Regarding sexual harassment and domestic violence, judges indicated that

- Domestic violence cases were rarely reported;

- Violence perpetrated by a husband would mostly not be perceived as a crime;

- A victim's family would probably pressure the domestic violence victim not to leave/ seek divorce; and

- Sexual harassment and domestic violence cases do not come before the courts, except before a Family Court, if at all.

Judges also expressed their views on abduction of unmarried women/girl:

- There was a potential for abuse of court processes by family members who allege abduction of a girl/woman or may compel a girl/woman to file a case of abduction.

- Some judges took precautionary measures to ascertain if the complaints were genuine and to protect the safety of the girl/woman from retribution by her family.

Additionally, information gathered from a review of court files in Lahore discloses standardized generic reasons given by witnesses for resiling (footnote 3).

II. What Is Meant by Attrition?

The term "attrition" refers to situations when complaints or cases in the criminal justice system (both prior or during the court process) are withdrawn or do not proceed to trial, or if they do proceed to trial, does not proceed through to judgment or criminal conviction. The "attrition rate" is the percentage of overall cases of that type.

The attrition rate for GBV cases is generally extremely high in comparison with other offenses. This is a global phenomenon and not just true of Pakistan. In Pakistan, it is mostly due to female victims withdrawing or disengaging from the prosecution for reasons discussed below.

Attrition is looked at in three stages:

(i)   after a complaint is made and before it enters the District and Sessions Court system by delivery of the *Challan* (charge sheet);

(ii) between when a charge is framed and up to the date of trial; and

(iii) between the start of the trial and the outcome of that trial.

III. International Experience on Attrition

Attrition is a global phenomenon with many interrelated and overlapping factors, some of which are country-specific. The reasons for attrition fall into two major categories: (i) victim-related factors, and (ii) system-related factors.

A. Victim-Related Factors

The victim-related factors are twofold.

First, the general background of a country in which the victim lives, including societal, cultural, religious, and criminal justice system attitudes toward victims (see Chapter 2)

Second, the victim's personal background and circumstances, including the following factors:

(i)   **Knowledge about GBV and their ability to access free legal services.** The victim may have little knowledge about what to do if she is the subject of GBV, particularly domestic violence. A victim needs to have access to legal services; if they are not freely and easily available, these constitute impediments. Language and communication issues can also be a barrier to her getting the necessary advice to enable her to pursue a case.

(ii)   **Financial circumstances, housing, and dependence on an abuser.** These circumstances are highly relevant as to whether the victim will pursue a case, particularly in respect of domestic violence. The victim may have nowhere to go. Shelters are only a temporary measure. Although shelters are much needed and valued, they do not provide a long-term solution.

(iii) **Child responsibility status.** This is a very relevant issue for a victim in deciding whether to pursue a case because this may compromise care and custody of children. It affects whether a woman can leave home and rebuild her life elsewhere if she is the subject of domestic violence.

(iv)   **Past personal experiences and family circumstances.** This includes a victim's past experiences pursuing a GBV case. It includes whether she has a supportive family, for example, when she makes a complaint; whether the family pressures her not to complain at all; or to withdraw a complaint; or to resile at court.

(v)   **Family members are mostly responsible for women not pursuing cases.** A study undertaken on this topic across 48 countries and territories (including countries from Asia and the Pacific as well as the Middle East and North Africa) notes that family members rather than victims are responsible for 47% of withdrawal of cases at the police station and 52% of withdrawals at court.[4]

---

[4]   Z. Abdul Aziz and J. Moussa. 2013, reprint 2016. *Due Diligence Framework: State Accountability Framework for Eliminating Violence against Women*. Penang.

B. System-Related Factors

Many of the factors that contribute to attrition rates are issues related to the criminal justice system. They include

- whether there are mechanisms that allow women to feel safe in making complaints of GBV, including protection orders, eviction (of the accused) orders, access to shelter and refuge (short-term and medium-term);

- the responses they receive when they make a complaint, including all personnel involved in the legal processes and whether those persons imply or expressly place the blame on victims for the violence committed against them and other similar negative responses;

- matters not being pursued promptly through criminal justice system. Delays adversely impact the quality of evidence due to its effect on recollection and memory and the stress related to prolonged trial aggravated by the lack of finality; and

- lack of support for women to pursue redress in the court, including free legal, medical, psychological, and social (family, community) support.

IV. Why Attrition Matters

GBV attrition leads to offender impunity and the continuation of the cycles of violence against women. If offenders are not brought to justice, there is no specific or general deterrence; offenders—usually men—know they can get away with committing offenses.

V. Attrition and Resiling in Pakistan

Most allegations of GBV—except for domestic violence (see Chapter 3)—do not require a warrant to be taken out by the police before they can make an arrest. Also, most GBV offenses are not bailable except some "hurts" (Section 337 of the Pakistan Penal Code [PPC]) and "abduction of married women" (Section 496 of the PPC). The relevance of whether a case is bailable has a direct impact on whether the accused can be arrested and placed in custody at an early point of time. It affects whether an accused can be released, and if so, the terms upon which he obtains bail. Whether or not bail is granted and the terms upon which it is granted may impact upon the safety of victims and whether they will pursue their case. This is an important heightened time of risk of further violence against victims.

For example, if an alleged perpetrator is released on conditions, there may be issues as to whether they are likely to be complied with and the risk to the victim. Alternatively, if an alleged perpetrator has to remain in custody pending trial and there is a delay in getting to a trial, pressure may be placed on the victim by the accused and their family for her to withdraw her case, so that the accused is released.

Most GBV offenses are non-compoundable offenses (e.g., rape, gang rape, attempted murder, abduction of unmarried women, acid attacks, and outrage of the modesty). Compoundable offenses are murder (Section 302 PPC) and hurts (Section 337 PPC). However, even in cases involving non-compoundable offenses—such as rape, particularly those that are the subject of resiling—there is concern that there had been an out-of-court compromise or settlement of their cases as a result of pressure from the family, the perpetrator, or on behalf of the perpetrator.

The Punjab Commission on the Status of Women *2018 Gender Parity Report* indicates that the reasons for low conviction rates include

- women's unwillingness to pursue trial due to fear of being retraumatized by the process;

- prosecutors only being prepared to take cases they could win;

- rape cases being "mired with myths and stereotypes" about race, class, gender, and character of rape victims;

- lack of protection for the victims from retaliation;

- weak judicial procedures; and

- out-of-court settlements and compromises due to weak procedures and fears.[5]

Examination of court files undertaken by the ADB team reveals that there was a formulaic wording of resiling statements made by either a complainant or a victim, with no or inadequate investigation undertaken by prosecutors, or inquiry by the court through processes such as hostile witness examinations (see Chapter 12). The court files disclose that the generic formula frequently used was:

> I am the complainant of the instant case. I filed an application as Ex.PA which bears my thumb impression as Ex.PA/1 for registration of the case against the accused persons, present before the court. I registered this instant case, due to some misunderstanding and now the accused persons have given me satisfaction of their innocence in the presence of respectable of the locality. Therefore, I have no more interest to proceed with the matter against the accused persons and I have no objection, if the accused persons are acquitted from the charge.

The common features of the formula, given as the reasons for the resiling, were that the registration of the case was "due to some misunderstanding" that was not identified; and the accused persons had "given satisfaction of their innocence," whatever "satisfaction" and "innocence" may mean, "before the respectable of the locality," who was not named. The same basic wording was used irrespective of whether it was the complainant or the victim who had resiled. The implausibility of these resiling statements is overt, especially when it is repeated across many different cases including rape and abduction.

---

[5] Footnote 1, p. 184.

The reality is that

- either the complaint and the Section 164 statement made by the victim under oath were false from the start, or

- the resiling statements later handed up on the date of trial are false.

In either situation, a complainant and/or a victim are making false charges or giving false information, or misleading a court, which are offenses (see PPC Chapter XI). It is also critical to apprehend and punish any person(s) who had persuaded, compelled, threatened, or promised compensation or other forms of gratification (through a settlement/'compromise') to the complainant and/or victim to make the false statements or resile. This situation should not be ignored and should be the subject of thorough investigation by the police.

On this topic of falsehood, the Supreme Court case of *Criminal Miscellaneous Application No. 200 of 2019* in Criminal Appeal No. 238-L of 2013 is highly pertinent.

Criminal Miscellaneous Application No. 200 of 2019[6]

Facts: A man was ambushed, shot, and killed by an accused and others. Two persons who are closely related to the deceased, one brother and the other cousin (a police officer), gave evidence that they were at the scene of the crime and were witnesses. The accused was convicted and sentenced. On appeal to the Supreme Court, it was established that the cousin police officer was nowhere near the scene, and the brother—who gave evidence that he was with the cousin at the scene—was likewise lying. The Supreme Court acquitted the accused and referred the matter back to a District and Sessions Court judge for the purposes of proceeding against the cousin under Section 194 PPC for perjury.

Issue: A fundamental issue in the case was whether the rule *falsus in uno, falsus in omnibus* (false in one thing, false in everything) should apply in courts in Pakistan. This is a rule that applies in common law countries and permits a court to separate out and reject false evidence of a witness but accept other evidence of that witness as true.

Ruling: The Supreme Court, after canvassing case law in Pakistan and other religious references, reached the conclusion that the problem in Pakistan of persons giving false information and evidence was so grave, that the rule should not apply in Pakistan. The result is that it was no longer possible for a judge to accept that some evidence of a witness who is found to have deliberately given false evidence (perjury), can be rejected, but other evidence of the witness could be accepted. Then Chief Justice Asif Saeed Khosa summarized this situation as follows:

> 21. We may observe in the end that a judicial system which permits deliberate falsehood is doomed to fail and a society which tolerates it is destined to self-destruct. Truth is the foundation of Criminal Miscellaneous Application No. 200 of 2019 justice and justice is the core and bedrock of a civilized society and, thus, any compromise on truth amounts to a compromise on a society's future as a just, fair and civilized society. Our judicial system has suffered a lot as a consequence

---

6   PLD 2019 Supreme Court 527.

of the above-mentioned permissible deviation from the truth and it is about time that such a colossal wrong may be rectified in all earnestness. Therefore, in light of the discussion made above, we declare that the rule falsus in uno, falsus in omnibus shall henceforth be an integral part of our jurisprudence in criminal cases and the same shall be given effect to, followed and applied by all the courts in the country in its letter and spirit. It is also directed that a witness found by a court to have resorted to a deliberate falsehood on a material aspect shall, without any latitude, invariably be proceeded against for committing perjury.[7]

The relevance of this case to situations of resiling is that circumstances of resiling often overtly reveal that there is likely falsehood by witnesses, a complainant, and/or a victim. A thorough police investigation may also reveal that the victim was under pressure at one or other point of time and therefore exonerated from such an offense. In addition, the investigation may reveal an additional offense of compounding of offenses that are non-compoundable and collusion of several actors.

It is no longer appropriate for judges to turn a blind eye to potential abuse of the judicial system through manipulation of court processes by resiling statements. The former Chief Justice has spoken. The situation of resiling statements needs to be scrutinized.

In the case of *Opuz v. Turkey*, both the wife and her mother had withdrawn their several complaints of domestic violence against the husband due to threats from the husband.[8] The husband ultimately killed his mother-in-law. Before the European Court of Human Rights, the wife submitted that the State of Turkey had failed to protect her mother. The State of Turkey submitted that the prosecution was unable to proceed due to these withdrawals. The Court held that, "the more serious the offence or the greater the risk of further offences, the more likely that the prosecution should continue in the public interest, even if victims withdraw their complaints."[9]

The Court also found that the national authorities of the State of Turkey could not be considered as having exercised due diligence:

> [In] the instant case, further violence was not only possible but even foreseeable, given the violent behaviour and criminal record of H.O. [the husband], his continuing threat to the health and safety of the victims and the history of violence in the relationship [...].

> In the Court's opinion, it does not appear that the local authorities sufficiently considered the above factors when repeatedly deciding to discontinue the criminal proceedings against H.O. Instead, they seem to have given exclusive weight to the need to refrain from interfering with what they perceived to be a "family matter" [...]. Moreover, there is no indication that the authorities considered the motives behind the withdrawal of the complaints. [...]

> In these circumstances, the Court concludes that the national authorities cannot be considered to have displayed due diligence. They therefore failed in their positive

---

7   Footnote 6, para. 21.

8   Application No. 33401/02, [2009] ECHR 870.

9   Footnote 8, para. 139.

obligation to protect the right to life of the applicant's mother within the meaning of Article 2 of the Convention.[10]

Allied to resiling is witness tampering and interference with the course of justice, as discussed below.

VI. Good Practices to Increase Conviction Rates and Reduce Attrition and Acquittal Rates

Four examples of good practice to increase conviction rates and reduce attrition and acquittal rates are provided below.

A. The Practice Notes: Approach of the Court When Resiling Occurs

The *Practice Notes* aim to address falsehood and compounding of non-compoundable offenses.[11] Paragraph 42 of the *Updated Practice Note* suggests four alternative procedures or a combination of those four procedures to address this very serious issue.

In summary, the procedures are as follows:

- **Procedure 1** is a procedure that during training programs, a number of judges indicated that they had already adopted to try and find out why the victim had resiled, whether or not she had been exposed to any pressure, or whether there had been any compromise. The questions and answers are to be recorded. Thereafter the judge may make appropriate orders that may include protection orders for the victim. A number of judges indicated that when they had taken this procedure with a child who resiled, they were told by the child that they had been under pressure to change their testimony by a family member.

- **Procedure 2** suggests an adjournment to allow the victim or witness to consider their situation with appropriate protection if required.

- **Procedure 3** suggests that the Judge direct the Assistant Superintendent of Police/ subdivisional police officer of concerned area to investigate the matter, including whether the victim or other witnesses have been pressured into making full statements, and provide a report to the court within seven days. A pro forma to assist with the directions is set out in Appendix 5. This pro forma was developed by a judge of the

---

10   Footnote 8, paras. 142–143, and 149.
11   The *2018 Practice Note* (Appendix 2) was issued by the Lahore High Court on 1 February 2018. It was later discussed and refined by the District and Sessions Court judges in Lahore to include additional offenses and special procedures for child witnesses, and used for subsequent trainings (*Updated Practice Note*, Appendix 2A). The *2018 Practice Note* and the *Updated Practice Note* are collectively referred to as "Practice Notes" in this publication.

High Court of Lahore. The style of questioning in the direction is similar to that which would be undertaken in the course of a prosecutor undertaking a hostile witness cross-examination.

- **Procedure 4** is the one that most judges during the training programs conducted on the GBV Court processes, appeared to favor. This is to direct that the trial continue and enable the prosecutor to undertake a hostile witness cross-examination and continue with the remainder of the trial. There have also been examples where a child victim or witness has indicated that they no longer made an accusation against an accused, and paragraph 52 of the *Updated Practice Note* addresses that situation.

Some judges during the training programs mentioned that they saw no point in going on with trial when the victim resiles, because the victim could no longer be regarded as credible. With respect to that view, it should be noted that often, the victim may have previously given a truthful statement under oath in Section 164. If an effective hostile witness cross-examination is conducted by the prosecutor, it may elicit the improbability of the later resiling statement drawn up by the lawyer, being adhered to by the witness as accurate. Instead, the victim may stand by the Section 164 statement given under oath which implicates the accused, and indicate that they were under pressure from others to resile from it. There is no reason why the court could not accept the victim as being credible and the case made out. Further, other evidence may be available which corroborates the victim.

In addition to the procedures set out in the *Updated Practice Note*, there are two good prosecutorial practice strategies that have been utilized in a number of common law countries to increase conviction rates and reduce attrition in GBV cases. The strategies are referred to as "victimless prosecution" and "pro-prosecution policy" or "no drop policy."

B.   Victimless Prosecution

A "victimless prosecution" or "evidence-based prosecution" is a strategy that requires the active engagement of the police and prosecutors from the very start. This strategy depends on effective police investigation, as the case is to be prosecuted without the need to call the victim at trial, particularly in a domestic violence case. Therefore, the case rests on the prosecution presenting sufficient evidence to prove a case of GBV. This approach requires a thorough police investigation. It requires the police to have a different mindset and attitude to ensure that they treat the victim empathetically; to gather all available evidence on the premise that the victim may not be available to give evidence (e.g., use of photographic and video evidence from a crime scene including the home of the victim for domestic violence and her injuries); and to ensure that the victims and potentially other witnesses who corroborate the victim, be protected from retaliation by the accused or their family.

Examples of a victimless prosecution with reference to admissibility under the Qanun e-Shahadat Order 1984 (QSO) provisions are as follows:

- The police arrive at the scene and the victim runs up to them in tears saying her husband had attacked her and ran away as soon as she rang the police (Articles 19(a) and 21(f)).

- The police take photos of marks of a struggle on the ground and broken kitchen items (QSO Article 20(6)) and collect the broken items.

- They record a video of the victim narrating her injuries and take photos of the wounds (QSO Article 19(a) and 27) as an expression by the victim of bodily feeling.

- The police record video statements from neighbors who witnessed/heard the incident (QSO Articles 71 and 19(a)) and past incidences (QSO Articles 27(i), 27(k), and 28).

- The medical report recording the injuries and pain (QSO Article 27) as a statement of bodily feeling.

- Other witnesses who had seen the victim with injuries or in whom the victim had confided (e.g., work colleagues) (QSO Article 28).

- The combination of calling the evidence of the neighbors (direct witnesses to the crime) and the police (witnesses as to the call by the victim and her statement when they arrived) would then permit the corroborative evidence of the doctor to be called. The evidence could then be fortified by the videos of the scene and broken items all of which corroborate the commission of the crime by the accused.

Even if the victim cannot give evidence in court, due to reasons such as fear, illness, psychiatric condition, incapacity, or does not attend court on the day, the case could still be pursued. While from a technical point of view, it is preferable for the victim (often referred to as the "star witness") to give evidence herself, it does not mean that the case cannot be proved otherwise if another witness(es) gives evidence in the case.

Such a situation is predicated in the *Updated Practice Note* (para. 45) which states that the trial may proceed in the absence of the victim if there is sufficient evidence.

C.   Pro-Prosecution: No Drop Policy

Pro-prosecution policies encourage pursuance of GBV cases (particularly domestic violence cases) even without the victim's consent or even if the victim refuses to testify (so long as she is protected and safe). A number of common law countries have adopted such policies, including Canada, the United States, Fiji, Tonga, and other Pacific island countries.

In Fiji, a police No Drop Policy was established in 1995 because women who reported domestic abuse cases often returned to the police station shortly afterward to withdraw their complaints due to family/in-law/communal pressure. Under the No Drop Policy, once a complaint is lodged, the investigation must continue, and the case must be sent to the magistrate. This not only takes the burden of continuing a case off the woman, but it also discourages the police from taking matters into their own hands and refusing to receive complaints or attempting to reconcile the couple. Other countries have similar approaches.

In Canada, the police and prosecutors are required, pursuant to directives or guidelines, to charge and prosecute all incidents of spousal abuse where there are reasonable and probable grounds to believe an offense has been committed, regardless of the victim's wishes. It is to be noted that in Canada, the guidelines and directives occur in a context where there has been the establishment of dedicated domestic violence courts, services, and treatment programs for perpetrators. The Department of Justice in Canada, in 2000, set up a working group to report on the efficacy of the "no drop" and "pro-prosecution" approaches that have been operating since 1983 throughout Canada. The working group concluded that the pro-charging policies had increased the number of incidents reported to the police and the number of charges laid in spousal abuse cases, and had reduced the risk of harm of reoffending.[12] For instance, a 10-year study in London, Ontario found that prior to the adoption of a pro-prosecution policy, 38.4% of charges were dismissed or withdrawn; 2 years later (1983) after the adoption of the policy, that rate had decreased to 16.4%; and then at the end of 10 years (1990), the charges dismissed or withdrawn had decreased to 10.9% (footnote 12).

Both "no drop" and "pro-prosecution" approaches utilize rules of evidence which allow exceptions to the hearsay rule. These exceptions can be used to good effect in GBV cases if the police are alert to their potential when undertaking an investigation, and if prosecutors are alert to their potential use when they are reviewing the evidence.

In conclusion, victimless prosecutions recognize the control dynamics in GBV cases where threats, coercion, and negative financial concerns can result in victims refusing to testify. Observations suggest that the victim's initial reports are the most accurate. It also recognizes that initial reports tend to be more consistent with all the other evidence. Still, there is no single perfect solution, and balancing a victim's refusal to pursue prosecution, the public interest in pursuing grave human rights violations against women, and the accused's right to confront witnesses is a delicate balancing act.

D.   Witness Tampering and Protections for Witnesses

A further process to address resiling due to familial pressure is charging persons with witness tampering, interfering with the course of justice, and providing appropriate protections for those who are threatened.

Witness tampering refers to an attempt to cause a person to testify falsely, withhold testimony or information, or be absent from any proceeding to which the witness has been summoned. A person does not have to be a party to the criminal or civil action to be charged with witness tampering. Making improper threats against witnesses may amount to the common law offense of perverting the course of justice.[13] It is also perverting the course of justice to put pressure upon a witness to give evidence or to pay them money to testify in a particular way. Sometimes interfering with witnesses may also amount to common law contempt of court. There is also a separate common law offense of tampering with witnesses when one uses threats to persuade them not to give evidence.

---

[12]   Government of Canada, Department of Justice. 2002. *Final Report of the Ad Hoc Federal–Provincial–Territorial Working Group Reviewing Spousal Abuse Policies and Legislation.*

[13]   It is a common law offense in England and Wales. See *R v Kellett* [1976] QB 372.

There appears to be no specific offense of witness tampering or perverting the course of justice in the PPC or in the various laws related to witness protection.[14] These witness protection laws were passed primarily to curb the widespread terrorism in the country and encourage the witnesses to testify against terrorist organizations.[15] However, their provisions have potentially broader application. Using the Punjab Witness Protection Act, 2018 as an example, although there is no offense of witness tampering, Section 7 provides assistance to witnesses if they believe they are at risk of harm or intimidation as described in the section.

In some common law countries/territories (such as Australia, Canada, and New Zealand), there are statutory provisions creating the offense of obstructing justice or interfering with the course of justice. For example, Section 139 of the Criminal Code of Canada provides that a person shall be deemed to wilfully obstruct, pervert or defeat the course of justice in a judicial proceeding, existing or proposed if he:

(a) dissuades or attempts to dissuade a person by threats, bribes, or other corrupt means from giving evidence;

(b) influences or attempts to influence by threats, bribes, or other corrupt means a person in his conduct as a juror; or

(c) accepts or obtains, agrees to accept or attempts to obtain a bribe or other corrupt consideration to abstain from giving evidence, or to do or to refrain from doing anything as a juror.

In summary, it is suggested that far greater use can be made of witness protection legislation. Persons who interfere with witnesses may be charged with interfering with the course of justice (as a common law offense) or contempt of court. This approach would require (i) greater awareness at all levels—such as for legislators, police, prosecutors, and judges—of the potential use of witness protection legislation, and (ii) capacity to identify a situation when such an offense has been committed or when such protection needs to be provided to witnesses.

VII. Conclusory Remarks

If the police, prosecutors, and judges each take positive steps to better understand stereotypes of female GBV victims and improve their responses to GBV offenses in all aspects of their work, as discussed above, this will promote and enable fair, impartial, and just outcomes for GBV victims.

If judges and prosecutors take a strong stance on resiling statements, it gives greater credibility to the justice system. It could be seen that they are not prepared to accept manipulation of the court system by litigants and witnesses. Instead of simply accepting the false situation and getting

---

[14] Acts include Protection of Pakistan Act, 2014 (Sections 9, 10, and 13); Sindh Witness Protection Act, 2013; Balochistan Witness Protection Act, 2016; and Punjab Witness Protection Act, 2018. On a review of witness protection laws, see S. Bashir. 2019. Witness Protection and Judicial System of Pakistan in the Light of International Legislations and Best Practices. *International Journal of Arts and Commerce*. 8 (11).

[15] S. Bashir. 2019. Witness Protection and Judicial System of Pakistan in the Light of International Legislations and Best Practices. *International Journal of Arts and Commerce*. 8 (11).

on with the next case-to-case disposal numbers, more time will have to be spent on each case of resiling. Taking a strong approach will deter others from attempting a similar manipulation. Persons who are involved in giving or assisting others to give false information or evidence should be charged with criminal offenses. This includes everyone facilitating this process. To requote former Chief Justice Khosa, "...a judicial system which permits deliberate falsehood is doomed to fail and a society which tolerates it is destined to self-destruct" (footnote 6).

The Faisal Mosque in Islamabad, Pakistan.
In *Ghulam Ali v. Ghulam Sarwar Naqvi*,
the Supreme Court of Pakistan held that
"relinquishment" by a female of her inheritance
is contrary to public policy as understood in the
Islamic sense (photo by Syed Bilal Javaid).

Art and the law. Children and adults get ready to watch a puppet show on women's rights in Multan, Punjab (photo by Samar Minallah Khan).

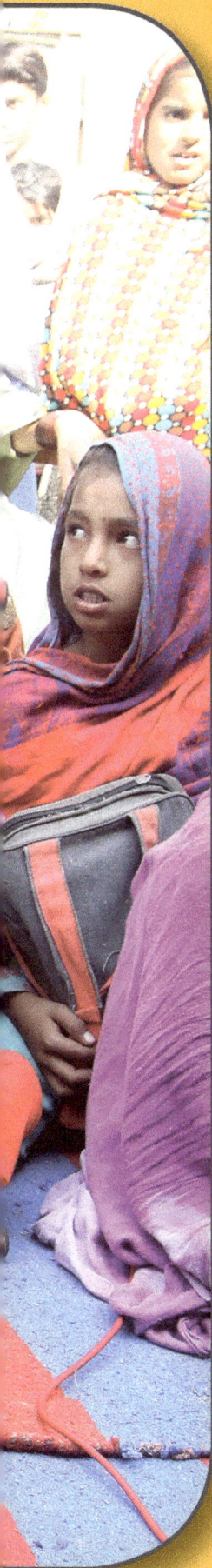

Chapter 13

INSTITUTIONAL PRACTICES, EVALUATION, AND MONITORING

I. Introduction

Addressing gender-based violence (GBV) is not confined solely to the courtroom. To thoroughly address GBV, the justice system must cooperate as a collective unit so that courts, the police, and the prosecution are united to work together to eliminate GBV in Pakistan. The justice system must also collaborate and work with civil society and organizations that provide legal aid, medical and psychological services, counselling, and shelters to victims.

As outlined in earlier chapters, the State has the overriding duty to investigate human rights violations, and GBV is a serious violation of human rights. Investigation of complaints needs to be without delay, thorough, impartial, and effective. The State needs to ensure that police and medical service providers have the requisite resources, and are sufficiently trained in collecting necessary evidence to facilitate and secure successful prosecutions.

In addition, it is essential that courts have sufficient resources to efficiently deal with cases and receive training on gender-sensitive approaches to interacting with victims who bring their cases to court. These three agencies—the court, the police, and the prosecution—need to take proactive and effective action to investigate GBV cases, provide protection to GBV victims, and punish any false practices that subvert the justice system.

II. Overarching Themes and Strategies

Research shows that good practice requires cooperative institutional practices that work to eliminate GBV and provide victims with safety and the ability to successfully uphold and pursue their rights. Good practice includes engaging with victims and responding to their needs through multiagency cooperation on a case-by-case approach. Without this common understanding, nothing will change, and each agency will simply work in a silo, without an appreciation of how collaborative work can produce better outcomes.

The following are factors that significantly influence whether women will pursue GBV complaints:

(i)   availability and accessibility of free victim support, legal advocacy, and information;

(ii)   cooperation between professionals in the justice system (police, prosecution, and courts);

(iii) early responses to protect the victim, including risk assessment and safety planning put in place early by the police, as well as throughout the progress of the case and after the case. This includes

    (a) availability of urgent safety measures,

    (b) restraining orders and arrest of the perpetrator,

    (c) shelter for victims and other services, and

    (d) early and continuing court orders to protect the victim;

(iv)   including court orders not only against the perpetrator but against family members of the perpetrator;

(v)   the efficacy of investigation and the quality and quantity of evidence collected independently of victim engagement. See further discussion on victimless prosecutions and pro-prosecution policies in Chapter 12; and

(vi)   professional attitudes of prosecutors and the judiciary in relation to GBV, including stereotyping, disbelief, victim blaming, and a lack of awareness of the needs of victims in the courtroom.

Figure 13.1 shows the seven linked strategies required for successfully pursuing the rights of GBV victims in court.

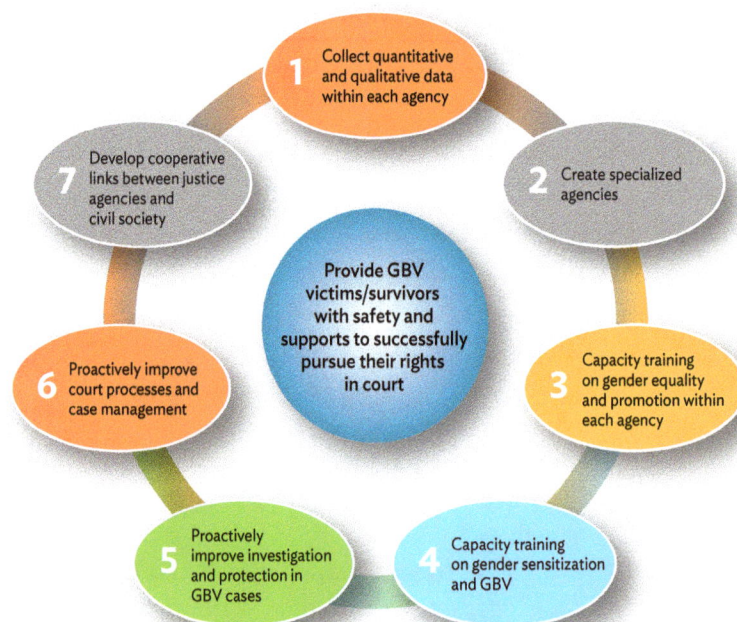

Figure 13.1: Seven Linked Strategies to Protect the Victim's Rights in Court

1 Collect quantitative and qualitative data within each agency

2 Create specialized agencies

3 Capacity training on gender equality and promotion within each agency

4 Capacity training on gender sensitization and GBV

5 Proactively improve investigation and protection in GBV cases

6 Proactively improve court processes and case management

7 Develop cooperative links between justice agencies and civil society

Provide GBV victims/survivors with safety and supports to successfully pursue their rights in court

GBV = gender-based violence.
Source: Authors.

III. Data Collection, Monitoring, and Evaluation

To fully understand the barriers victims face in coming forward to complain about GBV, it is necessary for each of the three agencies to collect data. This data, if not previously captured, provides a baseline measurement which is then regularly monitored and evaluated. Reliable, systematic, and regular data collection is crucial for understanding and improving responses to GBV cases.

Data collection is of two types:

- **Quantitative data** includes the number of complaints filed, how they progress through the justice system, and their outcome.

- **Qualitative data** captures issues such as how women are treated during the complaint process, whether the processes are efficient and sensitive to their needs, whether women obtain justice for the crimes that have been committed against them, and whether the perpetrators are appropriately punished for their crimes.

Each of the agencies need to obtain both quantitative and qualitative data. The collection of data is based on key indicators identified; the goal is to improve processes to ensure that victims are protected and have access to justice, and achieve improved outcomes of conviction and fair punishment.

The key indicators should include the following:

- **For quantitative data**—the number of complaints and date, the offense alleged, when the *Challan* (charge sheet) is delivered, the framed charge, outcome of the case, and punishment.

- **For qualitative data**—information from the victims on topics such as their perceptions of safety; attitudes taken by the police, prosecutors, and judges; the victims' experience in the court processes; and the outcomes achieved. This information should be collected via survey of victims or questions asked of them after the case, or conducted by/through nongovernment organizations (NGOs) and focus groups.

Thereafter, the data requires regular monitoring and evaluation to ensure effectiveness and to identify any gaps that need to be addressed, potentially by amending the key indicators.

A. Court Data

Data collection within the court system in Pakistan on matters related to GBV are presently somewhat haphazard. Some courts systematically collect information but there is no overall coherence within the provinces or territories. In 2019, a request was made to obtain data from all districts and the overall data from each province and territory. Unfortunately, the data was insufficient as it was not systematically collected and, therefore, was unable to provide a full understanding of the cases or their outcomes.

1. Quantitative Court Data

The current system of court files in Pakistan is still paper-based and kept in folders with pink tape. Going forward, a simple approach for improvement should be adopted, and, later, information can be transferred into digital form.

The front sheet on each file should contain the following information:

Dates

- complaint
- registration of the first information report (FIR)
- *Challan*
- delivery of the *Challan* to the District and Sessions Courts (DSC)
- framing of the charge
- hearings and progress of case in DSC to finalization

Number of hearings

- type and number of hearings, including adjournments and reasons

Finalization date and method of finalization

- judgement on the merits
- conviction
- acquittal
- resiling by victims and witnesses
- compromise
- withdrawal
- Criminal Procedure Code, Section 265K, acquittal
- plea of guilty
- also note "consigned to record" (referring to cases where the accused has absconded or cannot be located)

Sentence

- details of outcome

The collection of the above data does three things. First, it enables the pendency of cases to be traced from complaint to final verdict. Second, it allows the court to know how long it takes between the time a case comes to the court to when it is finally dealt with. Third, it identifies the manner of finalization and the extent to which there is resiling of victims and witnesses in cases, as well as the number of acquittals/convictions.

In addition to this data, further quantitative data should be collected on

- sex of the victims and the accused,
- age of the victim and the accused, and
- relationship between the victim and the accused.

2. Qualitative Court Data

A framework for gathering and analyzing qualitative data from each court must be developed. The framework should be a collaborative undertaking with the involvement of representatives from the court, prosecution, police, and NGOs. The framework should include key indicators that are to be monitored and assessed.

The relevant information includes pertinent data collected by way of surveys of judges and prosecutors about the processes in court. This information includes whether:

- The *Guidelines to be Followed in Cases of Gender-Based Violence* (*Guidelines*, Appendix 1) and *Practice Notes* (Appendixes 2 and 2A) are being followed;[1]

- Difficulties are encountered in following the *Guidelines* and *Practice Notes*, particularly in relation to responses of the defense counsel;

- Investigations undertaken by the police are sufficient and effective;

- Prosecution was effective in adducing of reasonably available evidence;

- Resiling procedures are effective; or

- The prosecution effectively responded to resiling, including hostile witness cross-examination.

The following information should be collected from the victims (via surveys conducted through NGOs or focus groups):

- their experience upon arrival;

- their overall feeling of security before and during the trial process;

- whether they felt they had been treated in a respectful and supportive manner by the judge, prosecutor, and defense counsel in the court, and if not, why not; and

- whether the sentencing outcomes were appropriate.

- monitoring and evaluation of quantitative data should be done yearly and qualitative data every two years.

B. Prosecution Data

Prosecution data is critical in understanding the effectiveness and efficacy of the criminal justice system. In their report on GBV processes, the Punjab Commission for Women (PCSW) often relies on prosecution data. It needs to be noted, however, that the way in which quantitative information is saved and stored is different from other sources, and not all offenses regarded as GBV offenses are captured.

---

[1] The *2018 Practice Note* (Appendix 2) was issued by the Lahore High Court on 1 February 2018. It was later discussed and refined by the District and Sessions Court judges in Lahore to include additional offenses and special procedures for child witnesses, and used for subsequent trainings (*Updated Practice Note*, Appendix 2A). The *2018 Practice Note* and the *Updated Practice Note* are collectively referred to as "*Practice Notes*" in this publication.

A common approach should be adopted across all relevant agencies regarding quantitative and qualitative data gathering and analysis of offenses to facilitate and enhance collaboration across agencies.

Quantitative and qualitative data, along with identification of key indicators, should be collected and monitored within Prosecution Departments. The key indicators can be identified through interaction between prosecutors, civil society, and the court. It is beyond the scope of this *Court Companion* to address that issue other than in broad terms, but more information is available in the *Handbook on Effective Prosecution Responses to Violence against Women and Girls* published in 2014 by the UN Office on Drugs and Crime.[2]

1. Quantitative Prosecution Data

Quantitative data should include the following:

- date of complaint, registration of the FIR, and the alleged crime;
- sex/gender of the victim and the perpetrator;
- age of the victim and the perpetrator;
- relationship between the victim and the perpetrator;
- whether the complaint is withdrawn before the delivery of the *Challan*, and if so, the date and the reason;
- date of delivery of the *Challan* to the DSC; and
- trial process to finalization including
    - whether there was an application to resile by complainant, victim, or witness;
    - what approach was taken by the court or prosecutor; and
    - whether there was a hostile witness cross-examination.

2. Qualitative Prosecution Data

Qualitative data should include information from victims (via surveys conducted through NGOs or focus groups) about their experiences and whether they felt they had been treated in a respectful and supportive manner by prosecutor communications at all stages—pretrial, trial, and post-trial. There are several key indicators that can be used as subject of data collection. See discussion and examples in the *Handbook on Effective Prosecution Responses to Violence against Women and Girls*.[3]

Monitoring and evaluation of quantitative data should be done yearly and qualitative data every 2 years.

---

[2]   United Nations Office on Drugs and Crime. 2014. *Handbook on Effective Prosecution Responses to Violence Against Women and Girls*. Vienna. pp. 161–166.

[3]   Footnote 2, p. 163.

C. Police Data

Police GBV data differs from the GBV data from courts and the prosecution office. Nonetheless, police data is required to complement the data obtained from other agencies such as courts and prosecutors. Police data should be both quantitative and qualitative.

Monitoring and evaluation of quantitative data should be done yearly and qualitative data every 2 years.

IV. Creating Specialized Agencies

Specialized agencies can help achieve greater victim satisfaction with delivery of services and engagement, reduce attrition, and increase conviction rates.

A. Special Judges for Gender-Based Violence Courts

As discussed in Chapter 8, establishing a specialized GBV Court is pivotal to improving outcomes for GBV victims. Only judges who have been trained on gender sensitization and GBV should preside in GBV Courts.

B. Special Prosecutors

Special prosecutors are equally pivotal to ensure the efficient and sensitive prosecution of GBV cases. Ultimately, prosecutorial discretion is what determines whether a case moves forward or not; the successful conviction of perpetrators rests on the prosecution's case.

Chapter 8 discusses the role and importance of prosecutors in GBV cases throughout the entire process. Chapter 5 presents good practice strategies that have been adopted in several common law countries to increase conviction rates and reduce attrition in GBV cases.

C. Special Police Cells/Investigators

When the first GBV Court in Lahore was set up, a High Court judge, Justice Aalia Neelum, worked with the police to establish a GBV cell at the Investigation Headquarters in the District of Lahore. A documentation of this undertaking is set out in Appendix 6. Gender-sensitive improvements were adopted and undertaken to develop the GBV cell. For example, a training program for investigating officers was initiated, there were meetings with NGOs to devise a joint strategy for elimination and investigation of GBV cases, the cell liaised with prosecutors, and improvements regarding processes for submission of DNA samples for forensic testing were undertaken.

In addition to the establishment of these special cells, all police officers, as part of their regular training, should be trained on gender sensitization and how to approach GBV cases. The reason for this is because almost all police officers are likely to have to deal with a GBV case frequently, or at least at some point in their career.

V. Capacity Building and Training on Gender Equality and Gender Promotion

An important strategy to eliminate GBV requires that the three agencies have a sound appreciation of the meaning and promotion of gender equality and gender sensitivity within their own organizations. This is an institutional issue.

Training on gender equality and gender promotion requires an analysis of the number of women who occupy positions in each of the three agencies and their specific job titles and roles. This entails a detailed and thorough investigation of all positions in the agency from the lowest to the highest levels. This investigation must include an assessment of why women are clustered in the lower levels of employment, how promotions work within each of the agencies, and whether such promotions are based on criteria or job functions that women are disproportionately unlikely to be able to fulfill. This disproportionate and skewed role of women in the workplace is oftentimes a result of gender stereotypes and/or gender roles due to prevailing social and cultural impacts including complex family obligations.

This situation calls for special training in each agency. This training includes an appreciation of the difference between formal equality (that refers simply to equal treatment) and substantive equality (that refers to providing equal opportunities to achieve equal outcomes) as discussed in Chapter 6. It also requires an understanding of special measures, laid out in Chapter 6, and the various ways in which such measures may be used to bring about substantive equality. Special measures may include targets or quotas to increase the number of women to be appointed to higher positions in each agency.

At the institutional level, achieving substantive equality for women within an agency requires sensitive and frank discussion between all judges, prosecutors, and the police to identify the barriers to women from taking on certain higher positions in each agency and tangible and realistic processes to overcome such impediments. An external facilitator may be useful to provide information and encourage discussion.

Achieving equality for women judges at all levels of the judiciary is an important goal, not only because it is right for women, but also because it strengthens the judiciary and helps gain public trust. As Judge Vanessa Ruiz, a Senior Judge of the Court of Appeals in the District of Columbia, United States, recently said:

> By their mere presence, women judges enhanced the legitimacy of courts, sending a powerful signal that they are open and accessible to those who seek recourse to justice.[4]

The type of capacity training to reduce inequalities in each agency will differ. An example of training undertaken with judges in Lahore on this topic in 2019 included training on promotion of gender equality and discussions by male and female judges together and separately about topics that they chose—such as attitudinal issues they each encountered in working with the other

---

[4]   V. Ruiz. 2019. *The Role of Women Judges and a Gender Perspective in Ensuring Judicial Independence and Integrity*. United Nations Office on Drugs and Crime.

sex, conduct or language which excluded the other, differences in duties and cases allocated to them, hours of work and flexibility, and how promotions occurred in the court system. These topics were recorded and discussions were conducted about ways to address the issues. Judges who attended the training agreed that such training should be included as part of the regular judicial training for all judges.

A similar approach could be undertaken for prosecutors and the police, as both agencies need to increase the participation of women at every level within the agency.

VI. Capacity Training on Gender Sensitization and Gender-Based Violence

To improve the outcomes and experiences of victims in courts, judges should receive specialized training on gender sensitization. There should also be specialized groups within prosecutors' offices and special police cells that focus on and are trained in gender sensitization.

Capacity training of all agencies on GBV includes examining the underlying and direct causes of GBV; understanding and promoting gender equality; understanding discrimination, gender roles, stereotyping, and the effects of these mindsets; and learning how to best support victims through the justice system processes. This training compels a change of mindset when dealing with a GBV crime. It is not just a business-as-usual approach as is used in other crimes. GBV crimes are a serious and pernicious form of discrimination based on gender, with women and girl children being the predominant victims of such crimes. The effect of these crimes on the victim, their families, and the community as a whole, is devastating.

Chapters 1, 2, and 3 of this *Court Companion* provide valuable information about the underlying and direct causes of GBV, and Chapter 4 tackles the responses required to eliminate those causes through the actions of judges and prosecutors.

This information needs to be provided, not only to judges in the court, but also to prosecutors and the police. The means by which this can be achieved is initially through a collective discussion between courts, the police, and prosecutors, as discussed below.

Training Topics for the Courts, Police, and Prosecutors

The types of training required for the three agencies include the following:

- a gender-sensitized approach for judges, prosecutors, and the police in all aspects of their work (mainstreaming gender sensitivity);

- the meaning of sex, gender, gender roles, gender identity, and gender stereotyping;

- why women and men conform to society's beliefs on the roles that are regarded as appropriate for each gender group;

- how culture, customs, and attitudes to religion impact upon the roles of women and men and their place within society;

- how these assumed roles adversely affect equality between women and men in society and how women in a patriarchal society have less equality and greater discrimination against them than men;

- how inequality, discrimination, and the greater power of men in society can lead to GBV and to domestic violence;

- different forms of GBV and how it becomes normalized and is often not regarded as a crime by society;

- how bias can adversely affect the outcome of GBV cases; and

- addressing how an understanding of these issues can be constructively used within the work of the agencies to better address GBV, support the victims in achieving justice, and punish the perpetrators for their crimes.

In Pakistan, more than 600 judges have been trained on those topics. Modules and handbooks have been created to allow judges to conduct their own training programs using the *Gender-Based Violence Court: Handbook and Training Manual for Judges,* either at the national or local level.[5] More than 100 prosecutors have also been trained about their work using similar modules and handbooks, in particular the *Gender-Based Violence Court: Handbook and Training Manual for Prosecutors* (Figure 13.2).[6]

Figure 13.2: Training Manuals for Judges and Prosecutors Handling Gender-Based Violence Cases

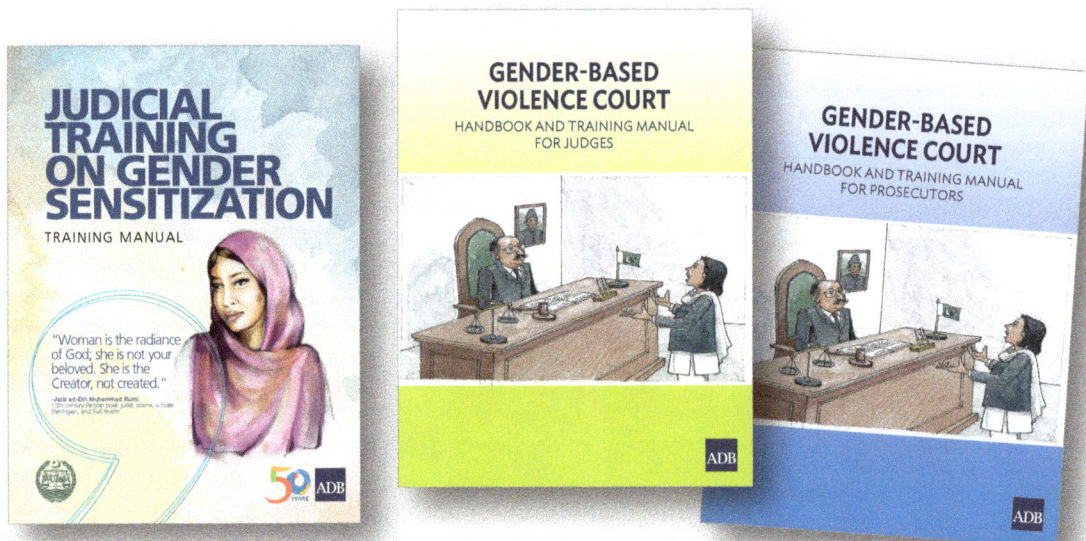

Source: Authors.

---

[5] Asian Development Bank (Office of the General Counsel). 2019. *Gender-Based Violence Court: Handbook and Training Manual for Judges.*

[6] Asian Development Bank (Office of the General Counsel). 2019. *Gender-Based Violence Court: Handbook and Training Manual for Prosecutors.*

A similar approach needs to be undertaken for the police with modules and handbooks that specifically address the different circumstances of their work.

VII. Proactively Improving Investigation and Protection in Gender-Based Violence Cases

Chapter 12 discusses good practices in addressing the common issues of victims not wishing to pursue cases due to fear of retaliation, incapacity, family pressure, or the prospect of the court processes. The chapter also discusses the problem of resiling and the need for a concerted effort by the police and prosecution to ensure that investigations of all GBV complaints are thorough, effective, and empathetically conducted. A thorough investigation also requires vigilance to ensure that if false information or evidence is given, then the purveyors of that information are fully investigated and prosecuted. There is also an emphasis on the need for early and effective protection orders for victims and witnesses. These are critical issues to be addressed if GBV victims are to achieve their right to access justice for the crimes committed against them.

VIII. Proactively Improving Court Processes and Case Management

Chapter 8 discusses the specific improvements needed to address the barriers and needs of victims in the court environment, prevent re-victimization to take place within the court process, and assist in increasing the extremely low conviction rates for GBV in the courts. One important aspect to be addressed is the systemic delay of the resolution of cases in the courts. This is a primary cause of attrition in GBV cases.

The length of time between complaint and finalization varies greatly among districts, provinces, and territories. Many factors can affect this, including population size. The purpose of case management processes is to reduce pendency and increase efficiency in disposal of cases, but it should not be at the expense of rushing justice inappropriately. Judges' effectiveness is frequently determined by the number of cases disposed of by them, which can have adverse effects on the quality of the judicial processes given to victims.

As described above, data is an essential tool for case management. Data will enable the court to have a better understanding of pendency issues and how they can best be addressed. Case management is judge-driven, judge-managed, and is best designed by the court after consultation and discussion with relevant stakeholders, as also discussed above.

There is no single system for court case management and this topic is simply being highlighted to enable judges to reflect on what may work in their court while simultaneously having an appreciation for the aforementioned gender-sensitive approaches to GBV cases.

IX. Developing Cooperative Approaches between the Courts, Police, Prosecutors, and Civil Society

Woven throughout the chapters are discussions about the needs of victims and the types of services they require. A best practice would be to adopt an overall framework for all the agencies, both government and nongovernment, to collaborate on ways to better address the victims' needs. Implementation of a joint approach will improve coordination among agencies and will help to better address GBV. Ideally, this approach includes a one-stop shop where a victim can obtain legal aid and medical/psychological services, including counselling and reference to a shelter.

Such an approach could be implemented on a district-by-district basis as these processes often work most effectively when close to the community so that they are able to best meet the community's particular needs. A national strategy would be ideal but sometimes that can take much longer to formulate.

X. Conclusory Remarks

When considering the effectiveness of the court system, often it comes down to the effectiveness of individual courts. For example, some of the best practices are honed by individual judges within a district who are committed to achieving better outcomes for victims of GBV who come before them. GBV best practices within these institutions require champions within the court to drive improvements to address GBV. These practices should also be shared between judges during training programs or through publications contributed to by judges and shared among them. Similarly, these approaches should be adopted by the prosecution agency and the police. Champions are also needed within each of the agencies to help drive change together and significantly improve safety and support for GBV victims to successfully pursue their rights in court.

Appendixes

Appendix 1   Guidelines to Be Followed in Cases of Gender-Based
              Violence (GBV)

Appendix 2   Practice Note For Cases in Gender–Based Violence Courts

Appendix 2A   Updated Practice Note Incorporating Underlined Refinements
              Suggested by the District and Sessions Court Judges in Lahore

Appendix 3   Questioning of Child Witnesses in Court—Some Helpful Hints
              Using Best Practices

Appendix 4   Suggested Procedure for Cross–Examination of the Victim
              by the Defense Counsel

Appendix 5   Direction to Police to Investigate Resiling Witness

Appendix 6   Direction to Establish a Gender-Based Violence Police Cell
              at Investigation Headquarters District Lahore

APPENDIX 1

Guidelines to Be Followed in Cases of Gender-Based Violence (GBV)

TO BE SUBSTITUTED FOR THE SAME NUMBER AND DATE

LAHORE HIGH COURT, LAHORE

Phone No. 042-99212951 Ext.274
E-mail: - lt.ddj@lhc.gov.pk
Fax No.   042-99212281

No. *22377*/HC/DDJ/DRIT
Dated *18*/October, 2017

From

The Director General,
Directorate of District Judiciary,
Lahore High Court, Lahore.

To

All the District & Sessions Judges,
In the Punjab.

Subject: -   **GUIDELINES TO BE FOLLOWED IN CASES OF GENDER BASED VIOLENCE (GBV)**

Dear Sir,

I am directed to refer to the subject cited above and to inform that **Hon'ble the Chief Justice** has been pleased to approve guidelines to be followed in cases of Gender Based Violence (GBV) in the light of **Salman Akram Raja Case (PLJ 2013 SC 107)**, however the word "chief examination" in para 2(5) has been substituted with **examination-in-chief** and word "sessions" in pars 2(6) has been omitted. The footnote has also been numbered accordingly.

2.   You are, therefore, requested to circulate these guidelines among all respected Judges working on Criminal side under your kind control, to comply with in letter and spirit.

Yours faithfully,

MUHAMMAD AKMAL KHAN
Director General
Directorate of District Judiciary

NUMBER & DATE EVEN

Copy is forwarded for kind information to: -

i.   *Principal Staff Officer to Hon'ble Chief Justice, Lahore High Court, Lahore.*
ii.   *Private Secretary to Hon'ble Justice Ayesha A. Malik, Judge, Lahore High Court, Lahore.*
iii.   *Staff Officer to Registrar, Lahore High Court, Lahore.*

Director General
Directorate of District Judiciary

GUIDELINES TO BE FOLLOWED IN CASES OF GENDER BASED VIOLENCE (GBV) IN THE LIGHT OF PLJ 2013 SC 107 (SALMAN AKRAM RAJA CASE)

1. And Whereas there is a need to build upon the directives given by the Supreme Court in Salman Akram Raja vs. The Government of Punjab through Chief Secretary, Civil Secretariat, Lahore and others[1] in respect of victims and vulnerable witnesses in rape trials, and extend them with suitable adaption to apply to women complainants, victims and vulnerable witnesses, such as women , children or persons with disabilities who are giving evidence in cases of violence;

2. The Lahore High Court, Lahore shall prioritize the gender-based violence cases. The courts shall conduct trials in a gender-sensitive manner and incorporate the directions of the Supreme Court in Salman Akram Raja vs. The Government of Punjab through Chief Secretary, Civil Secretariat, Lahore and others[2], Section 13 of the Criminal Law (Amendment) (Offences related to Rape) Act 2016[3]. The international best practices shall be followed in dealing with gender-based violence cases, such as a courtroom set-up responsive to the needs of women and other vulnerable witnesses. In particular, the courts shall act upon the guidelines issued by Lahore High Court, Lahore, as follows:

    1) *The magistrate unless there are compelling reasons shall record thestatement of the Victim under Section 164, Cr.P.C. in the day on which the application is moved by the Investigation Officer. The Magistrate before proceeding to record the statement shall ensure that the victim (child, women or any vulnerable person) is made comfortable and he/she is free of any extraneous pressure.*

    2) *If the victims of rape are reluctant to appear before a male magistrate as they cannot express their agony appropriately before them, therefore if requested the statement of victim be recorded before female Magistrate, where ever is available.*

    3) *An endeavor shall be made to commit such cases of offence to the Court of Sessions expeditiously and preferably within 15 days.*

---

[1] See note 9.

[2] Section 13 provides:

[3] "13. Amendment of section 352, Act V of 1898.-In the Code, in section 352, the existing provision shall be re-numbered as sub-section (1) of that section and after sub-section (1) re-numbered as aforesaid, the following new sub-sections shall be inserted namely:-

'(2) Notwithstanding anything contained in sub-section (1), the trial of offences under section 354A, 376, 376A, 377 and 377B of the Pakistan Penal Code. 1860 (Act XLV of 1860) shall be conducted in camera;

Provided that the Presiding Officer, if he thinks fit, or on an application made by either of the parties, allow any particular person to have access to, or be or remain in, the Court.

(3) Where any proceedings are held under sub-section (2), the Government may adopt appropriate measures, including holding of the trial through video link or usage of screens, for the protection of the victim and the witnesses.

(4) Where any proceedings are held under sub-section (2), it shall not be lawful for any person to print or publish or broadcast any matter in relation to any such proceedings, except with the permission of the Court.'"

4) *In such cases where a victim shall be given an opportunity to have a state counsel and in cases where a victim has a private lawyer, she may be allowed to retain the private lawyer.*

5) *That as far as possible examination-in-chief and cross-examination of the victim must be conducted on the same day.*

6) *The Court shall maintain a panel of psychiatrists, psychologists and experts in sign language etc. who would assist in recording the statement of victim are vulnerable as and when requested by the Court.*

7) *If it is brought to the notice of the Court from a support person/advocate/victim/Police/Prosecution department regarding threats received by the victim or his/her family members to compromise the matter, the Court shall immediately direct the Assistant Superintendent of Police to look into the matter and provide an action taken report before the Court within 2 days. The Court must ensure that protection is provided to the victim and her family.*

8) *In cases in which the witness is sent back unexamined and is bound down, the Court shall ensure that at least the travelling expenses for coming to and from for attending the Court are paid.*

9) *At the time of recording of evidence of the victim or vulnerable witness irrelevant persons be excluded from the Court. This may include an order that the accused is to be excluded from the court provided that the accused shall be able to see and hear the evidence given.*

10) *The proceedings of such cases be conducted in camera.*

11) *Conducting a trial after regular court hours where appropriate.*

12) *Where possible evidence of victim of violence should be recorded through video conferencing so that the victims do not need to be present in the Court*

13) *Availability of screens, one-way glass, or other arrangements such as closed circuit television so that a victim does not have to see the accused person in court when giving evidence.*

14) *Questions put in cross-examination on behalf of accused should be given in writing to the Presiding Officer who should put them to the victim or to a vulnerable witness in a language which is clear and not degrading.*

There are certain other international best practices and guidelines to be incrementally introduced into the courts: -

1) *A supportive person/Advocate may be allowed to the victim/survivors or witness' choice to be present while evidence is being given.*

2) *To make adjustments to the proximity of lawyers the dock and the witness box to the witness giving evidence in*

3) *Examination and cross examination of the victim/survivor are restricted to issue relevant to the case and are not frivolous or for the purposes of embarrassing or humiliating the victim/survivor including through the introduction of evidence of victim/survivor's past sexual behavior, history, or reputation.*

4) To develop practice guideline for the examination and cross-examination of such a witness to help ensure that questions are asked to the victim/witness using appropriate language manner and content.

5) Witness Care Video Link Rooms may be established to record evidence of the victim or vulnerable witness so that they feel comfortable in recording of their statement at a place where there is no physical interaction with the accused.

6) An audio-visual pre-recording of a statement or evidence of the victim may be allowed, either in part or in whole, to be replayed and admitted as their evidence at the trial. Such pre-recording can include the whole of the evidence of the victim; their evidence in chief cross examination, and re-examination.

7) Other procedural or practice guidelines to be developed where women or their relatives and representatives indicate their wish not to proceed with a case of violence or witnesses resile from their earlier statements;

8) Such other procedural or practical guidelines for other issues which ever so to overcome or remove constraints and barriers to women's access to justice in cases of gender-based violence.

MUHAMMAD AKMAL KHAN
Director General
Directorate of District Judiciary

APPENDIX 2

Practice Note for the Model Gender-Based Violence Cases Court, Lahore

---

LAHORE HIGH COURT, LAHORE
(Directorate of District Judiciary)

PH: 042-99212951-Ext.306
FAX: 042-99212281

From

The Director General,
Directorate of District Judiciary
Lahore High Court, Lahore

To

The District & Sessions Judge,
Lahore

No. 2053 /DDJ/P,D&IT/DR-IT   Dated: 01-02-2018

Subject: **Practice Note For the Model "Gender Base Violence Cases Court (GBV Court), Lahore**

Dear Sir,

I am directed to refer to the subject cited above and to state that Hon'ble the Chief Justice is pleased to approve the Practice Note (attached herewith) to be followed by the Model GBV Court Lahore. His lordship is further pleased to direct you to ensure implementation of the same.

2.   You are, therefore, requested to comply with the direction of his lordship in letter and spirit.

Yours faithfully,

(Judge Muhammad Akmal Khan)
DIRECTOR GENERAL

O/C

PRACTICE NOTE[1] FOR THE MODEL "GENDER-BASED VIOLENCE CASES COURT" ("GBV COURT")

THE PURPOSE OF THE GBV COURT

1. The purpose of the GBV Court is to enable cases which concern gender-based violence offences[2] to be prioritized and conducted in a gender- sensitive manner. The GBV Court applies to the victims of gender-based violence; these victims would include women, children, and other vulnerable witnesses[3] including persons who may regard themselves as having a different gender identity[4]. The purpose of GBV Court also recognises the fact that the victims of gender – based violence are mainly women (and girl children) and they often do not report violence against them for fear of retribution, humiliation, shame, social stigma and loss of honour. In addition victims are also fearful of coming to the court to give evidence because the court processes are intimidating and they feel re-victimised. The GBV Court and the Practice Note are a response to allow them to give their best evidence and minimise the trauma.

PURPOSE OF THE PRACTICE NOTE

2. The purpose of this Practice Note is to enable the "Guidelines to be followed in Cases of gender-based violence (GBV)" No. 22325 dated 17 October 2017 ("the Guidelines), to be implemented in practice with clarity and consistency.
3. At the same time the Practice Note is to be applied flexibly if particular situations require some modification in order to maintain the purpose and principles of the Guidelines.
4. The Practice Note will also apply to the treatment of other witnesses giving evidence in such cases, either for the prosecution or defense, and it includes the accused, with modifications as the situation may require. It is important for all witnesses in the court to have the best conditions be able to give their best evidence.

OUTSIDE THE COURT ROOM

5. On reaching the Court to precinct, the victim is to be met by a "Female Support Officer"[5], who will escort the victim to a protected place so as to avoid contact with the accused or their family or friends as well as the general public.

---

[1] This practice note replaces an earlier Practice Note No. 1 initially developed by the GBV Court.

[2] Gender based violence (GBV) is an act of violence that results in or is likely to result in physical, sexual, psychological or economic harm or suffering. It includes threats of such acts, coercion or arbitrary deprivations of liberty whether occurring public or in private and it includes domestic violence. The violence is primarily committed on the victim by reason of their sex or gender. Examples of gender based violence include offences under Section 332, 336A, 337, 337A1 – F1, 359-369, 376, 376 II, 302, 336 and 496A of PPC.

[3] Vulnerable witnesses would include also persons with mental or other disabilities.

[4] Persons who identify as being Lesbian, Gay, Bisexual, Transsexual or Intersex (LGBTI)

[5] A "Female Support Officer" is an employee of the court which is designated to fulfil this role.

6. The Female Support Person is to settle victim, but is not to talk about any of the details of the case.

7. The Female Support Person is to bring the victim either to the "*e*- court room" or to the court as required, and remain with the victim while the victim gives evidence.

8. The victim may be accompanied or spoken to by their private counsel or prosecutor as required.

9. The prosecutor or counsel for the victim should speak with the victim and find out whether the victim wishes to give evidence from the "*e*- court room", or in the courtroom with a screen, or in the court room without a screen. This may also be confirmed by the Female Support Officer.

THE SET UP OF THE COURT ROOM

10. Adjustments are to be made to the courtroom to improve the comfort for persons in the court which include, making adjustments to the witness box and the accused box so that the witnesses and the accused are able to sit and have water and tissues available to them during the trial process.

11. The lawyers, both prosecution and defence, are to be seated at a separate bar table during the trial process. Lawyers are to remain seated during the trial process unless they are speaking or are questioning the witnesses, in which case the counsel may either sit or stand.

12. If the victim gives evidence in the court room, it is required that the victim be allowed to enter the court room in the absence of the accused and be seated in the witness box behind a screen. When the accused returns to the court room, the accused should not be visible to the victim.

13. The victim will then give evidence with a screen which prevents the victim from seeing the accused and also the accused from seeing the victim, unless identification of the perpetrator is required. If identification is required then the victim may move away from behind the screen to also be able to view accused person. The female support person should be seated near to where the victim is giving evidence.

14. If the victim so chooses, the victim may give evidence in court without the use a screen.

15. Further, other arrangements may be made by the Judge in the court room according to the needs of the victim and having regard to the particular circumstances.

SET UP AND USE OF THE *e*-COURT ROOM

16. Video facilities are to be made available in the trial court room to permit evidence to be given by the victim from the *e* - Court room outside the trial court and be seen and heard on a screen in the trial court. This is to enable the victim to give evidence without coming into the trial court.

17. The positioning of the video camera should allow the victim to see the trial courtroom and particularly the Judge and counsel, but not the accused person, unless it is necessary for the victim to identify the person whom the victim says was the perpetrator of the conduct alleged.

18. If identification is required then the camera may be repositioned so as to include a view of the accused person.

19. The view that persons in the trial court will have is of the victim only, who will be seated unless there is, a need for identification or as per the requirement of the case.
20. Persons present in the e-Court room will be the female support officer and or any person such as an interpreter as required.
21. The Female Support Officer is to settle the victim in the room before commencement of their evidence.
22. If the victim is required to draw or identify certain objects then the Female Support Officer is to show this to the victim.
23. The Female Support Officer is also to inform the Judge if the victim indicates that they need a break because they are tired or need to take a break or becomes upset.

PROCESSES FOR THE TRIAL AND TAKING OF EVIDENCE

24. The Judge will usually list three cases on each day of hearing unless the circumstances suggest a different listing arrangement
25. The Judge at the commencement of the trial may acquaint counsel and the accused on matters related to the procedures to be followed in the Court.

PROCESS FOR TAKING OF THE EVIDENCE OF THE VICTIM AND THE WITNESSES

Settling the victim and witnesses

26. The judge shall decide the procedure to be followed, which in his/her opinion is most appropriate for both prosecution and defence with modification as required including evidence of the victim.
27. The Judge will introduce himself or herself to all including the victim and explain who the other persons in the court room are.
28. Questions asked by the Judge would include the following from the witnesses including the victims:
    a. asking whether they have any concerns about security for themselves or their family in relation to the case and may make orders as may be appropriate.
    b. asking questions to settle them and to ensure that they are comfortable for the giving of the evidence, including whether they are comfortable with giving evidence, from the "e-court, or in the court with or without the screen as they choose;.
    c. explaining to the witness the importance of their telling the Judge if they do not understand the questions and that is not shameful to say they do not understand;
    d. explaining to the witness that it is very important to know if the witness does not understand as the witness may give an unintended answer;
    e. informing the witness that if they feel tired or need a break they should tell the Female Support Officer.
29. A similar overall procedure should also be followed by the Judge with other witnesses as well as the accused if this is appropriate, with modification as required.

Trial process

30. The trial is to proceed and be completed without any adjournment where possible. Adjournment is only be permitted by the Judge for good reason. In particular, the whole of the evidence of the victim, including examination, cross examination and re-examination, is as far as possible to be conducted on the same day.

31. The Judge is to ensure that all questions asked of the victim are to be done with gender sensitivity and in appropriate language having regard to the victim's age, educational level, cultural background, physical or mental disabilities as well as being asked in an appropriate manner and tone. (Qanun-e-Shadat, Order 1984 (QSO) Arts 146 and 148).

32. In addition the court may also limit questions asked of the victim where that is appropriate and it includes unnecessarily repetitive questions.

33. In accordance with the Guidelines, questions put in cross-examination on behalf of the accused should be given in writing or as the court think fit according to circumstances of the case, the Judge who should put them to the victim or to a vulnerable witness in a language which is clear and not degrading. The Judge may give directions as to the manner in which this is to be undertaken.

PROTECTION ORDERS.

34. When the Judge orders that a summons be issued to the victim or witnesses, the Judge may include a further direction endorsed or attached to the summons form which asks the victim or witness "Do you require any police protection for yourself or family prior to the trial"

35. The process server is to be directed to ask this question of the victim or witness.

36. If the victim indicates "yes" by a signature or mark, the process server is then to arrange that protection requested be provided by the relevant SP cell. The SP Cell without any delay inform to the court of arrangements done.

37. The process server is then to report back to the court on the process, which was followed, and the protection, which was arranged.

38. Any person-receiving summons who is related to the case including victim or witnesses may file an application to the court through their counsel as early as possible for protection.

39. The Judge may at any time make orders to provide specific protection and arrangements in order to give security for the victim/witnesses and or other relevant family or persons. Further the Judge may direct that the SP Cell to arrange for any person related to the case applying for protection.

PROCEDURES WHEN THE VICTIM OR OTHER WITNESSES RESILE FROM PREVIOUS STATEMENTS

40. Having regard to the concerning number of cases involving non-compoundable offences in which on the date of trial, the victim resiles from earlier statements and further where other witnesses also resile from their statements, the Judge may adopt any of the following procedures or a combination of such procedures or another procedure which the Judge considers appropriate to address this issue.

a. **Procedure 1.** The Judge may clear the court of all persons (including the accused) leaving only the victim and a court reporter person or alternatively the Judge may bring the victim and a court reporter into chambers. The Judge may then ask questions of the victim as to why she has resiled and ascertain whether the victim has been exposed to any pressure and further whether there has been any compromise of the case through family pressure or agreement between the accused and the victim's family. These questions and answers are to be recorded. The Judge may thereafter make appropriate orders as to the process of the case and this may include making appropriate protection orders.

b. **Procedure 2.** The Judge may adjourn the case until the following day or some other early suitable day, and make appropriate protection orders and arrangements to protect the victim and or other relevant family or persons. On the resumed day the Judge may undertake Procedure 1.

c. **Procedure 3.** The Judge may adjourn the case to another day. The Judge may direct that the Assistant Superintendent of Police/Sub-Divisional Police Officer of Concerned Area, look into the matter including whether the victim and/or other witnesses have been pressured into making a false statements and provide a report on the actions before the court within 7 days, or such further extension as the Judge may order. The Judge may make appropriate protection orders.

d. **Procedure 4.** The Judge may instead direct that the trial continue and that the victim and other witnesses be required to give evidence either on that day or another early day with appropriate protection orders. If this Procedure is directed by the Judge, then the following processes would apply:
   i. The victim and other witnesses who seek to resile are to be informed about the process which will take place in the court them to give evidence.
   ii. If the victim is declared hostile, the cross examination of the victim by both the prosecutor and the defendant is not required to be in writing in the manner indicated in the Guidelines and Practice Note No. 2 paragraph 33.
   iii. Particular care needs to be taken by the Judge to ensure that the victim is not subjected to undue pressure by the nature and manner of this procedure.
   iv. After all of the relevant evidence in the case is called, the facts and the findings of the Judge will be assessed and based on the totality of the evidence.

PROCEDURES WHERE THE VICTIM DOES NOT ATTEND COURT

41. If the victim does not attend Court on the day set for hearing, the case may be adjourned to another date and a further summons may be issued for her attendance as provided in sections 87 and 88 Cr P.C

42. If a further summons is so issued, then the Judge should give directions on the manner in which the victim is to be brought to the court, so as to ensure this is undertaken sensitively.

43. If the victim cannot be found or again does not attend, the prosecution may still proceed with the trial if there appears to be sufficient evidence which can be called to prove the commission of the offence, even without the attendance of the victim, subject to the Judge deciding that the accused should be acquitted pursuant to S 265K Cr P.C.

COURTS POWER TO ASK QUESTION, CALL WITNESSES ETC.

44. In relation to the cases which come before the court, in particular in relation to cases where there is resiling or where the victim does not attend court, it is important for the court to appropriately utilise its powers given pursuant to Sections 540 CrP.C and 161 QSO

45. Pursuant to Section 540 CrP.C the Judge is empowered to summon any person as a witness, or examine any person in attendance, although not summoned as a witness. The Judge may also recall and re-examine any person already examined, if the evidence of such a witness appears to be essential to the just decision of the case.

46. Pursuant to Article 161 QSO. In order to discover or to obtain proper proof of relevant facts, the Judge may ask any question the Judge pleases, in any form at any time, of any witness, or of the parties about any fact either relevant or irrelevant. In addition the Judge may order the production of any document or thing. Neither the parties nor their agents shall be entitled to make any objection to any such question or order, nor, without the leave of the court, to cross examine any witness upon any answer given in reply to any such question. This is subject to the proviso contained in that section

47. This would include processes of the prosecutor giving up the victim and witnesses and having them declared hostile and then opening the victim and witnesses for cross examination by the Prosecutor and Defence Counsel.

(Judge Muhammad Akmal Khan)
Director General
Directorate Of District Judiciary

APPENDIX 2A

Updated Practice Note Incorporating Underlined Refinements Suggested by the District and Sessions Court Judges in Lahore

PRACTICE NOTE FOR CASES IN GENDER-BASED VIOLENCE COURTS ("GBV COURTS")

THE PURPOSE OF THE GBV COURT

1. The purpose of the GBV Court is to enable cases which concern gender-based violence offences[1] to be prioritized and conducted in a gender-sensitive manner. The GBV Court applies to the victims of gender-based violence; these victims would include women, children, and other vulnerable witnesses[2] including persons who may regard themselves as having a different gender identity.[3] The purpose of GBV Court also recognises the fact that the victims of gender-based violence are mainly women (and girl children) and they often do not report violence against them for fear of retribution, shame, social stigma, and lack of community support. In addition, victims may also not be confident or fearful of coming to the court to give evidence because the court processes are intimidating and they feel re-victimised. The GBV Court and the Practice Note are a response to provide court and judicial officials who are specialized and gender-sensitive regarding gender-based violence and include procedures to ensure cases are heard fairly and expeditiously and in a way that will avoid or minimize undue trauma to victims, children, and other vulnerable witnesses.

PURPOSE OF THE PRACTICE NOTE

2. The purpose of this Practice Note is to enable the "Guidelines to be followed in Cases of gender-based violence (GBV)" No. 22325 dated 17 October 2017 ("the Guidelines), to be implemented in practice with clarity and consistency.

3. At the same time the Practice Note is to be applied flexibly if particular situations require some modification in order to maintain the purpose and principles of the Guidelines.

4. The Practice Note will also apply to the treatment of other witnesses giving evidence in such cases, either for the prosecution or defense, and it includes the accused, with modifications

---

[1]   Gender based violence (GBV) is an act of violence that results in or is likely to result in physical, sexual, psychological or economic harm or suffering. It includes threats of such acts, coercion or arbitrary deprivations of liberty whether occurring public or in private and it includes domestic violence. The violence is primarily committed on the victim by reason of her/his sex or gender. Examples of gender based violence include offences under Sections 300-302, 310 - A, 315, 324, 332, 336-A and B, 337, 337-A – 337-Z, 354, 354A, 359 to 369, 362 to 374, 364 - A, 365- B, 376, 376(2) – 376(4), 371- A, 377, 496, 496 - A, 498 – A, 498 – B, 498 – C and 509 of PPC and Sections 3, 4, 11, 12,14,17 – 23 of the Prevention of Electronic Crimes Act.

[2]   Vulnerable witnesses would include also persons with mental or other disabilities.

[3]   Including persons protected under the Transgender Persons (Protection of Rights) Act, 2018.

as the situation may require. It is important for all witnesses in the court to have the best conditions be able to give their best evidence.

OUTSIDE THE COURT ROOM

5. On reaching the Court to precinct, the victim is to be met by a "Female Support Officer,"[4] who will escort the victim to a protected place so as to avoid contact with the accused or their family or friends as well as the general public.

6. The Female Support Person is to settle victim, but is not to talk about any of the details of the case.

7. The Female Support Person is to bring the victim either to the "e-courtroom" or to the court as required, and remain with the victim while the victim gives evidence.

8. The victim may be accompanied or spoken to by their private counsel or prosecutor as required.

9. The prosecutor or counsel for the victim should speak with the victim and find out whether the victim wishes to give evidence from the "e-courtroom," or in the courtroom with a screen, or in the court room without a screen. This may also be confirmed by the Female Support Officer.

THE SET UP OF THE COURT ROOM

10. Adjustments are to be made to the courtroom to improve the comfort for persons in the court which include, making adjustments to the witness box and the accused box so that the witnesses and the accused are able to sit and have water and tissues available to them during the trial process.

11. The lawyers, both prosecution and defence, are to be seated at a separate bar table during the trial process. Lawyers are to remain seated during the trial process unless they are speaking or are questioning the witnesses, in which case the counsel may either sit or stand.

12. If the victim gives evidence in the court room, it is required that the victim be allowed to enter the court room in the absence of the accused and be seated in the witness box behind a screen. When the accused returns to the court room, the accused should not be visible to the victim.

13. The victim will then give evidence with a screen which prevents the victim from seeing and being seen by the accused, unless identification of the perpetrator is required. If identification is required then the victim may move away from behind the screen to also be able to view accused person. The female support person should be seated near to where the victim is giving evidence.

14. If the victim so chooses, the victim may give evidence in court without the use a screen.

15. Further, other arrangements may be made by the Judge in the court room according to the needs of the victim and having regard to the particular circumstances.

---

4   A "Female Support Officer" is an employee of the court which is designated to fulfill this role.

SET UP AND USE OF THE e-COURTROOM

16. Video facilities are to be made available in the trial court room to permit evidence to be given by the victim from the e-courtroom outside the trial court and be seen and heard on a screen in the trial court. This is to enable the victim to give evidence without coming into the trial court.

17. The e-courtroom used for child victims or child witnesses should preferably be in a child court precinct if one is conveniently available, or if not, in a room which has a child friendly environment[5] and away from contact with adult court participants.

18. The positioning of the video camera should allow the victim to see the trial courtroom and particularly the Judge and counsel, but not the accused person, unless it is necessary for the victim to identify the person whom the victim says was the perpetrator of the conduct alleged.

19. If identification is required then the camera may be repositioned so as to include a view of the accused person.

20. The view that persons in the trial court will have is of the victim only, who will be seated unless there is, a need for identification or as per the requirement of the case.

21. Persons present in the e-courtroom will be the female support officer and or any person such as an interpreter as required.

22. The Female Support Officer is to settle the victim in the room before commencement of their evidence.

23. If the victim is required to use communication aids[6] to assist in giving their evidence or to draw or identify certain objects then the Female Support Officer is to show this to the victim.

24. The Female Support Officer is also to inform the Judge if the victim indicates that she/he needs a break because she/he is tired or becomes upset.

PROCESSES FOR THE TRIAL AND TAKING OF EVIDENCE

25. The Judge will usually list three cases on each day of hearing unless the circumstances suggest a different listing arrangement.

26. The Judge at the commencement of the trial may acquaint counsel and the accused on matters related to the procedures to be followed in the Court.

---

[5] A child-friendly environment is a space, even if small, which includes removable toys and decor which are age appropriate to help the child feel more comfortable when giving evidence.

[6] Communication aids include paper, markers, anatomically detailed drawings or dolls or toys, or cards which give short answers or other means as required for the witness and to include requirements for a child as well as persons with mental or physical or other disabilities.

PROCESS FOR TAKING OF THE EVIDENCE OF THE VICTIM AND THE WITNESSES

Settling the victim and witnesses

27. The judge shall decide the procedure to be followed, which in his/her opinion is most appropriate for both prosecution and defence with modification as required including evidence of the victim. Additional or modified requirements are to be made for child victims and child witnesses as set out below under "Child Victim and Child Witness Requirements"

28. The Judge will introduce himself or herself to all including the victim and explain who the other persons in the court room are.

29. Questions asked by the Judge would include the following from the witnesses including the victims:

    (a) asking whether they have any concerns about security for themselves or their family in relation to the case and may make orders as may be appropriate.

    (b) asking questions to settle them and to ensure that they are comfortable for the giving of the evidence, including whether they are comfortable with giving evidence, from the "e-court, or in the court with or without the screen as they choose;.

    (c) explaining to the witness the importance of their telling the Judge if they do not understand the questions and that is not shameful to say they do not understand;

    (d) explaining to the witness that it is very important to know if the witness does not understand as the witness may give an unintended answer;

    (e) informing the witness that if they feel tired or need a break they should tell the Female Support Officer.

30. A similar overall procedure should also be followed by the Judge with other witnesses as well as the accused if this is appropriate, with modification as required.

Trial process

31. The trial is to proceed and be completed without any adjournment where possible. Adjournment is only be permitted by the Judge for good reason. In particular, the whole of the evidence of the victim, including examination, cross examination and re-examination, is as far as possible to be conducted on the same day.

32. The Judge is to ensure that all questions asked of the victim are to be done with gender sensitivity and in appropriate language having regard to the victim's age, educational level, cultural background, physical or mental disabilities as well as being asked in an appropriate manner and tone. (Qanun-e-Shadat, Order 1984 (QSO) Arts 146 and 148).

33. In addition the court may also limit questions asked of the victim where that is appropriate and it includes unnecessarily repetitive questions.

34. In accordance with the Guidelines, questions put in cross-examination on behalf of the accused should be given in writing or as the court think fit according to circumstances of the case, the Judge who should put them to the victim or to a vulnerable witness in a language which is clear and not degrading. The Judge may give directions as to the manner in which this is to be undertaken.

35. Additional or modified requirements are to be made for child victims and child witnesses as set out below under the "Child Victim and Child Witness Requirements."

PROTECTION ORDERS

36. When the Judge orders that a summons be issued to the victim or witnesses, the Judge may include a further direction endorsed or attached to the summons form which asks the victim or witness "Do you require any police protection for yourself or family prior to the trial"

37. The process server is to be directed to ask this question of the victim or witness, or in relation to a child, the parent or guardian of the child as appropriate.

38. If the victim indicates "yes" by a signature or mark, the process server is then to arrange that protection requested be provided by the relevant SP cell. The SP Cell without any delay inform to the court of arrangements done.

39. The process server is then to report back to the court on the process, which was followed, and the protection, which was arranged.

40. Any person-receiving summons who is related to the case including victim or witnesses may file an application to the court through their counsel as early as possible for protection.

41. The Judge may at any time make orders to provide specific protection and arrangements in order to give security for the victim/witnesses and or other relevant family or persons. Further the Judge may direct that the SP Cell to arrange for any person related to the case applying for protection.

PROCEDURES WHEN THE VICTIM OR OTHER WITNESSES RESILE FROM PREVIOUS STATEMENTS

42. Having regard to the concerning number of cases involving non-compoundable offences in which on the date of trial, the victim resiles from earlier statements and further where other witnesses also resile from their statements, the Judge may adopt any of the following procedures or a combination of such procedures or another procedure which the Judge considers appropriate to address this issue. Additional or modified requirements are to be made for child victims and child witnesses as set out below under "Child Victim and Child Witness Requirements."

    (a) **Procedure 1.** The Judge may clear the court of all persons (including the accused) leaving only the victim and a court reporter person or alternatively the Judge may bring the victim and a court reporter into chambers. The Judge may then ask questions of the victim as to why she/he has resiled and ascertain whether the victim has been exposed to any pressure and further whether there has been any compromise of the case through family pressure or agreement between the accused and the victim's family. These questions and answers are to be recorded.

    The Judge may thereafter make appropriate orders as to the process of the case and this may include making appropriate protection orders.

    (b) **Procedure 2.** The Judge may adjourn the case until the following day or some other early suitable day, and make appropriate protection orders and arrangements to protect the victim or witness and or other relevant family or persons. On the resumed day the Judge may undertake Procedure 1.

(c) **Procedure 3.** The Judge may adjourn the case to another day. The Judge may direct that the Assistant Superintendent of Police/Subdivisional Police Officer of Concerned Area, look into the matter including whether the victim and/or other witnesses have been pressured into making a false statements and provide a report on the actions before the court within 7 days, or such further extension as the Judge may order. The Judge may make appropriate protection orders.

(d) **Procedure 4.** The Judge may instead direct that the trial continue and that the victim and other witnesses be required to give evidence either on that day or another early day with appropriate protection orders. If this Procedure is directed by the Judge, then the following processes would apply:

(i)   The victim and other witnesses who seek to resile are to be informed about in an appropriate sensitive manner of the process which will take place in the court them to give evidence.

(ii)   If the victim or witness is an adult and is declared hostile, the cross examination of the victim by both the prosecutor and the defendant is not required to be in writing in the manner indicated in the Guidelines and Practice Note No. 2 paragraph 33.

(iii) Particular care needs to be taken by the Judge to ensure that the victim is not subjected to undue pressure by the nature and manner of this procedure.

(iv)   After all of the relevant evidence in the case is called, the facts and the findings of the Judge will be assessed and based on the totality of the evidence.

PROCEDURES WHERE THE VICTIM DOES NOT ATTEND COURT

43. If the victim does not attend Court on the day set for hearing, the case may be adjourned to another date and a further summons may be issued for her attendance as provided in sections 87 and 88 CrPC.

44. If a further summons is so issued, then the Judge should give directions on the manner in which the victim is to be brought to the court, so as to ensure this is undertaken sensitively.

45. If the victim cannot be found or again does not attend, the prosecution may still proceed with the trial if there appears to be sufficient evidence which can be called to prove the commission of the offence, even without the attendance of the victim, subject to the Judge deciding that the accused should be acquitted pursuant to section 265K CrPC.

CHILD VICTIM AND CHILD WITNESS REQUIREMENTS

Settling the child victim and witness

46. The questions asked to settle the child should be open questions which are short, simple, one topic at a time, using language and expressions which are appropriate to age, educational level, cultural background, physical or mental disabilities of the child.

47. The questions should be limited in number and not connected in any way to the circumstances of the alleged offending.

48. The manner of questioning should be empathetic but not overly friendly and allow the child to respond in their own way.

49. The answers to these questions will assist the judge in understanding the communication capacity of the child and also the ability of the child to know the importance of telling the truth when giving their evidence.

Trial process for child victim and witness

50. In additions to items 31 to 34, best practice indicates that every child should be given a break at least after 45 mins of questioning, or earlier if they appear tired or stressed.

51. It is critical that item 34 is followed and that questions to be asked in cross examination are put in writing first by counsel and then asked by the Judge. Preferably the questions should be open questions which allow the child to respond in their own way.

Resiling of child victim or witness

52. If the victim or witness is a child then the Judge is to discuss the process to be followed with prosecution and defence counsel, in particular in relation to Item 42 Procedure 4 so that questions are still in writing with modifications to ensure that the best interest of the child is taken into account in the questioning process.

COURTS POWER TO ASK QUESTION, CALL WITNESSES ETC.

53. In relation to the cases which come before the court, in particular in relation to cases where there is resiling or where the victim does not attend court, it is important for the court to appropriately utilise its powers given pursuant to Sections 540 CrP.C and 161 QS0

54. Pursuant to Section 540 CrP.C the Judge is empowered to summon any person as a witness, or examine any person in attendance, although not summoned as a witness. The Judge may also recall and re-examine any person already examined, if the evidence of such a witness appears to be essential to the just decision of the case.

55. Pursuant to Article 161 QSO. In order to discover or to obtain proper proof of relevant facts, the Judge may ask any question the Judge pleases, in any form at any time, of any witness, or of the parties about any fact either relevant or irrelevant. In addition the Judge may order the production of any document or thing. Neither the parties nor their agents shall be entitled to make any objection to any such question or order, nor, without the leave of the court, to cross examine any witness upon any answer given in reply to any such question. This is subject to the proviso contained in that section

56. This would include processes of the prosecutor giving up the victim and witnesses and having them declared hostile and then opening the victim and witnesses for cross examination by the Prosecutor and Defence Counsel.

APPENDIX 3

Questioning of Child Witnesses in Court— Some Helpful Hints Using Best Practices

The content and style of questioning depends on the age of the child and other factors. Broadly speaking, the following processes are considered a best practice.

Commencement of the Child's Court Appearance

1. **First, relax the child and build rapport.**

    *   Ask for their name, what name they like to be called, their age, and date of birth. Do not ask for their address; this may be important for security reasons.

    *   Encourage the child to give a narrative about matters unrelated to the offense both in breadth and in depth (see below). A general technique is to incorporate the child's own words or answers and then prompt the child to greater elaboration by asking further questions.

    *   Use open ended questions which begin with what, where, who, which, and why.

    *   Ask them some easy-to-answer questions about themselves. For example:
        -   Tell me something about yourself.
        -   What do you like to do for fun?
        -   What did you do this morning?
        -   What things do you like to do that make you feel happy?
        -   What year are you in school?
        -   What subjects do you like?
        -   What is your favorite food?

    *   **Questions by depth.** The answers to those simple questions could be followed up by asking further detail. For example: "You have told me [...] in answer to my question earlier. Can you tell me more about that? What [...]? Who [...]?" (This is called open questions by depth.)

    *   **Questions by breadth.** Ask for more information about an object, a person, a location, details of an activity, or a particular period of time. For example: "You have told me about [...], and then what happened?" or "What happened next?" or "You have told me that you like to do [...], what else do you like to do?" (This is called open questions by breadth.)

    *   These questions and answers also allow you to have a better understanding of the child's linguistic skills, ability, and style.

2. **Move toward the substantive issues.**

    *   Introduce who you are and who the other people in the court are, and briefly what each of you does.

- You may, if it is appropriate for the child, tell them how you and others could be called or referred to. It may be easy to tell the child that they can refer to you and the counsel as "Sir" or "Madam" or whatever is easy for them. Otherwise saying nothing about this is fine.

- Ask the child something like, "What are you here to talk to me about today?" This brings them into why they are in the court and it will give you some information about their understanding.

- Follow-up with something like "That is right" and "When you talk about that, I would like you to tell me everything about it and don't leave anything out."

- Talk to the child about what will happen. For example, you may say:
  - **First,** you will be asked questions by (the prosecutor) and you will be asked to give answers. Sometimes I may also ask you questions.
  - It is important to let me know if you don't understand a question. It is all right to say, "I don't know" or "I don't understand that question." It is important that you do not answer a question if you are not sure what it means.
  - When answering questions, you do not have to give a "yes" or a "no" answer. You can answer in your own words.
  - If you need a break either because you are tired or upset, or you need to go to the toilet or something else, please let me know. Or tell the support person near you.
  - [In order to check whether the child understands what you have said, you may ask something like] If you do not understand the question, what do you say? [and] If you do not know the answer to a question, what do you say?
  - **Second,** you will be asked questions by (the defense). The same situation applies if you do not understand a question or you do not know the answer to the question.
  - I will talk more about this later before you are questioned by (the defense).

- Then ask questions about whether the child is comfortable, whether they can see and hear you, whether they have tissue paper and water, and whether the female support officer is nearby, among other things. Say, "I will try and make this as comfortable and as easy for you as possible and you can have a break if you need one."

- Note that generally young children need a break of about 5 minutes every 20 minutes or so. Sometimes they may just want to get on with it and not take a break; if that is the case, keep your eye on them. When tired, a child may simply keep answering "I do not know" to every question with a flat expression.

3.   **Move to the prosecutor for examination in chief.**

- Invite the prosecutor to ask the child some questions first.

- At the end of the examination in chief, it is likely that you will take a short adjournment before commencing the cross-examination.

- This process should also be explained to the child.

- During the adjournment, you may wish to discuss the process for cross-examination of the child with the counsel for the defense and go through the list of questions. If this is to take any particular length of time, some indication of time should be given to the child through the female support officer so that they would not worry during the break. This is all part of keeping the child informed.

4. **Move to cross-examination by the defendant.**

- Before the cross-examination starts, explain the process of cross-examination and that you will be asking the questions that the accused wants to ask and that you are asking them on behalf of the defendant.

- A suggested approach is that you could indicate something along the following lines to the child:

  - "XXX (the accused) has given me a list of questions in writing that he/she wishes to ask you. I will read out these questions on his/her behalf. They are not my questions. I will ask for your answers to each of the questions."

  - "Again, as I said earlier, if you do not understand the questions, please tell me. If you do not know the answer, please tell me. Also, when answering questions, you do not have to give a 'yes' or a 'no' answer, you can give the answer using your own words."

  - [You may also say] "In giving your answers, please tell me everything about it even if you have said it to me before." [This is to take account of the fact that children feel that if they are asked the same or a similar question it is because they were not believed the first time.]

- When you see the list of questions, there may be a pattern to questions that may contain phrases or words that the child may not readily understand. For example, questions may commence with "I suggest [...] that [...]" or "I suggest to you that...." The child may not understand what this phrase means.

- You may need to explain to the child that the accused does not agree with their answers and wants to put his/her own version and ask whether the child agrees with his/her version. This is done through questions that use the words "suggest." You may explain that the child may agree or disagree with the accused's version.

- You may want to ask questions to see whether the child understands each of these steps

Alternative approaches

- When the defense wishes to put an alternative version to the child in cross-examination, a best practice indicates that open questions should be asked. The variations are great and it is not possible to make other than broad suggestions.

- It is important that the questions be put in cross-examination and not simply alternative assertions which do not ask a question.

- Ideally an alternative version question ends in, for example, "What do you say happened?" or "What do you say to that?" which allows the child to respond in their own words, rather than a question that asks for a strict "yes" or "no" answer which may be limiting, particularly if the answer is not appropriately either a straight "yes" or "no" but something in between. It may be partly right or partly wrong.

- Endings such as "Do you agree? or "That's right, isn't it?" or questions ending in "did you?" or "did it?" tend to limit the answers to a "yes" or a "no" and the child will need to remember in those difficult moments that they are not confined to saying either "yes" or "no."

- It is best to have endings that allow the child to say what happened when the alternative proposition is put to them. Some possible approaches are as follows:

  The most open questions are—

  - You have said that XXX happened, I suggest that is not right and that YYY happened. What do you say about that?
  - The (accused) says that XXX happened, what do you say happened?
  - The (accused) says he/she was not there on that night. What do you say about that?
  - I suggest that (the accused) was not there. What do you say about that?

  The more closed questions are—

  - Do you agree that it was very dark on that night?
  - I suggest to you that XXX happened on that day. Do you agree? [or] Do you agree that XXX happened on that day?
  - I suggest that (the accused) did not do XXX. Do you agree?

  I suggest that (the accused) was not there. Do you agree?

  - The most closed questions are—
  - You never did XXX on that day, did you?
  - You never saw XXX on that day, did you?
  - You are unsure about who was there on that night. That's right, isn't it?

- Generally speaking, a child should not be accused of 'lying' or 'telling lies,' unless the defense case is that the child has 'deliberately told untruths' about what happened. Instead, the child could be asked "Are you sure you are telling me the truth about that?"

- The main point is to make the cross-examination fair so that the accused can challenge the evidence of the child, and at the same time the child is able to put their view in their own words in answer to questions that contradict their version of events.

5.   Re-examination of the child

- Situations may arise where the child has said XXX in examination in chief and YYY in cross-examination, and such differences have not been resolved. The child should have an opportunity to clarify the situation by being re-examined by the prosecution.

- The approach should be similar to the process of questions in cross-examination. There is no one approach. For example:

  - "In answer to my questions, you said that XXX happened, and later when you answered questions from (the accused), you said that YYY happened. Do you think your answers are different? [If the child says yes, then you may ask] "Why did you give different answers?" or "What do you say happened?"

6.   At the end of the child's evidence

- Thank the child for giving evidence and release them to go with the female support officer.

- Ask the female support officer to ask the child whether they feel safe and obtain information on that.

Additional Information

Competency Testing and Questions about Telling the Truth

In so far as this is relevant in any case, here are some suggested questions:

Q.   Do you know what it means to tell the truth?

Q.   Do you know what it means to tell a lie?

Q.   Is there any difference between telling the truth and telling lies?

Q.   What do you think is the difference?

Q.   Is it important to tell the truth?

Q.   Why is it important to tell the truth?

Q.   Do you see X (refer either to a police officer or clerk being a person whom the child can see on the CCTV)?

Q.   If somebody said to you that the woman/man is wearing glasses [or "not wearing glasses" whichever is inaccurate], is that true?

Q.   If somebody said to you that the woman/man is wearing a [...] [something which is accurate], is that true?

Q.   If someone said to you that you were in Grade X [different grade from what the child expresses], would that be the truth?

Q.   Do you think it is important for you to tell the truth in court?

Q.   Why do you think it is important?

APPENDIX 4

Suggested Procedure for Cross–Examination of the Victim by the Defense Counsel

The procedure suggested below mainly recognizes that the judge is the conduit for asking the questions in cross-examination sought to be put on behalf of the defense. This is not the usual process followed in cases, and every attempt should be made to ensure that (i) the defendant is able to properly and fairly conduct a defense; and (ii) the questions which the defense counsel seeks to ask of the victim are asked, so long as they are relevant and appropriate (see *Updated Practice Note* [Appendix 2A], paras. 32 and 33).

Paragraph 2(14) of the *Guidelines to Be Followed In Cases of Gender-Based Violence* (Appendix 1) and paragraph 34 of the *Updated Practice Note* provide:

> In accordance with the Guidelines, questions put in cross-examination on behalf of the accused should be given in writing to the Judge who should put them to the victim or to a vulnerable witness in a language which is clear and not degrading. The Judge may give directions as to the manner in which this is to be undertaken.

This process requires a number of steps. The following is an example of the process that could be followed and conveyed to the defense counsel:

Step 1

1. The defense counsel is to hand over the list of questions that he/she seeks to have the judge ask the victim.

2. The judge should look at the cross-examination questions and assess their suitability for asking the victim (see *Updated Practice Note* paras. 32 and 33). The judge may adjourn the court for a short time to review the questions in a suitable place such as in chambers.

3. If upon looking at the questions, the judge has a concern about the suitability of the cross-examination questions, the judge should take this up with the defense counsel.[1] The ruling should be done in an open court and recorded without the content of the questions being revealed in advance.

Step 2

4. The judge should resume the trial and ask the victim the cross-examination questions in a language that is clear and not degrading and suitable for the victim, especially a child.

---

[1] Note that this may sometimes be done in chambers and not in open court if the defense is concerned that it may prematurely disclose aspects of their defense. The defense counsel may agree with any changes suggested by the judge. If not, the judge would need to make a ruling on the suitability of the questions.

5. At the end of the list of cross-examination questions, the judge could ask the defense counsel whether there are further questions that they wish to ask the victim. If the defense counsel seeks to ask further questions, then they could be indicated and the judge could ask those questions. It would not be necessary for these to be in writing if they are short and can be done straight away. This is just a pragmatic, sensible variation of the procedure which otherwise requires them to be in writing.

Step 3

6. The prosecution counsel should be asked whether there is any re-examination of the victim.

ADDITIONAL NOTES

7. If during the process of the judge asking the questions to the witness as in Step 2 (4), there are answers by the victim for which the counsel wishes to ask additional question(s), the defense counsel could indicate directly to the judge as to what the questions are.[2] The judge may grant permission and then immediately ask those additional questions to the witness. It would not be necessary for these to be in writing if they are short and can be done straight away.

8. However, it is important that the process of requiring the list of questions should not be unduly modified. If for some reason some bigger issues arise that cannot be addressed by asking questions at the end, defense counsel should seek to amend the written list of questions.

9. It is important to ensure that fairness is given to the defendant in putting a defense at every stage in this process.

---

[2]   If necessary, in chambers.

APPENDIX 5

Direction to Police to Investigate Resiling Witness

DIRECTION TO THE ASSISTANT SUPERINTENDENT OF POLICE/SUB–DIVISIONAL POLICE OFFICER OF....

In the matter of ...., the victim [name] (and the complainant [name], where applicable) has (have) deposed before the court on [date] that she/he is (they are) "no more interested to proceed further with the matter against the accused [name]" and have "no objection, if the accused is acquitted from the charge." They indicate that the case was registered against the accused "due to some misunderstanding" and that the accused "has given satisfaction of his innocence in the presence of respectable of the locality."

In light of this indication, I direct you to undertake an investigation in relation to the following matters and report back to the court on or before [date].

Purpose of the Investigation

The primary purpose of the investigation is to question the victim and the complainant and any other person to obtain information on the following:

The Victim

- Why does the victim seek to resile?

- What specific parts of the Section 164 statement does the victim seek to resile from and why?

- Has there been any pressure, coercion, inducement, offer or threats to the victim or to any member of her family at any time in relation to the victim providing the Section 164 statement? If so, provide details.

- Is there any advice, pressure, encouragement, coercion, inducement, offer, or threats to the victim or complainant or to any member of her family which have led to the victim resiling?

- In a case where the complainant has also resiled, has that resiling influenced the victim to resile? If so, how?

- Has there been any compromise or deals done between the victim and/or complainant (and/or their families) with either the accused or the accused's family or someone on behalf of the accused at any time? If so, when? Give also the details of the compromise whether in writing or otherwise.

- In relation to the resiling deposition of the victim—

  - What is the nature of the 'misunderstanding' to which the victim has deposed and when did the victim realize it? Include details of when and how.

- What is the 'satisfaction' that the accused gave of his innocence? Include details of when and how.
- Who is the 'respectable of the locality' referred to in the deposition? Include details of when and other relevant facts. Where possible, obtain the statement of the 'respectable of the locality.'
- Take a full statement from the victim with all the details as to what the victim now says occurred and include the answers to the above questions.

A caution should be given to the victim before questions are asked of her about the possibility of being charged with giving false evidence if either her resiling statement or her Section 164 statement is false, and that it is important for her to disclose any advice, pressure, encouragement, coercion, inducement, offer or threats to her by any person in relation to giving either of the statements. Further the victim should be asked whether she requires any security protection in relation to the case.

The Complainant

- Why does the complainant seek to resile?

- What specific parts of the statement for registration of the case against the accused does the complainant seek to resile from and why?

- Has there been any pressure, coercion, inducement, offer or threats to the complainant or to any member of his/her family at any time in relation to the complainant providing the statement for registering the case? If so, provide details.

- Is there any advice, pressure, encouragement, coercion, inducement, offer or threats to the complainant or to any member of his/her family which have led to the complainant resiling?

- In a case where the victim has also resiled, has that resiling influenced the complainant to resile? If so, how?

- Has there been any compromise or deals done between the complainant and/or the victim (and/or their families) with either the accused or the accused's family or someone on behalf of the accused at any time? If so, when? Give also the details of the compromise whether in writing or otherwise.

- In relation to the resiling deposition of the complainant—

  - What is the nature of the 'misunderstanding' to which the complainant has deposed and when did the complainant realize it? Include details of when and how.
  - What is the 'satisfaction' that the accused gave of his innocence? Include details of when and how.
  - Who is the 'respectable of the locality' referred to in the deposition? Include details of when and other relevant facts. Where possible, obtain the statement of the 'respectable of the locality.'
  - Take a full statement from the complainant with all the details as to what the complainant now says occurred and include the answers to the above questions.

A caution should be given to the complainant before questions are asked of him/her about the possibility of being charged with giving false evidence if either the registration of the case or the resiling statement is false, and that it is important for him/her to disclose any advice, pressure, encouragement, coercion, inducement, offer or threats to him/her by any person in relation to giving either of the registration of the charge or the resiling statement. Further, the complainant should be asked whether he/she requires any security protection in relation to the case.

Direction to Establish a Gender-Based Violence Police Cell at Investigation Headquarters District Lahore

SUBJECT: ESTABLISHMENT OF GENDER BASED VIOLENCE CELL AT INVESTIGATION HEADQUARTERS DISTRICT LAHORE

Respectfully Sheweth,

INTRODUCTION

It is an alarming situation that number of the Gender Based Crime is increasing day by day in our society and this situation has created a chaos in the public at large. It has become the first and foremost priority of the four pillars of the state to curb this evil and to put the criminals behind the bars involved in this shabby crime at its earliest. New legislation is underway, new Court to tackle the Gender based violence/crimes has been established and the special cell to investigate such cases is being utilized to free the society from this apprehension.

DIRECTION OF HON'BLE JUSTICE MISS. AALIA NEELUM

On the guidelines & directions of Hon'ble Justice Miss. Aalia Neelum of Lahore High Court, Lahore regarding improving the quality of investigation in the cases of Gender Based Violence/Crime a meeting was held on 11.01.2018 at Lahore High Court, Lahore in the supervision of Hon'able Justice Miss. Aalia Neelum. Following officers/officials attended the same:-

1-   Mr. Sultan Ahmad Chaudhry, DIG Investigation, Lahore.
2-   Mr. Ghulam Mubashir Maken, SSP Investigation, Lahore.
3-   Mr. Muhammad Waqas Anwar DPG, Lahore.
4-   Mr. Muhammad Akhlaq, DPG, Lahore.
5-   Rana Muhammad Latif, SP Legal CCPO Office Lahore.
6-   Mr. Nasir Abbas Panjutha, DSP Legal Investigation, Lahore.

The participants considered different parameters and feasibility of the above said cell, several issues were explored comprehensively in this meeting about the functioning of the Gender Based Violence Cell.

ESTABLISHMENT OF SEPARATE SPECIAL CELL (GBVC)

A separate Cell of Gender based Violence cases keeping in view the sensitivity and modesty of the effectees, comprising of 06 Sub-Inspectors and 06 Lady Sub-Inspectors of the Investigation Wing, Lahore has been established under the direct supervision of SSP/Investigation, Lahore their names are as under:-

Sr.No.	Name and Rank of Male Officer	Name and Rank of Female officer	Division
1.	Nazir Ahmad SI No.1152/L	TSI Ayesha Azam	Saddar
2.	TSI Ahmad Tabasam	TSI Ambreen Rehman	Iqbal Town
3.	TSI Khalid Liaqat	TSI Sadaf Rasheed	Model Town
4.	TSI Ishtiaq Noor	TSI Jiaba Mansoor	City
5.	SI Ibrar Hussain No.1678/L	TSI Misbah Hafeez	Civil Lines
6.	SI Ashraf No.L/197	TSI Sadia Mehboob	Cantt:

After filling up all the post at the Divisional level, all kinds of logistic support in terms of vehicles/motorcycles with fuel and subordinates (Head Constable & Constable) with each I.O have been disbursed. System of leave and welfare of the I.Os has also been devised.

HIERARCHY

SSP/Investigation

↓

Divisional SsP

↓

Concerned DSPs/SDPOs

↓

In-Charge GBVC

↓

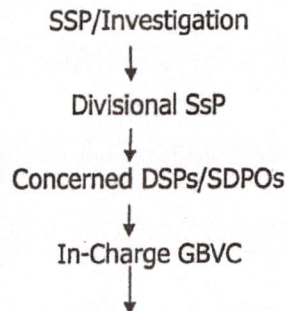

City Div.	Sadar Div.	Cantt Div.	Model Town Div.	Iqbal Town Div.	Civil Line Div.
01 SI (Male) 01 SI (Female) 02 HC, 02 FC, 01 lady Const.	01 SI (Male) 01 SI (Female) 02 HC, 02 FC, 01 lady Const.	01 SI (Male) 01 SI (Female) 02 HC, 02 FC, 01 lady Const.	01 SI (Male) 01 SI (Female) 02 HC, 02 FC, 01 lady Const.	01 SI (Male) 01 SI (Female) 02 HC, 02 FC, 01 lady Const.	01 SI (Male) 01 SI (Female) 02 HC, 02 FC, 01 lady Const.

TRAINING OF THE IO'S.

The Learned Judge of Gender Based Violence Court delivered the lectures to the IOs and share their views amongst them to tackle the Gender based Violence/Crime and preparation of Police File and report u/s 173 Cr.P.C. in his chamber. Afterwards 03 days workshop to enhance and develop the investigation skills of the IOs was held at Investigation HQrs: Lahore in which expert investigating officers of Investigation Wing delivered the lectures to the participants regarding Gender Based Violence/Crime. The guidelines and check-lists regarding

Gender based violence cases have been prepared, circulated and communicated to all relevant staff.

GUIDANCE

Separate meetings with the learned Judges of District Lahore, NGOs like "Aurat Foundation" "Bedari Foundation" "APWA" in Pakistan and "UNDP" are going to be conducted so that the awareness can be created in the society and such violence be discouraged and to devise joint strategy about elimination and investigation, of Gender based Violence cases. Their recommendations will be considered with zeal and zest.

FLAWS OF INVESTIGATION

To eradicate the lacunas in investigation of Gender based violence/crimes cases are being corrected. In this regard consultation is being made Prosecution Department and guidance is being taken from the Judgments passed by the Hon'ble Judges in various cases of Gender based violence/crimes in which the accused persons were awarded rigorous imprisonment. A proposal has also been forwarded to appoint at least two special prosecutors at Gender based violence/crimes Court to assist the learned Court and to deliver guidance to the IOs of the special Cell.

RECOMMENDATION FOR INCREASING THE COST OF INVESTIGATION

It has been opined that cost of investigation be raised up to Rs. 10,000/- per case in addition to already disbursing amount to the IOs so that they can conclude the case without any hindrance of lack of funds.

SUBMISSION OF SAMPLES IN PFSA

Meeting are being arranged with the high-ups of Forensic Lab Punjab, a mechanism is being developed to facilitate the IOs so that procedure for submission of DNA-samples can be made trouble-free, manageable and less time consuming. The IOs have already been directed to expedite and clear the pendency.

FUTURE ACTION PLAN

1- Meetings with the Prosecutors and learned Judges and the coordination with the Prosecution Department right from proceedings 154 Cr.P.C. till end of the trial.

2- Coordination with the PFSA authorities for early submission and generation of reports regarding samples (DNA/Swab etc)

3- Training of the witnesses in the cases of Gender based violence/crimes.

4- Appointment of the Pervi Officer in the Gender based violence/crimes Court.

5- Awareness programs with the liaison of NGOs on electronic and print media.

**Sr. Superintendent of Police,
Investigation, Lahore.**
17-1-18

Glossary

Amicus curiae	friend of the court
Arsh	compensation specified in Chapter XVI, Pakistan Penal Code to be paid to the victim or her/his heirs
Asian Development Bank	a regional development bank that promotes social and economic development in Asia and the Pacific
Avaaz lagana	a Pashtun custom where a man declares that a girl is engaged to him without her or her family's consent. Also known as *ghag*
Awf	waiver and forgiveness, one of three categories of punishment or consequences for committing *jinayat*
Badal-i-Sulh	compounding, one of three categories of punishment or consequences for committing a crime. Traditionally, women and girls are sometimes given in marriage to compound a crime, including murder. Girls, often minors, are handed over to the aggrieved family as reparation. This is now illegal and prohibited under Section 310 of the Pakistan Penal Code
Bazo	to settle blood feuds
Biradari	patrilineal clan or paternal lineage. A person who marries outside his *Biradari* is considered to have accepted an inferior status. Preferential marriages are cousin marriages from the father's family (e.g., father's brother's daughter). Also spelled as Baradari
Challan	charge sheet
Convention on the Elimination of All Forms of Discrimination against Women (CEDAW)	an international multilateral treaty that was adopted in 1979 by the United Nations General Assembly. It is one of the core international human rights instruments. Its main purpose is to establish public institutions that ensure women protection from discrimination. Pakistan ratified CEDAW in 1996 and is therefore obligated to implement CEDAW
Convention on the Rights of the Child (CRC)	an international multilateral treaty adopted in 1989 by the United Nations General Assembly. It is one of the core international human rights instruments. It provides for the protection of every child's civil, political, economic, social and cultural rights regardless of race, religion or ability. Pakistan ratified CRC in 1990 and is therefore obligated to implement CRC

Criminal Procedure Code	lays out the legal procedure in relation to investigation, collection of evidence, apprehension and arrest, court hearings, and determination of innocence or guilt and punishment
Daman	compensation determined by the Court to be paid by the offender to the victim for causing hurt not liable to *arsh*
Dar ul aman	shelter
Dhatun-nitaqain	two-belted woman, in reference to Asma who took food and water to the Prophet (PBUH) when he was hiding in Saur cave
Diyat	compensation
Falsus in uno, falsus in omnibus	a Latin phrase meaning "false in one thing, false in everything"
Fasad-fil-arz	the principle where the Court may, having regard to the facts and circumstances of the case, punish an offender against whom the right of *qisas* has been waived or compounded under Section 311 of the Pakistan Penal Code
Fiqh	Islamic jurisprudence
gender-based violence (GBV)	any form of violence that is committed against an individual because of that individual's biological sex or gender. GBV does not have to be physical abuse. It also includes threats, verbal abuse, emotional abuse, economic deprivation, and harassment, among other things
Gender-Based Violence Court (GBV Court)	the first GBV Court was established on 23 October 2017 by the Lahore High Court upon the directions of Supreme Court Justice Syed Mansoor Ali Shah, then Chief Justice of the Lahore High Court, with the technical support of the ADB team. About 100 pending GBV cases were then transferred to the GBV Court and the court commenced hearing cases in November 2017. The then Chief Justice of Pakistan, Justice Asif Saeed Khan Khosa, subsequently directed that GBV Courts be set up throughout Pakistan
Ghag	a Pashtun custom where a man declares that a girl is engaged to him without her or her family's consent. Also known as *avaaz lagana*
Ghairat	honor, i.e., in the name of honor
Hudood	offenses for which punishment is described in the Qur'an
Jinayat	offenses of homicide and bodily harm
Jirga	a village council
Katchi	literally "half-baked," i.e., an incomplete First Instance Report (FIR)
Lahore High Court	the apex court in the province of Punjab. It was instrumental in facilitating the judicial training programs. It also established the first gender-based violence court in Pakistan. Also known as the Punjab High Court

Mehr	dower
Nikahnama	marriage contract
Pait likhi	betrothals of girls at birth to a male member of the family
Pakhtu	unwritten social norms
Pakistan Penal Code 1860 (PPC)	Pakistan's criminal code that is meant to cover most offenses
Panchayat	a village council
Perdah	the practice of segregating women either physically or through attire
Pighore	societal scorn and taunts
Qanun e-Shahadat Order 1984 (QSO)	Pakistan's laws of evidence that are applied in cases of domestic and/or gender-based violence
Qatl	causing death of a person
Qatl-i-amd	the crime defined under Section 310 of the Pakistan Penal Code: "Whoever, with the intention of causing death or with the intention of causing bodily injury to a person, by doing an act which in the ordinary course of nature is likely to cause death, or with-the knowledge that his act is so imminently dangerous that it must in all probability cause death, causes the death of such person, is said to commit *qatl-i-amd*"
Qisas	law of retaliation (*lex talionis*)
Qisas and *Diyat*	law of retaliation (*lex talionis*) and compensation, one of three categories of punishment or consequences for committing *jinayat*
Rawaj	custom
Sarpaisa	a form of bride price that is demanded from the groom's family or kin to ratify the marriage. Also known as *Wulvur*
Suo moto cases	cases where the court, relying on its inherent powers, initiates the hearing
Swara	a form of compensation marriage practiced to resolve disputes, often murders. Girls, often minor, are handed over to the aggrieved family as reparation. Also known as *wanni*, *vani*, and *badla-e-sulha*
Ta'zir	offenses for which the punishment is within the discretion of the State or the judge
Taana	scorn with sarcasm

United Nations (UN)	an intergovernmental body established after the Second World War to maintain international peace and security. The UN Charter states that one of its main purposes is the promotion and encouragement of "respect for human rights and for fundamental freedoms for all without distinction as to race, sex, language or religion." The UN Human Rights system traces its origins to the adoption of the Universal Declaration of Human Rights in 1948. Thereafter there have been numerous multilateral human rights treaties. Nine of these treaties are designated as core international human rights instruments. The UN has also established mechanisms for monitoring compliance of State parties of their human rights obligations
Universal Declaration of Human Rights (UDHR)	a document that was adopted by the United Nations General Assembly in 1948. It is the primary international articulation of the fundamental and inalienable rights of all members of the human family. Every individual is entitled to these protections that should not be violated. UDHR is not a treaty so there are no signatories to the UDHR. However, universal compliance to it has elevated its stature to customary international law
Vani	a form of compensation marriage practiced to resolve disputes, often murders. Girls, often minor, are handed over to the aggrieved family as reparation. Also known as *swara, wanni*, and *badla-e-sulha*
violence against women (VAW)	defined by the 1993 UN Declaration on the Elimination of Violence against Women as an act of gender-based violence that results in, or is likely to result in, physical, sexual, psychological or economic harm or suffering to women, including threats of such acts, coercion or arbitrary deprivation of liberty, whether occurring in public or in private life. VAW is violence directed at a woman because she is a woman or that affects women disproportionately
Wali	a person entitled to claim *qisas*
Wanni	a form of compensation marriage practiced to resolve disputes, often murders. Girls, often minor, are handed over to the aggrieved family as reparation. Also known as *swara, vani*, and *badla-e-sulha*
Watta satta	a form of bride exchange, mostly endogamous marriages involving blood relatives, caste or clan
World Health Organization (WHO)	founded in 1948 to promote and protect international public health, it works to promote health, keep the world safe, and serve the vulnerable
Zakat	Muslim annual payment calculated based on income and specified property. The payments are used for charitable purposes
Zina	illicit intercourse, or fornication/adultery

About the Authors and Contributors

(in alphabetical order)

Zarizana Abdul Aziz

Zarizana specializes in legal and policy reform on gender equality, family law, and gender-based violence, focusing on intersections between international human rights, gender, culture, and national legislative frameworks.

Zarizana is a legislative drafter. She has drafted legislations; reviewed and revised laws on gender equality, violence against women, and family law in several countries; and trained legislative drafters, academics, and scholars on legislative drafting.

Zarizana is a researcher. Her recent seminal research includes a 40-country, multiyear research on gender-based violence based on which findings, she developed the *Due Diligence Framework on State Accountability for Eliminating Violence against Women*; a five-country research on information and communication technology (ICT)/online gender-based violence; and an 11-country research on Christian Personal Status Laws in Asia, the Middle East, and North Africa from a gender and human rights perspective. She co-authored a research paper on *COVID-19 and Violence Against Women: Unprecedented Impacts and Suggestions for Mitigation* (Routledge, 2021) and is undertaking an eight-country research into ICT/online gender-based violence in the Middle East and North Africa.

Zarizana is also a trainer. She has conducted trainings with judges, prosecutors, parliamentarians, and diverse stakeholders in government and civil society alike. From 2017 to 2020, as principal capacity development consultant for the Asian Development Bank, Zarizana conducted judicial training and capacity building in Afghanistan and Pakistan, and provided technical assistance in setting up Pakistan's first ever Gender-Based Violence Court.

Zarizana was a human rights fellow and a visiting scholar at Columbia University, New York and a visiting scholar and an adjunct professor at Northeastern University School of Law, Boston. She is currently an adjunct professor at George Washington University, Washington, DC and director of the Due Diligence Project, a global initiative dedicated to reimagining effective implementation of women's human rights.

Irum Ahsan

Irum Ahsan completed her legal education from the London School of Economics and Political Science, United Kingdom. Prior to joining the Asian Development Bank (ADB), Irum practiced on contentious and non-contentious legal matters in Pakistan. She also taught law at various prestigious institutions. At ADB, Irum provided legal advice on multisectoral development projects in Asia and the Pacific and negotiated hundreds of international finance agreements with various governments.

Currently, Irum is the Advisor of the Office of the Compliance Review Panel at ADB. She previously led ADB's Law and Policy Reform Program, which is based on the premise that a functioning legal system, anchored on the rule of law, is an essential component of sustainable development. Her projects focused on environmental and climate change adjudication and enforcement, sustainable development issues, gender equality laws and access to justice for women, corporate governance, energy laws, and regional cooperation.

Irum contributed to the establishment of the Asian Judges Network on Environment. Her work with Supreme Court judges across Asia proved instrumental in the establishment of more than six green courts in the region. In addition, the Legal Literacy for Women technical assistance that she had led assisted the Chief Justice of the Supreme Court of Pakistan in establishing 100 Gender-Based Violence Case Courts in the country, the first of such courts in Asia. Irum has been a judicial educator, and together with her team, trained more than 1,000 judges on environment and climate change laws and more than 500 judges and prosecutors in Afghanistan and Pakistan on laws related to violence against women.

Irum has also published her work in various journals and presented at several platforms. She is a member of ADB's governance, gender, environment, and climate change thematic groups. Irum is an active advocate for climate rights and gender consciousness and passionately steers the gender and climate discussions in ADB and at various international forums.

These accomplishments led her to receiving the (i) Lexis Nexis 2020 Global Inspiration Award for contributions to the Sustainable Development Goals, (ii) 2018 Financial Times Most Innovative In-House Legal Team Award and Innovation in Rule of Law and Access to Justice Award, (iii) ADB's 2019 Governance Award for Outstanding Knowledge Sharing and Collaborative Initiatives, and (iv) 2017 ADB's Vice-President Award for Exceptional Contributions to the Law and Policy Reform Work.

Samar Minallah Khan

Since obtaining her Master of Philosophy in Anthropology and Development from the University of Cambridge, United Kingdom, Samar has been challenging child marriages and various forms of culturally sanctioned forms of violence against women and girls. This she does by reaching out to different audiences through training programs and screenings of documentaries. She has been part of training programs at the National Judicial Academy, National Police Academy, and Civil Services Academy.

Referred to by the media as 'The Savior of Soul,' 'Women who Rock the World,' and 'The Crusader with the Camera,' she continues to advocate against child marriages.

In parts of Pakistan, girls are given away as compensation to settle disputes or to pay for crimes committed by men in their family or tribe. The family receiving the girl can make her a child bride, enslaving her for the rest of her life. *Swara*, as this custom is known, was practiced in parts of Pakistan for generations—until one woman, Samar Minallah Khan, used a camera to catalyze change.

In 2003, Samar created a documentary on *Swara*. Her goal was to raise awareness of the horrific custom and mobilize policymakers to abolish it. Thanks in part to her campaign, *Swara* was made illegal in Pakistan in 2004. Dozens of girls were rescued.

She did not stop there—she made sure that the law was implemented. She took the cause to Pakistanis of all backgrounds, even convincing truck drivers to paint anti-*Swara* slogans on their vehicles.

She sees her documentaries as a way to give voice to those who are seldom heard. Her films are made in regional languages and screened locally, so that people can relate and see themselves through her stories. She uses her lens to focus on unsung heroes within rural communities, such as Pakistani fathers who take enormous risks to stand up for their daughters. She believes in engaging men in order to end violence against women.

Samar has won several national and international awards: Commonwealth Secretary General's Innovation for Sustainable Development Awards 2021, Vanguard Award 2015, DVF Award 2015, Women with Wings 2014, Vital Voices Global Leadership Award (2012), Asia Foundation's Chang Lin Tein Fellowship (2010), Pakistan Women's Day Award (2010), Roberto Rossellini Award (2009), Canon Premio Internationale (2009), The Asia Society Young Leader (2007), and Asia Society's Perdita Huston Award (2007). Her latest film, *Out Swing*, won the Best Foreign Language Short at the 2021 Moscow International Film Festival, the Best Sport Film at the 2021 Toronto Women Film Festival, and Best Short Documentary at the March 2021 Florence Film Awards. A previous campaign she led also won four awards at the 2019 Cannes International Festival of Creativity.

Saima Amin Khawaja

Saima Amin Khawaja is a partner of Progressive Advocates and Legal Consultants. She was formerly a partner of Afridi, Shah & Minallah, Advocates and Legal Consultants and prior to that, she was an associate at Surridge & Beecheno, Advocates and Legal Consultants.

Saima did her Master of Laws from Kings College, London. Her initial experience was in corporate and constitutional litigation, which subsequently expanded to transactional work and consultancy relating to legal reforms and development.

Her areas of interest include the environment, constitution, corporate governance, regulatory laws, land acquisition, not-for-profit laws, and public interest litigation. She has handled numerous development consultancies which vary from environment enforcement, development of small and medium enterprises, improvement in the Lower Judiciary, to development of legal and regulatory framework for not-for-profit organizations. Her work has helped bring policy change in regulatory framework of taxation regime, improve urban development, address governance and corruption issues in water and sanitation, and implement reforms in acquisition laws. She has received special training in environment laws from M.C. Metha Foundation Rishkish, India. She has also been trained in mediation and is an accredited mediator. She has taught various subjects at the Institute of Legal Studies, Universal College Lahore, Lahore University of Management Sciences, Civil Services Academy, and the Judicial Academy.

She has been an amicus and part of many commissions at the High Court, and presently part of the Climate Change Commission constituted by the Lahore High Court. She is also a board member of LUMS Board of Trustees. Concurrently, she is part of the Board of Governors National Management Fund, Gurmani Foundation, The Citizens Foundation and Bali Memorial Trust.

Robyn Layton

Robyn Layton is a former Supreme Court Judge of South Australia. Prior to her Supreme Court appointment, she was a barrister and Queen's Counsel, then a Judge in the South Australian Industrial Court, and later a Deputy President of the Commonwealth Administrative Appeals Tribunal. As a judge in Australia, she was involved in developing and delivering judicial training courses on issues such as vulnerable witnesses including children and women in court. She and other judges produced a Bench book for all judges in Australia on children as witnesses.

Robyn was a member and later the Chair of the Committee of Experts on Application of Conventions of International Labour Organization (ILO), Geneva, from 1993 to 2008. She has been an ILO consultant since 2000 to the present time, delivering training for judges and lawyers in labor law and human rights standards internationally, particularly in Asia (Bangladesh, India, Indonesia, Malaysia, the Philippines, and Thailand).

Currently, Robyn is an adjunct professor at Justice and Society, University of South Australia. She holds a Master of Laws from the University of Adelaide and is a Doctor of the University of South Australia. She regularly trains students and lawyers on advocacy skills. She is an accredited judicial educator and a fellow of the Commonwealth Judicial Education Institute in Canada. She also works independently as a judicial education and program development consultant. She has been a consultant for the Asian Development Bank on a number of projects including a Gender Development Poverty Reduction Project for Women in Cambodia, Kazakhstan, and the Philippines and is currently a consultant on Strengthening Women's Resilience to Climate Change and Disasters in Fiji, the Lao PDR, and Mongolia. Her recent relevant publications have been as a co-author of a book on *Evidence Law in Australia* in 2017 and two publications on equal remuneration and the gender pay gap.

Robyn has been nationally recognized for her work relating to law, human rights, women, children and indigenous peoples. She has received the following awards: Member of the Order of Australia (OA) (2012); The South Australian, Australian of the Year (2012); Life member of the Law Society of South Australia (2012); Justice Award Law Society of South Australia (2013) and Australian Woman Lawyer Award (2016). She is a patron of numerous prestigious organizations and serves as a board member or chair of other organizations.

Maria Cecilia T. Sicangco

Maria Cecilia T. Sicangco is currently a senior legal officer at the Asian Development Bank (ADB). She is involved in the design, processing, and implementation of the Law and Policy Reform Program portfolio, which covers key areas such as environment and climate change law, international arbitration, gender-based violence and access to justice, commercial law and private sector development, digital economy, and Islamic finance.

Cecille works with development partners across Asia and the Pacific to promote the rule of law and establish an enabling environment for sustainable development. She has in-country experience in Afghanistan, Bhutan, Cambodia, Fiji, India, Myanmar, Pakistan, the Philippines, and Samoa. Her work has been published in the Yearbook of International Environmental Law (Oxford University Press) and the Human Rights Education in Asia-Pacific Journal. She authored the International Climate Change Legal Frameworks volume of the *Climate Change, Coming Soon to a Court Near You* report series. She also co-authored the National Climate Change Legal Frameworks volume, which synthesized the climate legal and policy frameworks of 32 countries in the region and analyzed key legislative trends and climate-relevant constitutional rights. Under ADB's *Legal Literacy for Women* technical assistance, she put together knowledge resources and compiled training manuals for judges and prosecutors handling gender-based violence cases in Pakistan and Afghanistan.

Cecille holds a Bachelor of Applied Economics and Accountancy double degree (cum laude) from De La Salle University and a Bachelor of Laws degree (cum laude, salutatorian) from the University of the Philippines. Thereafter, she pursued a Master of Laws in International Legal Studies degree at New York University, where she was the Starr Foundation Global Scholar, Hauser Scholar, and Thomas M. Franck Scholar in International Law.

Cecille is a Philippine- and US-qualified lawyer (admitted to the bar in the State of New York), and a certified public accountant. She is a member of the World Commission on Environmental Law.

Sohail Akbar Warraich

Sohail Akbar Warraich holds a Master of Laws in Law in Development from the University of Warwick. He has been working for over 25 years on law and policy reform relating to issues of violence against women. With extensive experience as a farmer, a journalist, a field researcher, and a human rights activist, he brings to the field of law a strong interest in the interrelationship between the principles of law and the realities of people's lives.

He was appointed as member of the National Commission on the Status of Women from 2016 to 2019, where he was chair of the Commission's Committee on Law and Policy. In this capacity, Sohail made extensive contribution in legislation related to women by making recommendations and comments on proposed bills. The notable laws that he worked on include amendments in criminal law (substantive i.e., Penal Code and procedural) on sexual violence against women and children, honor crimes, law on rights of transgender persons, and law on prevention of trafficking of person, especially of women and children.

He has researched and published on matters relating to law and women, specifically, *Special Mechanisms to Address Violence Against Women in Punjab: A Study of GBV Court in Lahore & Violence Against Women Centre in Multan*, commissioned by the Punjab Commission on the Status of Women (PCSW) in 2019; *Access to Justice for Survivors of Sexual Assault*, a research study published by the National Commission on Status of Women in 2017; Remedies for Forced Marriage in Pakistan, a chapter in *Remedies for Forced Marriage: A Handbook for Lawyers*, edited by Sara Hossain and Lynn Welchman, published by Interights, London in 2014 (available at interights.org); and Through the Looking Glass: Demise of Pakistan's Hudood Rape Laws, a chapter in *Criminal Law Reform and Transitional Justice, Human Rights Perspective for Sudan* published by Ashgate in 2011.

Sohail is an experienced trainer and has conducted training programs on human rights instruments, fundamental rights, family laws, and other domestic and international laws for jail officials, lawyers, and community-based rights groups, and on investigation of gender-based violence matters for police officials.